The Role of Revelation
in the World's Religions

The Role of Revelation in the World's Religions

BEVERLY MOON

McFarland & Company, Inc., Publishers
Jefferson, North Carolina, and London

Dao De Jing, I.25, from *Tao Te Ching*, translated with an introduction by D. C. Lau (Penguin Classics, 1963), 82. ©1963 by D. C. Lau. Reprinted by permission of Penguin Group (UK).

"Locks of shining red hair...," by Mahadeviyakka, from *Speaking of Siva*, translated with an introduction by A. K. Ramanujan (Penguin Classics, 1973), 120. ©1973 by A. K. Ramanujan. Reprinted by permission of Penguin Group (UK).

Excerpts from *The Essential Rumi* by Jalal al-Din Rumi and translated by Coleman Barks (HarperCollins, 1996), 3; 16; 132 f.; 137; 178 f.; and 191. © 1995 by Coleman Barks. Reprinted by permission of Coleman Barks.

Excerpts from *The Collected Works of St. Teresa of Avila*, vol. 1, translated by Kieran Kavanaugh. ©2001 by Washington Province of Discalced Carmelites, ICS Publications, 2131 Lincoln Road, N.E., Washington, DC 20002-1199 U.S.A. Reprinted by permission of ICS Publications (www.icspublications.org).

LIBRARY OF CONGRESS CATALOGUING-IN-PUBLICATION DATA

Moon, Beverly, 1945–
    The role of revelation in the world's religions / Beverly Moon.
    p. cm.
    Includes bibliographical references and index.

    ISBN 978-0-7864-4948-4
    softcover : 50# alkaline paper ∞

    1. Revelation.   2. Religions.   I. Title.
    BL475.5.M66   2010
    212'.6—dc22   2010022126

British Library cataloguing data are available

©2010 Beverly Moon. All rights reserved

No part of this book may be reproduced or transmitted in any form or by any means, electronic or mechanical, including photocopying or recording, or by any information storage and retrieval system, without permission in writing from the publisher.

Cover images: ©2010 Shutterstock

Manufactured in the United States of America

McFarland & Company, Inc., Publishers
  Box 611, Jefferson, North Carolina 28640
    www.mcfarlandpub.com

In memory of
Mircea Eliade and
Joseph M. Kitagawa

Table of Contents

Acknowledgments ix

Preface 1

PART ONE. A PHENOMENOLOGY OF REVELATION

1. Finding Common Ground:
The Experience of Revelation 7

2. Expressing Revelation: Sacred Art,
Sacred Place, and Sacred Time 26

3. Seeking Revelation:
Worship and Spiritual Discipline 43

4. Ways of Receiving Revelation 67

PART TWO. A TYPOLOGY OF REVELATION

5. Visions and Voices 83

6. Divination 102

7. Spirit Travel 120

8. Spirit Mediation 137

9. Mystical Union 155

10. Divine Incarnation 174

Glossary 193

Notes 195

Select Bibliography 209

Index 213

Acknowledgments

I wish to express my gratitude to those many people who have helped to make this book possible; above all I thank my teachers. I have been lucky to have studied with many exceptional professors of religion, both at the University of Chicago and at Columbia University. In Chicago I studied the History of Religions with Mircea Eliade, Joseph M. Kitagawa, Frank Reynolds, Charles H. Long, Jonathan Z. Smith, Gösta Franzén, and others. Later, as a student in the joint program for the academic study of religion at Columbia University and Union Theological Seminary, my research into the history of early Christianity brought me into contact with Cyril C. Richardson, Richard A. Norris, Jr., and Elaine Pagels. Finally, I would include among my teachers Claude B. Conyers, project editor of *The Encyclopedia of Religion*: first, he inculcated his editorial assistants with the skills necessary for publishing any encyclopedia; and second, Mr. Conyers provided a working environment that allowed each scholar — young and old — to contribute his or her own knowledge to a collective project. For nearly a decade he led us in a dynamic and constructive seminar on the nature of religion in all its manifestations.

Second, I wish to thank those few individual persons who have contributed to the publishing of the present study, a phenomenology and typology of revelation. Serinity Young, a scholar with a broad range of knowledge about religion, carefully read the original draft with a critical eye. I am indebted to her for her insights and suggestions. I thank Brian Romer, too, for his efforts in promoting the book.

Further, during the several years when I was researching and writing this book, I was supported by the United Methodist Church through the agency of the General Board of Global Ministries. I am grateful to all those connected with this church: the individual members of congregations all

Acknowledgments

over the United States as well as the staff in New York and Atlanta. As a commissioned missionary, I have been teaching world religions in Taiwan. This opportunity has deepened my understanding of Asian religious traditions. And so I would like also to express my thanks to the leaders and members of the Methodist Church in the Republic of China for their invitation to work in Taiwan and their unfailing hospitality.

Finally, I must acknowledge my debt to my father. A United Methodist minister whose ancestors were Quaker, he taught me to respect all religious traditions. Carroll M. Moon was the founder of the College Religious Center, which for many years served the faculty and students of Fresno State College (now California State University, Fresno). The center provided a place for students of different cultures and religious traditions to meet and work together. Our living room — and likewise, our cabin in Yosemite — seemed to function as extensions of the College Religious Center, in the sense that students of all faiths and backgrounds often gathered and socialized there. Thus, ever since I can remember, I have been guided by my father's patient appreciation for all people, no matter what their religious beliefs might be.

Preface

The idea for this book emerged around 1980 when I was working at Macmillan Publishing Company as an associate project editor on *The Encyclopedia of Religion*.[1] Jeremiah Kaplan, president of Macmillan, had invited Mircea Eliade, a scholar of the history of religions at the University of Chicago, to be the general editor of a wholly new encyclopedia reflecting in 16 volumes the current academic study of religions. The project editor, and my boss, was Claude B. Conyers. In consultation with Eliade and his team of scholars, Conyers put together the plans for the encyclopedia, which comprised three categories: articles on the historical religions; articles on religious phenomena; and articles that discussed religion and various aspects of culture.

One religious phenomenon that received our attention was revelation. We wrote a scope description for the main essay on "Revelation" and then did the same for related articles: "Prophecy," "Oracles," "Divination," "Inspiration," and "Enthusiasm." Later, while teaching a class on world religions in an interfaith classroom at a college in New York City, I discovered the usefulness of beginning the semester with the topic of revelation and its various types: regardless of religious background, each student was able to participate in the discussion with some sense of their own ability to contribute. For example, they learned that the experience of revelation is expressed through various art forms as well as in the establishment of sacred places and festivals. Illustrating this aspect of religion, one Chinese student, who had grown up in Hawaii where she had studied hula dancing with a traditional artist, performed for her classmates a dance that used movement to tell a sacred Polynesian myth.

Soon, however, I grew frustrated with the "related topics" that we had designated in planning the encyclopedia. Sometimes two different terms actually refer to the same type of revelation: oracles and divination are often synonymous, as are inspiration and enthusiasm. In addition, prophecy is actually a complex tradition that includes more than one form of revelation. So, I began to identify my own list of the different types of revelation, trying to avoid using any theological language that might bind the type to a specific tradition. This effort resulted first in a paper presented at an academic conference,[2] eventually a college-level class focusing on revelation and its types, and now this monograph.

By focusing on the experience of revelation as a human experience that is subjectively interpreted to be a message from the spirit world (however that world is envisioned), we are able to see the relationship between spirituality (personal religious experience) and the historical religions, which give symbolic form to and preserve the fruits of human spirituality. By showing the interplay of personal religious experience and the sacred traditions, a clearer picture of human culture emerges.

Some people say they are "spiritual" and not "religious." Perhaps they feel alienated from religious institutions. But this absolute opposition of the terms *spiritual* and *religious* appears to be misleading. By focusing on the spiritual foundations of the sacred traditions, we recognize the necessary connection between personal inner life and the religious heritage that is shared by all who are born into a human community

The book is divided into two parts. "A Phenomenology of Revelation" analyzes the human experience of revelation into three components. Chapter 1 introduces the experience of revelation, presents an operating definition for *revelation*, and gives examples of revelations that have led to the establishment of major religious traditions. The guiding view of revelation here derives from Mircea Eliade's discussion of religious revelation as hierophany, that is, "something sacred appears to someone." By itself, the term *revelation* merely suggests that something hidden becomes apparent; the specific nature of what is hidden is not indicated. So Eliade uses *hierophany*, because the Greek *hieros* contributes the dimension of the supernatural to the term. It is something supernatural that appears.

Chapter 2 shows the main ways by means of which people lend form to their experiences of revelation. Sacred art embraces all forms of art: images, books, film, dance, and so on. Sacred places include holy mountains, rivers, and caves as well as human-made shrines of all kinds: temples, churches, synagogues, mosques, and so forth. Sacred time refers to religious ritual, simple and complex, as well as holy days, both seasonal festivals (the New

Year and the birthday celebrations of divine beings) and those festivals that commemorate divinely wrought miracles, such as Passover and Easter.

Chapter 3 describes the two ways by means of which people orient their lives in response to revelation: in worship, they cultivate a relationship with the source of revelation; while spiritual discipline (asceticism) refers to those techniques that people practice in order to transform themselves and become more pleasing to that source. The differentiation of worship and spiritual discipline may be helpful to many who think of spiritual discipline (asceticism) as some kind of "self-punishment" (austerities) rather than as techniques for self-transformation.

Chapter 4 provides a transition to the second part by exploring two different metaphors for *religion*: religion as a house that provides a "home" and protection; and religion as a path that leads to the divine presence. Both metaphors are useful. Further, the image of religion as a house leads us then to conceptualize the many ways people encounter messages from the spirit world. Just as people have phones, computers, the postal service, and so forth, allowing them to receive messages from other humans in multiple ways, so, too, there appear to be different ways of receiving revelations.

"A Typology of Revelation" is the second part, presenting in chapters 5 through 10 the six different ways of receiving revelations. In Visions and Voices, Chapter 5, the human being receives messages from the spirit world by means of the body and the imagination. In Divination, natural events and random patterns are interpreted as messages from the spirits. In Spirit Travel, the spirit (mind, soul, consciousness) of the human being leaves the body in order to travel to the spirit world and then return with new knowledge.[3] In Spirit Mediation, a non–human spirit borrows a physical body for a short time in order to communicate with people. Mysticism refers to any tradition that has as its goal Mystical Union (Chapter 9), the union of the human and the divine (or ultimate reality). Finally, in Chapter 10, Divine Incarnation, a non–human spirit chooses to have a human life in order to help people.

Revelation is the common ground that underlies all religions, polytheistic or monotheistic, modern or archaic. Modernism often disregards such forms of experience because they are subjective rather than objective. Nevertheless, the conviction that the spirit realm is actively communicating with the human realm is precisely what makes people feel that something sacred and holy is happening. Thus, one cannot truly understand religion apart from revelation.

It is, in fact, possible to speak rationally about our subjective lives, even about a complex phenomenon such as religion. By analyzing the basic components of the experience of revelation and by exploring the six different ways that revelations are received, we come to understand how people are motivated to create cultural traditions, such as art, rituals, and beliefs, in order to express their religious experience. At the same time, we see how people develop forms of worship and spiritual discipline in order to live in relationship with the spiritual source of revelation.

This book has the general goal of discerning what it is that all religions have in common. Certainly, each sacred tradition will have its own unique history. Books such as *The World's Religions*,[4] Huston Smith's thoughtful and clear presentation of certain major religions one by one, can be consulted to see each tradition as a whole. In contrast, this study does not seek to give the history of any single tradition. Here, because the focus is on one theme — revelation — it includes examples of religious phenomena found in the major religions while at the same time introducing traditions that might be less well known, such as ancient Scandinavian religion or Tenrikyo, a new religion of Japan. Recognizing what religions have in common helps people overcome misconceptions about forms of religious expression that might be new or foreign. For example, an analysis of spirit mediation shows that so-called spirit possession, which is found in three-quarters of the societies worldwide, and Christian inspiration are related. One is a form of spirit mediation where the spirit is in full control of the human medium; the other, where the medium remains conscious and in control but has the option of allowing the spirit to influence his or her life.

Recognizing revelation as common to all faiths is furthered, too, by presenting each type of revelation without any personal judgment. In this study, I do not ask what is true or what is better. Instead of judging the value of various sacred traditions, the effort is towards description of what exists and a corresponding deeper understanding of our neighbors and ourselves.

Finally, I seek to avoid a Western bias by not slanting towards a monotheistic perspective; nor is the religion of any elite the lens through which all of religious experience is seen.

Part One.
A Phenomenology
of Revelation

Chapter 1

Finding Common Ground: The Experience of Revelation

What would we learn if, like interested and well-meaning travelers, we were to ask religious people all over the world and throughout time: "What is your religion and where does it come from?" Would a religious person be able to accept theories that say, "Your most valued beliefs are nothing more than 'psychological crutches' or 'social control mechanisms'"?[1] Not likely. What religious people tell us is something quite different: "Our religion consists of beliefs and traditions based on teachings and sacred knowledge that we have received through divine revelation."

What does this mean? What is a revelation and what makes it divine? We must explore the answers to these questions if we are to begin to understand the human experience that defines each and every religion. Finding this common ground will provide us with a place from where we can then approach any religious tradition, both respectfully and thoughtfully. Standing on this common ground, we soon discover that each religious tradition is valued as sacred precisely because of its origin in what is felt to be a message from an invisible realm of spirit.

For example, many of the sacred beliefs and rituals of the Lakota[2] were given to them by White Buffalo Calf Woman in the early days of their people. Black Elk (1863–1950), a Lakota holy man,[3] relates how certain customs of his people developed in response to her revelations.[4] Central to the religious life of this Native American people is the sacred pipe. Sitting in a circle they share the pipe. Each one inhales the smoke and then passes the pipe along to his or her neighbor. By means of this ceremony the Lakota participate in a community made up of the people and their gods. As the smoke goes up to heaven, it connects them with the spirits, such as Wakan Tanka, the Great

Spirit.[5] As they pass the pipe around, the smoke connects them to one another.

According to Black Elk, this religious rite is not something that people made up on their own. No, the Lakota are faithfully following the teachings of White Buffalo Calf Woman, a wakan woman who brought them the pipe and taught them how to use it. A wakan woman is what the Lakota call a goddess. The word *wakan* means both "holy" and "powerful." White Buffalo Calf Woman is one of the names for the Lakota goddess Falling Star, the daughter of the Moon and the Sun, a goddess who appeared to the people first as a beautiful woman and then later as a buffalo.

One day long ago two young hunters were in the forest searching for game when they came upon a lovely maiden, standing alone in the midst of the trees. Her beauty was so remarkable that each responded according to his nature: One young man wanted to possess her; blinded to the sacredness of the one standing before him, he felt only lustful longings arising within him. The second young man, on the other hand, felt humbled by what he saw; recognizing that she was a wakan woman, he paid homage to the maiden.

The woman invited the first young man to come closer. As he approached her, the two figures were surrounded by a cloud and disappeared from view. When the cloud lifted, the woman stood alone. At her feet lay the bones of the man, covered with snakes.

She then turned to the second young man, telling him to remember all that he had seen. He should return to his chief, Standing Hollow Horn, and ask him to set up a large tipi as a meeting place for all the people. As soon as they were gathered together in this place, she would come to share with them an important teaching.

All proceeded according to her wish, and the spirit woman appeared before the chief and his people. Upon arriving, she gave to Standing Hollow Horn a pipe. The bowl of the pipe was red stone; its stem, wood. Hanging from the stem were twelve feathers representing the eagle and all the birds. The maiden handed the pipe to the chief, saying that it was a sacred pipe that would carry the prayers of the people to the highest god, Wakan Tanka.

> The *wakan* woman then touched the foot of the pipe to the round stone which lay upon the ground, and said: "With this pipe you will be bound to all your relatives: your Grandfather and Father, your Grandmother and Mother. This round rock, which is made of the same red stone as the bowl of the pipe, your Father *Wakan Tanka* has also given to you. It is the Earth, your Grandmother

1. Finding Common Ground: The Experience of Revelation

and Mother, and it is where you will live and increase.... All of this is sacred and so do not forget! Every dawn as it comes is a holy event, and every day is holy, for the light comes from your Father *Wakan Tanka*; and also you must always remember that the two-leggeds and all the other peoples who stand upon this earth are sacred and should be treated as such.[6]

On this first visit to the ancestors of Black Elk, the goddess not only gave them the gift of the pipe, she also taught them how to care for the dead. She told the people that when a person dies, that day becomes a holy day and must be treated as such; moreover, for the next seven days the soul of the deceased must be prepared by means of rituals for final liberation, that is, a return to the spirit world.

After imparting this teaching, the woman departed. She circled the tipi and then walked some distance before sitting down in the high grass. When she stood up again, she no longer had the form of a woman. Now she appeared as a young red and brown buffalo calf. This calf walked a little ways, lay down, and then stood up as a white buffalo. Once more the white buffalo rolled on the ground and became a black buffalo, which bowed to the four directions and then disappeared.

Black Elk tells us that this is just one example of how his people received the many sacred traditions that they practice.[7] Other teachings were received through other revelatory experiences, especially visions. We see how both the pipe and the teachings of White Buffalo Calf Woman are sacred to the Lakota because they come from a holy source, from the spirit world that includes the wakan woman and Wakan Tanka.

It is in this way that religions differ from ideologies, which are not regarded as holy nor associated with revelation. An ideological tradition, such as positivism or Marxism, may also include many rituals and beliefs. It may even be a compelling way of life. Based on an idea — a human insight into the nature of reality — an ideology, however, makes no claims to divine guidance. Thus, any philosophy that rejects revelation can serve as the foundation of a way of life without being a religion.

For example, according to positivism, true knowledge can only be based on empirical experience, that is, events known by means of the bodily senses: touch, taste, sight, hearing, and smell. Science, not religion, should provide humankind with its values and goals. Auguste Comte (1798–1857) was first to speak of a "positive philosophy," a philosophical system and way of life based on explicit facts and observable phenomena.[8] He called himself an atheist (one who believes that gods do not exist) and proposed a new "religion of humanity," with its focus on meeting the earthly needs of all human beings.

In a similar way, Marxism also rejects revelation. Through an analysis of history and the various factors that appear to control social realities, Karl Marx (1818–1883) articulated a model for all of human life: scientific socialism.[9] His goal was the creation of a paradise on earth, that is, to establish peace and equality among humankind while providing for the physical and social needs of the individual person. In a way, Marx continued to express an eschatological vision[10] common in Western religions — something like the kingdom of God, found in the teachings of Jesus. However, Marx removes the idea of faith in God from his socialist utopia, and in its place we find a reliance on human reason, the ability to identify problems and solve them without recourse to supernatural help.

The goal of any ideology is to solve problems with the help of human skills, such as objective reasoning, rather than with the help of the gods. Religious people see things differently: in direct contrast to the ideologists, they tell us that subjective experiences can also be important, even sacred. Disclosing a reality beyond the material world that we know through our senses, revelations can show us how to live and how to find meaning in our lives. The value of subjective experience was challenged during the eighteenth century, commonly known as the European Enlightenment, or Age of Reason, a time when ancient Greek philosophical theories explaining the nature of religion reappeared. At first, the emphasis lay on discovering rational forms of religion and rejecting all that appeared to be irrational. Deism, a philosophical system that saw God as the divine craftsman, who created the world according to scientific principles and then withdrew to allow it to function on its own, is representative of this attitude towards religion. At the same time, it became popular to use the word *superstition* when referring to religious beliefs and practices that supposedly lacked any "rational" basis.[11]

The Evolutionists, for example, argued that superstition, like magic, was characteristic of so-called less evolved religions. The more evolved a religion, the more rational and ethical it became, in their eyes. Applying the theories of the English naturalist Charles Darwin (1809–1882), which described the evolution of plants and animals from simpler to more complex forms, the Evolutionists decided that religions, too, must have evolved. As a result they set out to determine what the so-called evolutionary stages of religion might be. They argued about what the religion of prehistoric peoples must have been like. Were the earliest humans polytheists, monotheists, or perhaps animistic — that is, seeing soul (Latin, *anima*) at work in all natural phenomena, as defined in the theory of English ethnologist Edward Burnett Tylor (1832–1917)? Tylor was one of the first to use the model of biological evolution to interpret the history of religions generally. In his *Primitive Culture*, he theorizes that early humans had no scientific understanding of the workings of nature and so they imagined that soul-like beings caused all things to happen.[12] He thus coined the word *animism* to denote what in his view is the earliest form of religion, from which all others evolve.

Tylor also set forth the theory that contemporary small societies resemble in kind the earliest societies of humans. As a result, he thought it possible to study small societies that had long existed in isolation in order to know more about early human communities. Of course, this idea is no longer generally accepted, but at the time, it did have one very positive effect on the study of religion. In a way, Tylor was the founder of what we now call the anthropology of religion. His students actively left home to live in small societies throughout the world, studying the languages and religious traditions of these groups with the conviction that they were simultaneously learning about prehistoric cultures. What these scholars then learned in the field has vastly changed our understanding of religion in general.

Another Evolutionist was John Lubbock (1834–1913), who assumed that prehistoric humans were naturally atheistic and lacked religion altogether.[13] His model for the evolution of religion shows five stages developing one after the other out of this primary, non-religious condition.

1. atheism (earliest human societies)
2. nature worship
3. magic
4. polytheism
5. monotheism
6. moral atheism

Nature worship, in his view, exists when people begin to worship cosmic forces — such as the sun, fire, and the ocean — recognizing their power to determine natural events. This is then followed by a period dominated by magic, the human attempt to use non-rational activities in order to control supernatural forces. Polytheism (worship of many personal deities) and monotheism (worship of one personal God) are, in his mind, more sophisticated ways of imagining supernatural beings, because the gods and goddesses exhibit the best qualities found in human nature: justice, love, and wisdom. Finally, Lubbock suggests that the stages of religion will ultimately give way to an age of secular morality, based on reason, not faith.

Influenced by the thinkers of the Enlightenment, who regarded any non-rational activity as degenerate, Lubbock felt that the only important contribution of any specific religion to social life lay in its ethics — the teachings of how to live a moral life. So he identifies morality as the final achievement in the evolution of religion.

The traditions of Black Elk's people probably would have been explained by the evolutionist E. B. Tylor as evidence of their "pre-scientific" or "animistic" thinking. John Lubbock might have placed the Lakota in the evolutionary stage of polytheism, which, he argues, is less evolved than both monotheism and some kind of purely ethical system.

In contrast, twentieth-century scholars of religion began to view non-rational forms of religion in a less condescending manner. Rejecting derogatory terms, such as *superstition* and *animism*, they recognized the essential role of subjective experience at the heart of all religions. Thus, in 1917, a German scholar by the name of Rudolf Otto (1869–1937) wrote a book entitled *Das Heilige* (literally, "The Holy"),[14] wherein he urges modern scholars of religion to recognize and understand the value and necessity of non-rational forms of religion. Although trained as a Christian theologian, Otto learned Sanskrit and translated numerous Hindu scriptures. Having traveled widely in both Asia and the Near East, Otto recognized that the feeling that a religion is sacred simply cannot occur without some kind of direct experience of what he called the Holy (or the *numen*, to use a comparable Latin term). By using non-personal terms to refer to the divine, Otto was able to redirect the discussion away from an exclusive focus on the monotheistic experience of one God so as to include in it the great variety of religions. For Otto, religion is both rational and non-rational. It begins with the immediate, subjective experience of the divine, which draws people into worship and compels them to transform their lives. This is then followed by thoughtful interpretation of revelation by religious thinkers and the systematic development of theology and ethical teachings.

Rudolf Otto, we can imagine, would find in Black Elk's story of White

1. Finding Common Ground: The Experience of Revelation

Buffalo Calf Woman both rational and non-rational elements: On the one hand, her teaching has an ethical component that embraces all of creation and prescribes as sacred the "rational" ideas of compassion and respect for all living beings. At the same time, the meeting with White Buffalo Calf Woman is visionary and miraculous. The people feel her sacredness (she is wakan), and she changes her form quite easily, from woman to buffalo in the blink of an eye. Otto's work supported a new approach to religion, one that could view both rational and non-rational forms of religion as essentially integral.

Like Otto, the Romanian historian of religions Mircea Eliade (1907–1986) utilized non-theological terms so as to provide a neutral language when talking about more than one tradition. To refer to revelation, or the experience of the divine, he used the term *hierophany*, which derives from two Greek words that together mean "the appearance of something supernatural."[15] The term does not signify the actual existence of a supernatural entity but only the fact of the experience. The human being *feels* the presence of something holy, sacred, divine. The subjective experience is real, regardless of whatever caused it to happen.

Eliade then goes on to identify the great variety of religious phenomena that make up the human response to the hierophanies: these are the universal religious themes, such as creation myths, new year festivals, rituals of initiation, funerary beliefs and rituals, and so on. He would probably have referred to White Buffalo Calf Woman as belonging to the category of "culture heroes and heroines." These are mythical beings[16] who are said to have taught the people how to live. Culture heroes may participate in the creation of the world, but more importantly, they appear after the creation of the first ancestors, to whom they give the tools of civilization: White Buffalo Calf Woman gave the Lakota the pipe and its sacred power to connect the people with the spirit world.

In this study, I am indebted to both Otto and Eliade for their emphasis on the value of both rational and non-rational forms of religion. Further, following Eliade's method of identifying and explicating universal religious themes, it is my goal to examine more closely the hierophany itself—that is to say, the experience of revelation—analyzing its structural components and identifying its different types. Furthermore, both scholars have demonstrated the usefulness of developing a "neutral" language for talking about religion. In this way a variety of traditions can belong to the discussion at the same time. As far as I can, I try to employ terminology that is not overly laden with theological meaning or religious bias towards any one culture. Or else I try to make it clear how I am using a term, perhaps differently from its original intent.

Defining Revelation

So let us begin with a definition of revelation, one that might be recognized by all religious people as both useful and meaningful.

> A revelation is a human experience that is interpreted subjectively as a message from the spirit world.

The terminology of our definition is important enough for us to examine in detail:

a. *human experience:* All that we know about a revelation is based on what people tell us about their own experiences. We cannot make metaphysical claims, either for or against the "reality" of a revelation. We cannot prove whether the vision of White Buffalo Calf Woman was "true" in any objective way. The truth of the experience is personal: whatever happens to us affects our being, regardless of the nature of the event. Thus, a dream can be deeply disturbing or inspiring. A friendship can transform our lives. Human beings have an inner life that has truth inaccessible to science.

b. *subjectively interpreted:* This refers to the relativity of revelation. Two people might experience the same thing but interpret it differently. We are subjects of our experience and interpret what happens to us according to our own personal pasts and the traditions by which we live. Thus, if a young American woman were to have a dream in which White Buffalo Calf Woman appeared and asked her to participate in a sacred pipe ceremony, she might interpret the dream in a variety of ways. If she were Native American, she might want to learn all she could about the Lakota and perhaps visit them to understand better her dream. If she belonged to a monotheistic tradition, such as Judaism or Islam, she might consider the images insignificant and forget the dream soon after awakening.

c. *message:* The content of the revelation is interpreted to be some type of message, a communication of some kind. It has meaning.

1. Finding Common Ground: The Experience of Revelation

d. *from:* The message is interpreted as coming from some spirit being or spirit reality. It is not a message to be sent to that reality: that would most likely be a prayer. People pray to the gods; they receive revelations from them.

e. *spirit world:* Every culture contains some visualization of the spirit world. This is the result of the revelatory experiences of the people over time. For example, many Christians see the spirit world as comprised of God, Jesus, and the Holy Spirit, together with all the saints in heaven. Mahayana Buddhists envision the spirit world populated with bodhisattvas and buddhas. There are many ways that different peoples describe the spirit world. In fact, these symbolic visualizations are always changing — sometimes slowly, imperceptibly; at other times, quickly.

This last characteristic of revelation requires a little more discussion at this time. It is difficult to talk about the great variety of religious traditions, because there are so many different ideas about the make-up of the "spirit world." If we take the time now to acknowledge this difficulty, it may then allow us to speak generally about the "spirit world" knowing more specifically to what this general term then refers.

Perhaps the scholarly term that applies here is *cosmology*, which derives from two Greek words: *kosmos* and *logos*. *Kosmos* means beautiful order; it is the Greek word for the universe. A word that has many meanings, *logos* is best translated in this context as "study." Thus the cosmology is the study of the universe. Each culture has a cosmology, which is the way the people visualize the world in which they live. In a predominantly scientific context, cosmology refers to the science of the universe and its origins; in traditional religious societies, it refers to a universe that comprises both the realm of humans *and* the realm of spirit (or the spirits).

Traditional cosmologies include descriptions of the cosmological map (where the ancestors live, for example) while identifying the various inhabitants of the universe (gods, ancestors, humans, animals, and so on). Thus, the cosmological map of a given culture might begin with the domain inhabited by human beings; and there is a certain consistency to this, as humans live on the earth. Jungle, desert, mountain, or island — these homelands differ, but all are recognizable to us as part of the earth. It is in ideas about where the spirits live that there are such great differences.

In some cultures, the spirits are close at hand, living in the land, the stream nearby, the grove of trees over the hill, and so on. The Chinese *Classic of the Mountains and Seas* (c. 300 BCE to 200 CE) introduces the reader to the ordered realm of early Chinese peoples, surrounded by foreign lands filled with strange human-like creatures. Occupying the center of the world, ancient China is depicted as consisting of 447 mountains, from which flow myriad rivers. Especially the mountains are the dwelling places of spirit beings, such as Mount Jade, the home of the Queen Mother of the West: "In appearance, Queen Mother of the West looks like a human, but she has a leopard's tail and the fangs of a tigress, and she is good at whistling. She wears a victory crown on her tangled hair. She presides over the Catastrophes from the Sky and the Five Destructive Forces."[17]

Elsewhere, it is the sky that is the home of the spirits. The inhabitants of ancient Sumer (modern-day Iraq) believed that the gods lived in the heavens and that the celestial lights were actually the bodies of such spirits. Scholars refer to their belief as astral religion — the worship of stars as divine beings. For the Sumerians the most important deities appeared in the sky as the sun, the moon, and the morning star (the planet Venus). These celestial bodies were observed every day and every night. Their movements were recorded by astrologers in order to discern any messages that the gods might have for humankind.[18]

Common also is the belief that the home of the gods lies in the underworld, below the surface of the earth. Among the Hopi there are tales of a creator goddess called Spider Woman, who shared the primordial reality with Tawa, the Sun God. "All the mysteries and power of the Above belonged to Tawa, while Spider Woman controlled the magic of the Below. In the Underworld, abode of the gods, they dwelt and they were All."[19]

Sometimes the gods or spirits live in a world under the ocean. Knud Rasmussen in his *Intellectual Culture of the Iglulik Eskimos*[20] describes a ritual in which the spirit of a shaman leaves the body and journeys to the bottom of the ocean where he finds the palace of Takánakapsâluk, the Mother of the Sea Animals. Especially when his people have no success in hunting, he will visit the goddess to learn the cause and to appeal to her for help. For those who participate in Vodou, an African-American form of Christianity found in Haiti and the United States, the ancestors go to live under the ocean. One of the spirits that they honor is Lasyrenn, who appears as a mermaid — part woman and part fish. "When people catch a glimpse of Lasyrenn beneath the water, they feel her beckoning them to come with her back to Ginen, … the ancestral home and the dwelling place of the *lwa* [spirits]."[21]

1. Finding Common Ground: The Experience of Revelation

Indeed, the spirits can live anywhere: on the edge of the world, in caves, even in volcanoes. And cosmologies are both simple and complex. Elaborate cosmologies, such as that of the ancient Scandinavians, will present a map of reality with different realms connected by a cosmic tree or mountain. The *Voluspa*, or Prophecy of the Seeress, depicts the ancient Norse account of the universe — its creation and its destiny.[22] At the center is the cosmic tree, Yggdrasill, a gigantic ash, whose branches spread out over both the heavens and the earth. Its three roots reach far down into the underworld: one leads to the home of the Aesir, one race of gods; another provides shelter for the frost giants; and the third root serves as a road to the land of the dead, where the goddess Hel is queen. But the gods are not restricted to living in the underworld: some live in the sea, others in the mountains, and many build great fortresses in the sky. Nor are the gods, frost giants, and ancestors the only spirit beings in Scandinavian cosmology. There are also elves, dwarves, and the World Snake, whose body encircles the ocean, as well as many other strange and wonderful creatures.

Contradictions often appear in any given map of the cosmos. Perhaps this happens when more than one tradition attains authority. For example, early Christians held two beliefs concurrently about God's dwelling place: on the one hand, there was the idea that God's dwelling place lay in an eternal realm above the fixed stars, in heaven; at the same time, other Christians believed that the kingdom of God would be a paradise on a newly created earth (sort of a restored Eden) after the present world was first destroyed by fire. This contradiction reflects the historical context of early Christianity, which began within the Jewish traditions of Palestine but ultimately survived in its non–Jewish form because of the missionary activity of early Christians, such as Paul and Peter. The restoration of paradise links us to Jewish traditions about the Garden of Eden; whereas the Hellenistic view of a celestial realm where death does not exist is the source of Christian ideas about a heaven.

The Hellenistic view is commonly referred to as the Ptolemaic cosmology. It predominated in the West from the time of the Alexandrian astronomer Claudius Ptolemaeus (c. 100–170), who recorded the generally accepted Hellenistic cosmology in his *Almagest*. According to this view, the earth was situated in the center of seven concentric spheres, each one moved by a heavenly being (the sun, the moon, and the five visible planets). Below the moon — with its changing appearance — existed birth, growth, and death;

above the moon was the eternal realm where there was no change, hence no death. The Scientific Revolution of the seventeenth century led to a complete revision of this cosmology, placing the sun in the center and denying the existence of two distinct realms following different laws. Instead the law of gravity governs everywhere, below and above the moon.

Apart from the great variety of cosmic maps, there are as many if not more visions of the inhabitants of the spirit world. Monotheists, such as Jews, Christians, Muslims, and the Baha'i, believe in the existence of one God only. But they may also recognize the reality of angels, and even devils, as well as heavenly saints and martyrs. Elsewhere, among polytheists, the number of spirit beings can seem uncountable. Very often there is a belief in the ancestors. From Africa to China and Japan, the close relationship between the living and the deceased members of a family are central in daily ritual life. Ancestors are more powerful than the living; they can serve as intermediaries with other, even more powerful spirits.

Spirit beings can take on many forms when they make themselves known to humans. Especially common are animal forms, human forms, and even a mixture of the two. The San (Bushmen) of southern Africa envision their gods in the form of animals. The writer Laurens van der Post (1906–1996), whose childhood nanny was part San, has recorded many of their sacred stories.[23] Especially, prominent are the tales of Mantis and Eland. Mantis, who takes the tiny form of a preying mantis, is a creator god. He often sits between the horns or toes of his beloved Eland (having the appearance of an African antelope), whom he calls his son.

The wakan woman who gave the Lakota the gift of the sacred pipe so that they could communicate with the gods appeared both as a woman and as a buffalo. In a similar fashion, for the people of ancient Egypt it was quite usual to envision their gods sometimes in animal form, sometimes in human form, sometimes as a combination of both. For example, the goddess Hathor became associated with the royal family already during the second dynasty (prior to 2700 BCE). In Egyptian iconography she appears often as a wild cow nursing the young king, or as a woman with the horns of a cow. Perhaps the combination of human and animal characteristics more immediately conveys the sense of an "other than natural" being: like the human, like the animal, but actually neither. It suggests something supernatural, monstrous.

Originally the word *monster* carried the meaning of its Latin parent, *monstrum*: "pointing to" something extraordinary. Rehabilitation of the term

1. Finding Common Ground: The Experience of Revelation

allows us to call any creature of the imagination — one that cannot be found in nature — as a monster. Thus, there are both positive and negative monsters: angels, for example, are often shown to be human-like beings with the wings of birds. Yet they are, as messengers of the gods, always in service of what is good. The wise and good Queen Mother of the West, teacher of immortality, appears as we have noted already in the form of a woman with leopard and tiger characteristics. Of course, monsters can also signify evil spirits, such as "the great red dragon with seven heads and ten horns" who appears in the John's apocalyptic vision and whom John identifies as the embodiment of the Devil.[24]

While religious visions filled with symbols of all kinds are common, not all revelations include such imagery. There is also the ineffable experience of the divine reality as encountered by the mystics. For example, some Christian mystics speak of the "godhead" to suggest a sense of the reality that lies beyond any image or symbol for God; and in India, there is the expression Nirguna-Brahman, which means Brahman (or the Absolute) without qualities. This is the divine in so far as it is indescribably beyond all opposites. Further, both Hindus and Buddhists may use the term *nirvana* to refer to the ultimate reality. This impersonal and rather abstract term points to a reality that transcends all images.

In this study, we will use the term *spirit world* to refer to any and all of these very diverse ways of naming the realm where revelations originate. The word *spirit* is particularly apt here since it can be imagined as an individual spirit capable of manifestation and also it can refer to undifferentiated spirit reality.

Additional Examples of Revelation

Let us now look at further examples of revelations as they appear in literary religious traditions and the world religions. These cultural settings differ from that of the Lakota, who might be classified as having an oral religious tradition.

I am using the expression *oral religious traditions* to refer to those traditions of small societies that lack a written language: such as the Lakota, the pre–Christian Scandinavians, the San of South Africa, and many, many more. Because there is no written text, the account of each revelation is memorized and taught to succeeding generations. Often different versions of the same basic tale are all deemed quite acceptable.

In literary traditions, it is common for important or official revelations to be preserved in writing. Societies that have a written language usually also have a complex economic system that includes specialized occupations: rulers, soldiers, farmers, artisans, and so forth. Sometimes there is even a group of people whose job is to preserve the religious tradition: the priesthood. Ancient Sumerians had both priests and astrologers, who recorded the movements of the star gods. Other peoples that have sacred writings still in use today include the Jews as well as those who live in India or China. Often, however, as soon as a written form of a revelation exists, there is a tendency to see it as authoritative. Ongoing revelation may continue to be vital, but the written text serves as the guiding standard for what is orthodox, or acceptable.

In China, for example, the literary tradition associated with Daoism is both complex and ancient. Daoism refers to both early mystical texts, such as the *Dao De Jing* attributed to Lao Zi and the *Zhuang Zi*,[25] as well as to various religious movements that teach the people how to attain immortality. There are many sacred Daoist writings, and so we can speak of it as a literary religious tradition. In these writings the word Dao, often translated as "the way," refers to the ultimate source of all things:

> There is a thing confusedly formed,
> Born before heaven and earth.
> Silent and void
> It stands alone and does not change,
> Goes round and does not weary.
> It is capable of being the mother of the world.
> I know not its name
> So I style it "the way."[26]

Tradition relates the story of the well-known Daoist Zhang Ling; also called Zhang Dao Ling, he lived in Sichuan at the end of the Han period (second century CE). In 142, while meditating in a mountain cave, Zhang experienced a vision of Lao Zi in his form as a god. Lao Zi complained that the people had lost sight of all that was true and just. Instead, they were being drawn into the worship of demons.[27] The god gave him a teaching called the "Doctrine of the Orthodox One [Resting on] the Authority of the Alliance," which announced the end of the demon-ruled Six Heavens and the establishment of a golden age under the dominion of the Three Heavens.

1. Finding Common Ground: The Experience of Revelation

In the vision, Lao Zi bestowed on Zhang a new name and a commission. Calling him Celestial Master, Lao Zi commanded him to reform the religion of the people. Henceforth, they must worship only the gods of the Alliance. Instead of animal sacrifice they must make offerings of cooked vegetables. Further, the religious leaders must not accept payment. These leaders were later called libationers, "an old term used in lay society for the chief notable who presided at local banquets and was first to make an offering of wine."[28] Eventually, Zhang succeeded in organizing a hierarchy of male and female libationers. Later, around 750, the Celestial Master School of Daoism[29] would move to the Dragon-Tiger Mountain of Jiangxi; and after the Communist revolution in China, on to Taiwan.

Some literary traditions are not identified with any one culture. These are the so-called world religions. They usually have a founder, such as Jesus of Nazareth, the Christ, in Christianity and Siddhartha Gautama, the historical Buddha, in Buddhism. Usually, the message of a specific world religion is expressed in such a way that it is easily accepted by people in very different societies. Other examples of world religions are Islam, Tenrikyo from Japan, and Bahá'í, originating in Iran. Most religious traditions exist as integral parts of a specific culture, and one is simply born into a community defined by that culture and religion. In contrast, one must "become" a member of a world religion. This may involve studying the teachings and practices of the religion and even sometimes, undergoing ritual initiation: for example, in Christianity baptism with water is the ceremony that begins the Christian's participation in the religion.

Often world religions begin as reform movements within a tradition from which they then separate. Perhaps this is the reason that they often make claims of exclusivity, insisting that the revelation experienced by the religion's founder is actually the final, or only, divine revelation. The Bahá'í followers of Mirza Husayn 'Ali Nuri (1817–1892), also known as Baha' Allah ("the glory of God"), believe — as he did — that God sends new prophets in every age. Thus, they recognize as valid the teachings of Moses, Jesus, and the Buddha. But at the same time, they claim that Baha' Allah is the prophet for this age. For the next thousand years or so, his teachings alone represent God's will for humankind.

A similar belief is found in Islam, where the prophet Muhammad ibn Abdallah (570–632 CE) is called the Seal of the Prophets. This means that Muhammad's teachings serve as a closing seal on what had gone before. Islam is found all over the world. As a world religion it has taken root in cultures as different as that of Iraq, Indonesia, and the United States. Like all sacred traditions, Islam is based on the experience of revelation: in this case, it is the visions of Muhammad that serve as the foundation of the religion.

In seventh-century Arabia, the prophet Muhammad heard the voices of Allah (Arabic, *al-Lah*, "God") and his angels. Although he himself could not write, he could recite aloud what he heard and others could then write down his words. Eventually these texts were collected and compiled and the revelations to Muhammad became the Qur'an, the sacred book of Islam.[30]

Muhammad was born in Mecca and until he was six years old he was raised by his mother and her family because his father was deceased. Then, when his mother died, he came first under the care of his paternal grandfather and then later, his father's brother. As an adult, he became a successful merchant and family man until one day he experienced a religious vision that changed his life. The religion of the Arabs at the time was polytheistic, that is, the worship of many gods and goddesses. The chief attraction of Mecca was that it possessed a shrine, the Ka'bah (Arabic, "cube"), which was the object of popular religious pilgrimage. Muhammad's vision would draw him away from polytheism and cause him to rededicate the Ka'bah to the "one true god," Allah.

When Muhammad was a grown man, he began to have strange dreams, so every year he would spend one month living in a cave in a nearby mountain praying and fasting. There he had a vision: An angel by the name of Gabriel appeared to him.[31] In Hebrew tradition, Gabriel (Hebrew, "God is almighty") is one of the four chief angels of God. In the Hebrew Bible, Gabriel appears to the prophet Daniel; in the Christian New Testament, he appears to both Mary, the mother of Jesus, and to Zachariah, the father of John the Baptist. Thus, he serves to link into one great tradition all three biblical religions.

Gabriel announced to Muhammad that he was a prophet of Allah and commanded him to "recite." But Muhammad was afraid. This happened many times. At one point, Muhammad wanted to kill himself, he was so afraid. But his wife Khadijah, in her wisdom, reassured him saying, "Rejoice, for by Allah, Allah will never put thee to shame."[32] Gradually, Muhammad accepted God's command and became the leader of a religious community that continues to thrive all over the world.

Visions are one kind of revelation. The Lakota have visions of White Buffalo Calf Woman, a sacred spirit (or goddess); Zhang Ling saw visions

1. Finding Common Ground: The Experience of Revelation

of Lao Zi, whose *Dao De Jing* serves also as one of the sacred texts in Celestial Master Daoism; Muhammad saw the angel Gabriel, who announced to him his role as God's prophet. In Christianity there are also many important visions, but the one that lies at the very heart of this world religion is the visionary experience of the risen Christ. The first Christians believed that Jesus of Nazareth was the Son of God and the king who would rule in God's kingdom, because they witnessed his return from death. This is called the Resurrection; in Christian thought, the resurrection of Jesus is a sign that death's power has been broken once and for all. It is celebrated with great joy and hope every spring in the Easter festival, the holiest day of the Christian year.

Jesus of Nazareth (c. 7/6 BCE–c. 30 CE) was a Jew who lived in Palestine during the period of the Roman Empire.[33] His father was a carpenter, and Jesus himself was uneducated. Still, he was well versed in the religious traditions of Judaism. At a time when many Jews were longing for independence from Rome, having suffered foreign rulers for over five hundred years, Jesus preached the imminent arrival of God's kingdom. Through his ministry of healing the sick in body and mind as well as his compassion for the poor and the outcast in society, he demonstrated his understanding of what it means when God rules in human lives. But his enemies saw in him some kind of threat — political or religious — and for this he was crucified, the Roman form of execution. His broken and lifeless body was placed in a borrowed tomb, because by then it was the Sabbath, or Jewish holy day. After the Sabbath, on the first day of the week, the women who befriended Jesus went to the tomb to prepare his body for burial. But the body was gone. Various accounts relate how Jesus then appeared to his followers.[34]

For example, chapter sixteen of the Gospel according to Mark describes how it was the women who were first to learn that Jesus was raised from the dead. Early Sunday morning three women from among his followers went to the tomb carrying aromatic oils in order to prepare his corpse for burial. They found that the protective stone placed at the opening of the tomb had been moved away, and the tomb was empty. Inside sat a youth dressed in white robes, who declared: "Fear nothing; you are looking for Jesus of Nazareth, who was crucified. He has been raised again; he is not here; look, there is the place where they laid him." Frightened, the women fled and kept silent.

Then the author of Mark tells about the first actual appearance of the

Part One. A Phenomenology of Revelation

risen Christ: "When he had risen from the dead early on Sunday morning [Jesus] appeared first to Mary of Magdala, from whom he had formerly cast out seven devils." Mary is not afraid. She tells the good news to the other followers of Jesus. However, they do not believe her.

Again Jesus appeared "in a different guise" to two of his followers as they were walking in the countryside. These, like Mary of Magdala, reported their experience. Still, no one believed them.

Finally, Jesus appears to his disciples while they are eating a meal. He reproaches them for their inability to believe that he could have returned from the dead.

Then, according to the Acts of the Apostles, which recounts the early history of the church, the resurrected Jesus remained for a while together with his disciples, who wanted to know when he would set up his kingdom. Jesus answered, "It is not for you to know about dates or times, which the Father has set within his own control."[35] In the meantime, they were to travel throughout the world and spread the good news of the Resurrection and all that it means for humankind. Thus, Christians believe that at the end of this age, Jesus will return and establish the kingdom of God. At that time, all human beings will be, like Jesus, raised from the dead, and those who love and follow him will live eternally in his kingdom.

Although visions are very common, they are by no means the only way that people receive revelations. One important type of revelation is the mystical experience, such as the enlightenment of the historical Buddha.[36] Unlike a vision, the mystical experience does not reveal a spirit being (deity, angel, and so on). In the mystical experience the consciousness of the human being merges with a larger reality; and the mystic perceives everything from a perspective that lacks the limitations of ordinary human perception. Some Christians and Muslims interpret this form of revelation as union with God; Buddhists call it nirvana, unconditioned reality.

The historical Buddha, founder of what we now call Buddhism, was Siddhartha Gautama, who lived in northern India perhaps from 566 to 486 BCE.[37] His title, the Buddha, means "the one who is awakened," and it refers to his experience of enlightenment, a transformation of consciousness that frees one from both death and all forms of suffering.

In his efforts to attain nirvana, Siddhartha studied with different masters and practiced extreme austerities for many years. These austerities included fasting, homelessness, celibacy, meditation, and breath control. Yet, despite

1. Finding Common Ground: The Experience of Revelation

his efforts, he failed to attain his goal. Finally, he decided to balance the austerities with more attention to the needs of the body. Feeling stronger, he then sat under the Bodhi Tree (or Tree of Enlightenment) and meditated all night. At dawn, "the great seer took up the position which knows no more alteration, and the leader of all reached the state of all-knowledge.... He thought: 'Here I have found freedom,' and he knew that the longings of his heart had at last come to fulfillment."[38]

After Siddhartha became enlightened, he spent the rest of his life teaching others. "Nirvana have I now obtained, and I am not the same as others are.... Having crossed the ocean of suffering, I must help others to cross it. Freed myself, I must set others free. This is the vow which I made in the past when I saw all that lives in distress."[39] Eventually, he founded a community of monks and nuns and taught them his method for attaining buddhahood.

These are but a few examples of human experiences that have been interpreted as messages from the spirit world. Over time and around the world, such revelations have served to guide people and teach them how to live meaningful lives. A revelation can be simple or dramatic; like a seed, it can seem small and insignificant, and yet give rise to a vast and complex tradition.

Chapter 2

Expressing Revelation: Sacred Art, Sacred Place, and Sacred Time

What happens once people have interpreted an event as a revelation? How do they feel, and how do they respond? Rudolf Otto tells us that in the presence of any kind of spirit, people typically feel two emotions: awe and fascination.[1]

Religious awe is a sense of being confronted with some reality that is both overwhelming and other-than-natural. One may feel a fear that is not exactly natural fear but rather a reaction to what is uncanny: "The awe or 'dread' may indeed be so overwhelmingly great that it seems to penetrate to the very marrow, making the man's hair bristle and his limbs quake. But it may also steal upon him almost unobserved as the gentlest of agitations, a mere fleeting shadow passing across his mood."[2]

The American psychologist William James (1842–1910) in his book *The Varieties of Religious Experience* focuses likewise on the feelings evoked by the experience of revelation. Sometimes dread is the dominating emotion, as in this example of a person who feels the presence of an invisible spirit:

> Quite early in the night I was awakened.... I felt as if I had been aroused intentionally, and at first thought some one was breaking into the house.... I then turned on my side to go to sleep again, and immediately felt a consciousness of a presence in the room, and singular to state, it was not the consciousness of a live person, but of a spiritual presence. This may provoke a smile, but I can only tell you the facts as they occurred to me. I do not know how to better describe my sensations than by simply stating that I felt a consciousness of a spiritual presence.... I felt also at the same time a strong feeling of superstitious dread, as if something strange and fearful were about to happen.[3]

2. Expressing Revelation: Sacred Art, Sacred Place, and Sacred Time

This account comes from a person who was not actively seeking any religious experience. Indeed, revelations quite often do happen to people who have no prior religious orientation.

As seen above, Muhammad, too, felt awe or dread, when the angel Gabriel appeared before him as he sat praying in his mountain cave. When the spirit spoke to him, Muhammad was frightened! He fled in terror. Only the wise counsel of his wife gave him the courage to face this messenger from God.

The second emotion that Otto ascribes to the encounter with the holy is fascination. Attracted to the spiritual reality manifested in the experience of revelation, the person feels emotions of joy, wonder, relief, and love. Mircea Eliade focuses on the feeling of fascination when he speaks of the sacred as being perceived as absolutely real and of ultimate value: "Religious man's desire to live *in the sacred* is in fact equivalent to his desire to take up his abode in objective reality, not to let himself be paralyzed by the never-ceasing relativity of purely subjective experiences, to live in a real and effective world, and not in an illusion."[4] The hierophany, or appearance of the sacred, acts like a magnet on the one who experiences it.

The sexual attraction between male and female is one of the symbolic themes used to lend expression to such feelings of fascination towards the divine. Mahadeviyakka, sometimes called Akka Mahadevi,[5] was a woman who lived in southwestern India (today's Karnataka) during the twelfth century. She was devoted to the Hindu god Shiva, a divinity who often appears as an ascetic practitioner of meditation. Mahadeviyakka dedicated herself to Shiva, seeing him as her divine husband, whom she also called the Lord White as Jasmine. Her poetry describes her fascination with Shiva, her longing to be united with him, her adoration and love.

> Locks of shining red hair
> a crown of diamonds
> small beautiful teeth
> and eyes in a laughing face
> that light up fourteen worlds —
>   I saw His glory,
> and seeing, I quell today
> the famine in my eyes.
>
> I saw the haughty Master
> for whom men, all men,
> are but women, wives.

Part One. A Phenomenology of Revelation

> I saw the Great One
> who plays at love
> with Sakti,
> original to the world,
>
> I saw His stance
> and began to live.⁶

In this poem, the devotee describes her vision of Shiva. She has witnessed both his form and his glory, his divine radiance. As she is drawn to Shiva, in the same way all men are attracted — like a devoted wife to her husband — to God. The experience of Shiva's presence marks the moment of her spiritual birth.

Contact with the spirit world can cause a woman to fall to the ground in terror or the hair on a man's head to stand on end. On the other hand, the person might be filled with feelings of great joy and longing. Regardless of the emotion, such an encounter can lead to a fundamental change in a human life. The French saint Thérèse of the Lisieux (1873–1897) tells how one of her visions of Jesus turned her life around. In this vision Christ appears to Thérèse in his form as the infant Jesus.

> [O]n Christmas Day in 1886, the Divine Child, scarcely an hour old, flooded the darkness of my soul with radiant light. By becoming little and weak for love of me, He made me strong and full of courage, and with the arms He gave me, I went from one victory to another, and began to run as a giant.⁷

The vision, which occurred to her during a church service when she was not yet fourteen years old, marked a transition in Thérèse's life. From that point on the young woman was certain of her desire to become a Carmelite nun. Although underage, with the help of others and her strength of conviction, she succeeded and entered the cloistered convent of the Discalced Carmelites in Lisieux at the age of fifteen.

Every divine revelation evokes emotion of some kind: the feeling of fear or peace, joy or courage. Fascinated, the person is convinced that he or she is in the presence of some supernatural reality: something more real, more powerful, and more valuable than ordinary events. This sense of the divine or holy character of the spirit world makes a great impression on the person who receives a revelation. Therefore, it is in this context that we can ask: "After having the experience of a divine revelation, what does the person want to do?" And clearly the most common response to revelation is the need to share it with others. Sometimes the need is felt immediately; at other

2. Expressing Revelation: Sacred Art, Sacred Place, and Sacred Time

times, as in the case of Black Elk, it is felt with the passing of time. Not only does he relate how his ancestors came to know White Buffalo Calf Woman, Black Elk, the Lakota holy man, tells also of his own visions.

When he was about four years old, Black Elk began to hear voices. From the first, he was afraid: "It was like somebody calling me, and I thought it was my mother, but there was nobody there. This happened more than once and always made me afraid, so that I ran home."[8] The next year, after his grandfather had given him a gift of bow and arrows, Black Elk was riding horseback alongside a creek in the forest, when he saw a kingbird sitting in a tree. He was about to shoot the bird, when it spoke to him. "'Listen! A voice is calling you!' Then I looked up at the clouds, and two men were coming there, headfirst like arrows slanting down; and as they came, they sang a sacred song.... 'Behold, a sacred voice is calling you; / All over the sky a sacred voice is calling.'"[9] Black Elk was afraid to tell anyone about this vision, but he says he liked to think about it from time to time.

When he was nine years old, Black Elk fell ill, during which time he had what he calls a Great Vision. While his body lay as if dead in his parent's tipi, his spirit soared to the heavens. There he met six gods holding council in a tipi with a rainbow door. The oldest of these told him that they were his grandfathers and had brought him there in order to teach him. Black Elk's initial reaction to the "grandfathers" was one of dread: "His voice was very kind, but I shook all over with fear now, for I knew that these were not old men, but the Powers of the World."[10]

Lasting the entire twelve days that young Black Elk lay ill in his parents' tipi, the vision consisted of two primary scenarios: within the rainbow tipi and outside it. Inside the rainbow tipi, the six grandfathers give him a new name, Eagle Wing Stretches, and gifts of power: a wooden cup of water to give life; a bow to destroy it; a white wing for healing; the herb of understanding; the sacred pipe; a sacred red flowering stick; and a hoop symbolic of the Lakota people. Outside the rainbow tipi, Black Elk rode a bay horse, accompanied by horses from the four directions: black horses in the color of the west; white horses in the color of the north; red horses of the east; and yellow from the south. Black Elk saw the future struggles of his people, and then, upon reaching the top of the world's highest mountain, he recognized the unity of all humankind: "I was seeing in a sacred manner the shapes of all things in the spirit, and the shape of all shapes as they must live together like one being. And I saw that the sacred hoop of my people was one of

Part One. A Phenomenology of Revelation

many hoops that made one circle, wide as daylight and as starlight, and in the center grew one mighty flowering tree to shelter all the children of one mother and one father. And I saw that it was holy."[11] When Black Elk finally awakened, his body was still swollen from the illness, but he felt fine. The next day his health was completely restored. Still, he was afraid to talk about his vision.

At the age of seventeen, Black Elk began to feel fearful and anxious. He kept on hearing voices telling him, "Now is the time; now is the time." All winter long, he seemed to be under the spell of his Great Vision. Finally, his parents asked an old medicine man to talk with him. To him Black Elk described his visit to the grandfathers in the rainbow tipi and all that had happened there. Immediately, the wise man knew what was wrong: it was time to share the vision with all the people. For it is a Lakota tradition that certain visions are meant to be performed for the benefit of all; they are not the possession of the individual person.

Thus was born the festival of the Horse Dance. A tipi of bison hide was constructed and on it were painted pictures depicting the scenes of the vision. Six elders played the grandfathers; horses of the appropriate colors, with riders, were gathered together. Black Elk spent one long night teaching the musicians the songs he had heard during his vision. The Horse Dance was not just dance, but included song and theater, even an art exhibit.

During the performance, Black Elk again had a vision of the rainbow tipi. Looking up into the sky, he saw the six grandfathers looking down towards him with their hands palms outward facing him in the manner of greeting.

At the end of the Horse Dance, the people gathered together to smoke the sacred pipe. Black Elk's feelings of anxiety and fear were gone. From that day forward, he was no longer treated as a child. He now joined in the councils of the medicine men.

When the Lakota first performed the Horse Dance, they were participating in an expression of Black Elk's Great Vision. What had been private and personal now belonged to the experience of all: revelation had become tradition. The English word *tradition* derives from the Latin *traditio*, "the action of handing over something." Once a revelation is expressed, it has been handed over to others. It becomes the possession of the society as a whole.

As time goes on, others might reenact a sacred dance or interpret it in

2. Expressing Revelation: Sacred Art, Sacred Place, and Sacred Time

their own way. Tradition suggests continuity but not necessarily conformity. For example, in *Wakinyan: Lakota Religion in the Twentieth Century*, Stephen E. Feraca offers a short description of innovations in the tradition of the Horse Dance.[12] By the 1940s the primary function of the Horse Dance was to bring rain. In addition, it might serve the spiritual life of an individual person: "those who dream of themselves 'dancing horses' will be assisted by a medicine man and may accomplish the dictates of the dreams with a minimum of spectators, or may wait for an opportunity such as that presented by a tribal or community fair or dance."[13] Further, the ceremony has become a ritual to aid in the healing of psychological distress: neuroses, psychoses, and nightmares.

The human attempt to share with others the experience of revelation results in three kinds of religious creativity: sacred art encompasses all the various aesthetic media that give the memory of religious experience a concrete form, from story telling to the construction of monumental temples; sacred space begins by marking those sites (mountain tops, rivers, trees and so forth) where the revelations occur; and sacred time comes into play when people commemorate with rituals and festivals the actual times when revelations have taken place.

Sacred Art

Perhaps the most obvious way to share the experience of revelation is to tell somebody. Myths are the sacred stories that result.[14] Here we are using the word *myth* in the early Greek way of referring to stories that depend on revelation — that is, stories about the various kinds of spirits and their interaction with human beings. There are many different kinds of myths: creation myths, myths about the gods and the goddesses, hero myths, and myths about the afterlife, to name but a few.

Every people, it would seem, has some kind of sacred story about the creation of the world.[15] For example, the Polynesian people of the Society Islands relate how Ta'aroa, supreme being and creator, emerged from a primordial egg. "Ta'aroa sat in his shell in darkness from eternity. The shell was like an egg revolving in endless space, with no sky, no land, no sea, no moon, no sun, no stars. All was darkness; it was continuous thick darkness." Ta'aroa breaks out of his shell, and for a while he swims around in empty space.

Then, he finds another shell and rests within it. This second shell, when he finally emerges from it, becomes the foundation for the world. "And the shell Rumia that he opened first, became his house, the dome of the gods' sky, which was a confined sky, enclosing the world then forming." This creation story was preserved within Polynesian oral tradition until outsiders wrote it down.[16]

In societies that have a written language, a sacred story may eventually be written down by those who belong to the tradition, or by their descendents even if they no longer accept the faith of their ancestors. The oral traditions of the ancient Norwegians survive today in their relatively late, written form. The written texts inform us that the universe was created out of the body of an immense giant named Ymir. This giant arose in the mist that formed between two primordial realms of fire and ice. Three gods emerged from the body of the giant and went to work, cutting up the body into pieces and using these various parts as building materials for the creation: Ymir's blood became the rivers and oceans; its skull, the heavens; out of its body the sun, the moon, and the stars were made, as well as all of the creatures of the earth.

This myth survived for centuries as part of an oral tradition until two Christian kings, Olaf Tryggvason and Olaf the Holy, transformed Norway into a Christian land during the tenth and eleventh centuries. With the new religion came a new attitude towards the uses of writing. Pre-Christian Norwegians considered writing too holy for everyday use. Runic letters were carved on memorial stones, amulets,[17] and other ritual objects, but they were not used to record either sacred stories or historical events. By the twelfth century, however, the sacred stories of pre–Christian Norway were beginning to be forgotten. Therefore, around 1220 one Icelandic scholar (Iceland had been settled by people from Norway) decided to write them down. Snorri Sturluson was both a poet and an historian. He recorded the old myths as a handbook for poets, and he called his book the *Edda*. Today it is known as the *Prose Edda* to distinguish it from a collection of poems with the same name (the *Poetic* or *Elder Edda*).[18] Most of what we know about pre–Christian mythology in Scandinavian countries comes from the two Eddas.

A written myth has certain advantages: literary texts are good for preserving the details of a given story. At the same time, however, there are also disadvantages: the story may become fixed in one particular form. As part of an oral tradition, it may have undergone alterations since the first telling, but once the story is written down it is harder to change it. People tend to forget that a written text has a long history of re-telling. In addition, they may start to believe, mistakenly, that the written story is a record of actual historical events.

In addition to story telling, the expression of a revelation may take the form of a poem or a song. The Islamic mystic Jalal al-Din Rumi (1207–1273) was originally a teacher, but after he came to know the mendicant holy man Shams, he discovered that he was a mystic, one who experiences God in a most immediate way. Sham's influence on Rumi was disturbing to Rumi's family, and eventually they forced the holy man to leave. As Rumi mourned the loss of his spiritual teacher, he found himself spontaneously writing poetry:

> Do you think I know what I'm doing?
> That for one breath or half-breath I belong to myself?
> As much as a pen knows what it's writing,
> or the ball can guess where it's going next.[19]

The poet attributes the poetry to some other source to which he now "belongs." The outpouring of inspired poetry continued unabated the rest of Rumi's life. Today both Muslims and non–Muslims alike read, recite, and sing his poems.

As a Sufi, or Islamic mystic, Rumi sought "annihilation in God" (*fana*). Sometimes this is expressed as a loving union with the Friend; at other times, the imagery suggests transmutation followed by absorption into the divine reality, as in the poem about the chickpea that is turned into a delicious soup for God.

> A chickpea leaps almost over the rim of the pot
> where it's being boiled.
> "Why are you doing this to me?"
> The cook knocks him down with the ladle.
> "Don't you try to jump out.
> You think I'm torturing you.
> I'm giving you flavor,
> so you can mix with spices and rice
> and be the lovely vitality of a human being.
> Remember when you drank rain in the garden.
> That was for this."
> Grace first. Sexual pleasure,
> then a boiling new life begins,
> and the Friend has something good to eat.[20]

Here the spiritual guide is likened to a cook and the mystic is a chickpea. At first the ordeal of spiritual discipline is both painful and difficult; but with a deeper understanding of the process of transformation, the initiate begins to welcome a change that will draw him into the very being of God, the beloved Friend.

Words are not always the best tools for sharing a revelation. There are many other ways to express a message from the spirit world. The Lakota re-enact the great visions of their people. This may involve dance as well as dramatization. In the past, temple women in India danced the stories of the gods, for example, the love and longing of Radha, the gopi,[21] for her divine lord Krishna.[22] On the other side of the world, the Spanish Franciscans used dance dramas to introduce the Christian Gospel to the indigenous peoples of the Americas.

People can also make a picture or statue of what they experience in revelation. Sacred images are found nearly everywhere: on the walls of caves, in temples, and in graves. Everywhere people depict their visions of the gods. For example, found in a gravesite in Ur, Iraq, a little statue (14 cm.) portrays a figure that has the body of a woman and the head of a snake. Nestled in her left arm is an infant.[23] This statuette is over five thousand years old. The combined symbolism — snake and woman — suggests that she represents something not found in nature, something supernatural. The fact that she was placed in a grave may mean that she represents a goddess who cares for the dead in some way.

Sometimes, however, there is the belief that fashioning pictures or statues of the spirits or the deities is against their wishes. For example, we call Judaism aniconic, which means "without sacred images," because in Jewish tradition God prohibits the making of religious images. This prohibition is found already in Leviticus, an early book of revealed laws found in the Hebrew Bible.

> You shall not make idols[24] for yourselves; you shall not erect a carved image or a sacred pillar; you shall not put a figured stone on your land to prostrate yourselves upon, because I am the Lord your God. You shall keep my Sabbaths and revere my sanctuary.[25]

Instead of sacred art, the emphasis here is on the Sabbath, the holy day of rest, a sacred time each week when Jews worship the God who created the world in six days and rested on the seventh.

Early Buddhists, too, were aniconic. "Because the Buddha as a personality was deemed to have passed outside of history altogether at his *parinirvana*, or death, his presence was instead symbolized by such motifs as the rich turban of the prince Siddhartha, the throne of the Blessed One, his footprints marked with the Wheel of the Law, the begging bowl, or the Bodhi Tree...."[26] One early Buddhist was Ashoka, the emperor of India (c. 270–230 BCE), who converted to Buddhism and sought to create a spiritual empire through missionary activity.[27] One the one hand, Ashoka sent ambassadors of Buddhism to the five Hellenistic rulers in the Greek empire. In addition, by means of inscriptions on rocks and pillars, he exhorted his subjects to follow the Dharma, or teachings of the Buddha. These Rock Edicts and Pillar Edicts include one at Sarnath, Uttar Pradish, India.[28] At the top stand four lions, each above a wheel; originally the four lions supported a fifth wheel. The lion here is a symbol for the historical Buddha; his teachings are symbolized by the wheel. In Sanskrit the meaning of *buddha* is "the one who is awake." Thus, just as the lion's roar awakens men and women in the jungle, so, too, the teachings of the Buddha awaken those who hear, so that they can follow the same path and become buddhas.

Sacred art is found everywhere. Whatever people use to express themselves can be employed to share their experiences of revelation. There are sacred gardens, such as the Zen Buddhist temple Ryoan-ji in Kyoto, Japan. The rock garden is composed of raked gravel surrounding 15 moss-covered boulders. It is generally believed that only the enlightened can see all 15 boulders at once. Further, movies and comic books are two very contemporary media today, and many artists turn to them in order to share their own interpretations of religious traditions. For example, Bernardo Bertolucci's "The Little Buddha" is a full-length film that presents both the story of the historical Buddha, Siddhartha Gautama, and an introduction to the Tibetan Buddhist belief in the tulku, or incarnating spiritual guide. In the Far East, Tsai Chih Chung and others have created graphic novels to present the teachings of Daoism and Buddhism for the Singapore series called Chinese Philosophies in Comics.

Sacred Space

Sacred space begins with a revelation in a particular geographical place, which then is deemed holy.[29] Many natural phenomena, such as rocks, rivers, mountains, and caves, are sacred sites associated with messages from the spirits. Often there is the idea also that the place is a "doorway" to the spirit world. The Hebrew Bible relates the story of Jacob, who dreamed of a ladder connecting heaven and earth; and so he marked the place where had slept as the gateway to heaven.[30]

Jacob was one of the twin sons of Isaac and Rebecca. His brother was called Esau. Their grandfather was Abraham, the man recognized as ancestor in four religions: Judaism, Christianity, Islam, and Baha'i. Esau was the first twin to be born, but Jacob was favored by their mother, Rebecca. Once, when Esau was hungry, Jacob gave him food in exchange for his birthright as eldest son. Later, when their aged father called for Esau in order to bless him, Rebecca helped Jacob deceive the father into thinking that he was Esau, and so he received the blessing and the birthright of the firstborn son. Esau vowed that as soon as their father died, he would kill Jacob and regain his birthright, and so Jacob had to flee. He traveled alone towards the land of his mother's family.

One night Jacob went to sleep in the wilderness with his head on a stone, and he had a dream. In the dream, there was a ladder connecting the earth and the heavens; angels moved up and down the ladder. At the top was God, promising Jacob that he would protect him and his family, granting to them the land all around the location where he had slept. When he woke up, Jacob declared: "Truly the Lord is in this place, and I did not know it.... How fearsome is this place! This is no other than the house of God, this is the gate of heaven."[31]

Jacob then took the stone on which he had rested his head and set it up as a holy pillar. He poured fragrant oil over it, anointing it and calling it Beth-El, which means House of God. In this way Jacob marked the site of his dream as a sacred place, a shrine for future generations.

The Yoruba of Nigeria believe that one of their rivers is divine. Osogbo is a Yoruba city associated with the goddess Osun. The founder of the town of Osogbo was a prince by the name of Laroye. Before he came to Osogbo, Laroye lived in a place where there was not enough water to support the lives of his people. So he sent out the hunter Timehin to search for water. Timehin walked until he came to a river. Finding a suitable site, he cut down a tree on the riverbank so as to remember the exact spot. Suddenly, he heard the river shouting at him: "You have destroyed my pots of dyes; you wizard of the forest, you are here again."[32] Of course, Timehin was quite frightened

2. Expressing Revelation: Sacred Art, Sacred Place, and Sacred Time

and wanted to flee. But before he could get away, a beautiful goddess emerged from within the river. She told him not to panic, but to return to Prince Laroye and invite him to live on the banks of her river. Later, when the town of Osogbo had been established, the goddess often appeared before the Yoruba people, or else she would send her messenger, Iko, a goddess in the form of a fish. For the people of Osogbo, the river itself is Osun, and every year they hold a festival to honor the river goddess.

Sometimes people build temples or tombs in sacred places. For Muslims, after Mecca and Medina, the holiest city is Jerusalem. There at Haram al-Sharif stands the Dome of the Rock, an octagonal structure with a dome of gilded lead. This oldest surviving Islamic monument was built in 691–692 CE out of stone, marble, and ceramic tile. The mosque commemorates Muhammad's ascent into the heavens where he had many wonderful visions. The story, sometimes called "the night journey," is shared by all factions of Islam. The tradition states that one night Muhammad journeyed mysteriously from Mecca to Jerusalem, where he stood on a rock that once had been part of the Jewish Temple. From there he ascended into Paradise and spoke with God. The dome of the present-day mosque lies directly over this sacred rock, where Muhammad stood before ascending into God's presence.

Often temples and tombs will resemble mountains. Indeed, it is the form of the mountain itself that makes it a suitable site for revelation. The mountain base is one with the earth, and yet its peak reaches into the heavens. Connecting both realms, the mountain enables communication between the spirits and the humans: it may serve as a location where revelations are received. Moses, the great prophet of Judaism, heard the voice of the God of his fathers on top of a mountain, where he lingered for many days to receive God's law, the Torah.

The pyramids of ancient Egypt are tombs that resemble mountains. The ancient Egyptians built the pyramids to mark the burial sites of their kings, whom they believed to be divine: the sons of gods and goddesses. Believing that the king would be reborn in the world of the gods, the people prepared him for the transition by building the pyramid and filling it with whatever the king might need in his future life.

Buddhist stupas likewise resemble hills. Stupas are not temples, or places of worship, but rather they house relics of the historical Buddha. Usually hemispherical in shape and built of stone, the stupa commemorates the sacred life of the mystic and teacher, Siddhartha Gautama. One example is the

Great Stupa at Sanci, Madhya Pradesh, India. Built between 100 BCE and 100 CE, the shrine is sometimes referred to as an "egg," since the funerary mound symbolizes the beginning of a new and eternal existence free from the cycles of birth, suffering, death, and rebirth.

Certain rituals are particularly associated with sacred places: among these are pilgrimage, circumambulation, and incubation. A pilgrimage is a journey to a sacred place. Circumambulation is a ritual in which the devotee walks around a sacred shrine, temple, or city. Incubation is the ritual of sleeping in a temple in order to receive a vision.

Like the Osun of Nigeria, the Ganga (the Ganges, in English) in India is a divine river.[33] Originating in the Himalayas at Gangotri, it flows 1,560 miles through the plains of northern India into the Bay of Bengal. The river is recognized as a manifestation of the goddess Ganga. According to the epics and many Puranas (mythological texts that include the lore of sacred places in India), Ganga's home is in the heavens. She came down to earth in response to the ascetic practices and prayers of King Bhagiratha. This king had sixty thousand sons, who accidentally disturbed the meditations of the great sage Kapila. The angry glance of the sage had turned the young men into ash. So King Bhagiratha petitioned Ganga to descend to earth in order to revive them.

When the goddess agreed to come to earth to help King Bhagiratha, it was feared that the forceful impact of her descent might actually harm the land. Thus, in order to break her fall, the god Shiva caught the river goddess in his eyebrows and then directed the course of her waters through his matted hair. For this reason Shiva is known as Ganga-Dhara, that is, the one who "holds Ganga."

According to Hindu belief, the waters of Ganga purify all that they touch. People from all over India journey as pilgrims to her riverbanks in order to drink a sip of her water, worship her, or chant her holy name. The pilgrims then return home with sealed jars of holy Ganga water. This they share with those unable to make the trip: offering the water to guests at weddings, giving it to the sick and the dying, and employing it in the sanctification of oaths.

The ancient city of Varanasi (Benares) lies on the Ganga River and provides temporary shelter for pilgrims. Some bathe in the river; others spend their last days looking at her, for even the sight of the river can cleanse one of all sins. Finally, the corpses of devotees may be brought to the ghats, broad flights of steps that line the river and provide access to the waters, especially for bathing. There they are cremated and their ashes placed in small bowls to be set afloat on the surface of the river.

Circumambulation — circling a sacred site on foot or even by walking on ones knees — is a ritual found in many traditions, such as the circumambulation of the Ka'bah in Mecca. The Ka'bah is the House of Allah, the principle Islamic shrine. Muslims say their daily prayers facing in the direction of the shrine. One of the five pillars of Islam is pilgrimage (*hajj*) to the Ka'bah. Every Muslim is expected to travel to this holy shrine once in his or her lifetime. The most important object at the Ka'bah is the Black Stone embedded in the outer wall of the shrine. Probably a meteorite, the stone was sacred already to the ancestors of Muhammad. The highpoint of the pilgrimage involves circumambulation of the Ka'bah and kissing the Black Stone, following thus in the footsteps of Muhammad the Prophet.

For the ancient Greeks, and later the Romans, incubation — sleeping in a holy place in order to receive healing dreams — was a common practice associated with the Greek god of healing, Asklepios,[34] whose temples were located as far west as Italy. Sometimes there was an immediate cure; this would be recorded on a stone tablet, describing the illness, the dream, and the cure itself. Other times, the god would recommend a long-term therapy, such as cold baths, attending the theater, making music, or writing poetry. In addition, he might prescribe herbs and other medicines, or even shock therapy of one kind or another.

The records inform us that the sick quite often saw the god himself in their dreams. Asklepios would appear as a tall, bearded man wearing a white robe and carrying his staff around which two serpents entwined (emblems of the healer, even today). He would address the dreamer with advice concerning the illness and the necessary treatment. Sometimes Asklepios was accompanied by his dog or members of his family, his wife or daughters.

Sacred Time

In addition to creating sacred art and marking sacred places, people often celebrate the time that a revelation takes place, the day or the season. Every culture has days that are considered to be holy — holidays. These days are set apart. One does not pursue ordinary work; instead, ceremonies of various kinds create an atmosphere that allows people to participate in the reality of the spirit world.[35]

One holiday is the New Year, which is celebrated all over the world in one form or another. The actual season of the New Year, however, differs from place to place. For example, it may be reckoned according to the solar year or the lunar calendar. One conception found in many archaic cultures is that the rotation of seasons is a characteristic of the cosmos itself. As the year appears in winter to get old and weak, the need for a renewal of the entire creation is felt. This is the New Year. The gods are invited to come to earth, to banish all that is evil and debilitating, and to restore life and energy to nature as a whole. The symbolism of the New Year is thus closely aligned with tales of creation.

The Celts who inhabited the British Isles celebrated Samhain as the first day of the solar New Year (November 1). On the evening before Samhain, the boundaries that separate the human and the spirit worlds were temporarily dissolved as if to return everything to the state of chaos that existed prior to creation. At this time, the souls of the dead as well as the spirits of gods and other supernatural beings were able freely to roam the earth. To protect themselves, the people offered the wandering spirits tributes of various kinds: especially gifts of beverage and foodstuffs. At the same time, human beings were able to penetrate into the spirit world. Thus, it was considered an opportune time to get information about the future or other hidden knowledge. Numerous techniques of divination were practiced on this evening.

The morning of Samhain brought with it a restoration of cosmic order. The boundaries separating the different realms of the world were again in place and the creation renewed.

Samhain continued to be celebrated in Great Britain even after the christianization of the Celtic people who lived there. Unable to do away with the Celtic New Year, the British church decided to incorporate the festival into the Christian liturgical year. Thus, Samhain was renamed the Feast of All the Saints, a day for remembering the known and unknown saints of Christian history. The eve of Samhain became the Vigil of All Saints, or Allhallows' Eve (Halloween). Still, the ancient meaning of the festival survives in the customs that continue to this day: people dress up in costumes and masks so as to represent supernatural beings and they travel from house to house demanding tributes of food and drink. The dread of the spirit world pervades the symbolism of the festival, with images of bats and owls, witches and ghosts everywhere.

Another day that is celebrated as holy is the birthday of a religious

2. Expressing Revelation: Sacred Art, Sacred Place, and Sacred Time

teacher or a divinity. For example, on the eighth day of the fourth lunar month, Buddhists celebrate the birthday of Siddhartha Gautama, the historical Buddha; the followers of Confucius likewise celebrate his birthday on the 27th day of the eighth lunar month. The ancient Romans celebrated the birthday of Sol, the sun god, on the 25th of December near the time of the winter solstice. During the second half of the fourth century, Christians in the Roman Empire began to celebrate the birthday of Jesus Christ on the same day. Accordingly, the festival was reinterpreted as the coming into the world of the Christian "light." The English term *Christmas* refers to the mass (Eucharist) on the day celebrated as Christ's nativity.

Finally, there are holy days that commemorate divine activity in history, that is, important revelatory events are remembered according to the context of their time or season. For example, every spring the Jews celebrate Passover, a time when they recall the liberation of their ancestors — the Israelites — from living as slaves in Egypt.[36] The Pharaoh did not give in quickly to the demands of Moses, the prophet of the Israelites, who asked for the release of his people so that they could go into the wilderness and worship the God of their ancestors there in a holy festival. Meeting great resistance, Moses finally threatened the Egyptian king, saying that if he would not free the Israelites, their God would kill the first-born child in every Egyptian household. That night the Israelites sacrificed lambs, placing the blood of each on the outside of the door, so that the spirit of death would "pass over" their homes. The next morning, in his grief and horror at the death of the children throughout his kingdom, Pharaoh allowed the Israelites to leave Egypt. Before he could change his mind, they were beyond his reach.

During this weeklong holiday (outside Israel, eight days), parents tell their children the story of the Exodus (literally, "the road out" of Egypt), and how God rescued their ancestors from slavery in a foreign land. The Seder, a festive meal celebrated in the home on the first night of Passover, includes reading and chanting the Haggadah ("telling"), a collection of stories, hymns, and poems about the Exodus. Passover is a time to thank God for deliverance from all forms of bondage.

Similar is the Bun Festival, celebrated for six days each summer (the exact date is selected annually by means of divination) on the small island of Cheung Chau, just south of Hong Kong. The festival honors the Daoist god, whose Cantonese name is Pak Tai, or Ruler of the North; his full title is Superior Divinity of the Deep Dark Heaven, True Soldier of the North.[37]

He obtained this designation when he successfully overcame the demon king who sought to lay waste the universe. Fighting in his bare feet with his hair flowing down over his shoulders, Pak Tai banished the demon king together with all his host, including the supernatural snake and turtle that had come to the aid of the demon.

The Bun Festival is a local festival associated with this important Daoist god. According to the people of Cheung Chau, at the turn of the nineteenth century there was an outbreak of plague on the island. Only when the statue of Pak Tai was carried in procession throughout the island did the illness loosen its grip on the islanders. This miracle, in which the god demonstrated his healing power, is celebrated during the Bun Festival. The two main events of the week are parades and the bun towers. On each of the last two days of the festival, a procession winds through the little streets of this island village, where there are neither cars nor motorbikes. The crowds witness the usual dancing lions and unicorns with their drummers, kung fu clubs with their banners, adult actors impersonating well-known mythological figures, and a band.[38] In addition, children between the ages of five and eight, dressed up to represent famous figures of history or myth, are carried through the streets on small platforms at shoulder height.

The bun towers consist of huge conical bamboo and paper towers, some as much as sixty feet tall, covered with steamed white buns. Each bun is marked in red with a Chinese character signifying good fortune. In the past, it was the custom on the last night of the festival for the young men to scramble up the towers in order to remove the buns as fast as possible. In 1977, however, one of the towers collapsed. Luckily, no one was hurt, but for many years, the midnight ritual was forbidden. During that time the lucky buns were distributed to all the islanders on the morning after the festival.

Much of what we call religion consists of sacred art, holy places, and holidays. Thus, one can readily say that religion is "human-made." It is people who tell the stories about the gods, build the temples, and join in the festivals. At the same time, however, it is important to remember that what we are witnessing is the human response to what has been experienced as divine revelation. For the religious person, the gods act first; the people then respond. This dialogue between the human and the spirit world is the inner life of any religion.

Chapter 3

Seeking Revelation:
Worship and Spiritual Discipline

Once a person has shared the experience of revelation with others, what does he or she want?—To have it again.

Contact with the spirit world gives people the sense that they have encountered something that is fundamentally more real, more power-filled, and more valuable than anything else. The contact with the holy gives the person a sense of being more alive and even more awake than usual. Sometimes there is fear; other times, joy. Always there is an intensity of emotion.

The experience can even be a healing one. Thérèse of Lisieux, the young Carmelite French nun who shared her spiritual life by writing an autobiography, tells about her visions of Jesus and numerous Christian saints. Once in a time of hopeless illness, gazing on a statue of the Virgin Mary, she appealed to the mother of Jesus for comfort: "I could find no help on earth, so I also turned to my heavenly Mother and beseeched her to have pity on me. Suddenly the Blessed Virgin glowed with a beauty beyond anything I had every seen. Her face was alive with kindness and an infinite tenderness, but it was her enchanting smile which really moved me to the depths. My pain vanished and two great tears crept down my cheeks — tears of pure joy."[1] Because of this vision, the ten-year-old child, who had lost her mother very early on, began to recover the strength to live.

The revelations that have such a strong influence on people's lives are of many different kinds, but there is always a sense of being connected to some powerful and meaningful dimension of reality. People are drawn to what they feel to be holy; they want to orient their lives around these "peak" experiences, and so they seek further revelation. Much of what we call religious ritual, or ceremony, has this role.

Ritual is a word we use to refer to symbolic actions. When a person does something that carries meaning over and above the actual act itself, it becomes symbolic. For example, shaking hands is a Western ritual that conveys equality, respect, and relationship; in Japan, bowing serves a similar function. Religious ritual comprises actions that carry religious meaning: such as prostration before the image of a deity; kneeling in homage before the spirit tablet of one's ancestors; or bowing one's head in prayer.

Ceremony is a related term that describes a formal series of rituals. Two different kinds of ceremony are fundamental in seeking closeness to the source of revelation. One is worship, by means of which the devotee cultivates an on-going relationship with the spiritual source of revelation. The second is spiritual discipline, which has as its goal the transformation of the man or woman so as to draw closer to the spirit in some way. Sometimes the goal of spiritual discipline is be become god-like or even divine.

Worship

Ceremonies of worship are one kind of response to the experience of revelation. In worship, people direct their attention and actions towards the source of revelation, reaching out to the spirit world in order to make some kind of connection — either temporary or more permanent.

In many religious traditions, ritual specialists lead the worship service. There are many terms used to refer to those persons who maintain the space used in worship and guide others in the actual ceremonies: priest, priestess, minister, pastor, rabbi, imam, and so on. They may be professionals or lay leaders. They may belong to large complex religious organizations or serve temporarily in smaller, loosely organized communities.

Ceremonies of worship may be performed individually or involve the entire community. Public ceremonies may be prescribed by a sacred calendar. For example, the idea of a week having seven days is based on the Jewish designation of every seventh day as a day of rest. The Sabbath, which literally means "that which stops," is holy because according to biblical tradition God created the world in six days and rested on the seventh, calling it a holy day of rest for humankind as well. Freed from other duties, the Jews are able to spend this day worshipping the creator.

As in other cultures, the Chinese have a calendar that is filled with holy

3. Seeking Revelation: Worship and Spiritual Discipline

days, beginning with the lunar New Year, or Spring Festival, the most important holiday of the year. Other holy days in the Chinese calendar include the Lantern Festival on the fifteenth day of the first lunar month; Dragon Boat Festival (fifth month, fifth day); the Hungry Ghost Festival (seventh month, fifteenth day); Mid-Autumn Festival (eighth month, fifteenth day); and the birthdays of numerous Chinese gods, goddesses, and religious teachers of the past. Very popular in southern Chinese communities is the birthday of the goddess Mazu, whose highest title is Celestial Empress; the birthday of Confucius is especially significant for scholars and officials.

Commonly the ceremony of worship will include three kinds of activities, all of which are directed towards sending a message of some kind to the spirit world: sacrifice, praise and homage, and prayer. It makes sense that these activities have something in common with the patterns of behavior that people will follow in their efforts to cultivate human relationships as well: giving gifts and sharing one's possessions with others; letting others know how much they are valued; and talking, conversing, creating dialogue.

Sacrifice. This English word derives from the Latin *sacrificium*, which means, "to make holy." Whatever is sacrificed is sent by ritual means to the spirit world. It is consecrated, that is, dedicated to a spirit being.[2] Sometimes the sacrifice is also called an oblation, which derives from the Latin word for "offering" (*oblatio*).

Anything can serve as the oblation, or gift: food, flowers, fragrance (incense), even words. For example, according to the ancient Vedic traditions of India, each home had a sacred fire kindled at the time of the wedding ceremony, a fire that was used only for sacrifice. Three times each day the father would offer the Pancha Mahayajna, which included both diverse gifts for other living beings as well as sacrifices for the spirits: (1) gifts of hospitality were offered to other human beings; (2) food was placed on the threshold of the home and tossed in the four directions for local spirits, animals, and outcasts; (3) burnt offerings were made as gifts to the gods; (4) food and water was offered to the ancestors; and (5) the recitation of sacred texts was offered as sacrifice to Brahman, the world spirit.

The form taken by a sacrifice, that is, the way the oblation is "sent" to the spirit world, can differ as well. Different rituals symbolize the transferral of the gift to the spirit world, depending on the domain of the spirits. For example, many peoples see their gods as living in the heavens. Especially nomadic peoples have historically worshipped celestial gods and goddesses, because the sky was the fixed point in their wandering existence. Sacrifice to a sky deity usually consists of burning the gift, so that through the transforming power of fire it becomes smoke that rises up into the heavens. Both the Semitic ancestors of the Jews and Indo-European ancestors of the Greeks and the Hindus offered burnt offerings in this way.

Agriculturally based cultures might develop a different vision of the spirit world, seeing the domain of the spirits as being situated under the earth's surface. In these societies, the most common form of sacrifice would require placing the gift close to the ground on a low table or in a cave. Or the gift might be buried. The libation, pouring a liquid such as wine or mead directly onto the earth, is a related form of sacrifice, sending the gift to the underworld. Ancient Minoan art, such as the images found on gems or jewelry, portrays the vessels that held liquids used in libations[3]; so it is not surprising to see that this practice was known as well to their successors, the Greeks. This is evident in the story of Odysseus, who, when seeking to communicate with the spirit of the dead seer Teiresias, "dug a pit of a cubit's length this way and that, and around it poured a libation to all the dead, first with milk and honey, thereafter with sweet wine, and in the third place with water."[4]

Sacrifices for the dead are often found in the grave or tomb of the deceased. Gifts to water spirits may be placed in wells, on riverbanks, or set afloat on the ocean. For example, among the Yoruba of western Africa, the river goddess Osun is savior and protector of the king. "Perhaps the main part of Osun's festival is the ritual procession and pilgrimage of the king, the Arugba (the young maiden who carries Osun's gifts to the river bank), and the Osogbo people to the Osun River to present their sacrificial offerings. The procession takes place amidst shouts of prayerful wishes to the goddess."[5]

> Whenever we hear a joyful music from the river,
> It is Osun who is dancing, Osun who is honored with a banquet after her melodious music.[6]

High places, such as mountains and towers, can also be the site of offerings to spirits that dwell in the atmosphere above the earth. Sometimes the mountain itself is believed to be the home of the spirits: Before the arrival of Buddhism in Japan, the Japanese believed that both the *kami* (gods or spirits)

3. Seeking Revelation: Worship and Spiritual Discipline

and the ancestors lived on the mountains, which were so holy that human beings were not allowed to ascend them.[7] Sacrifices, therefore, were brought to the foot of a mountain.

Sometimes the sacrifice consists of a shared meal with the ancestors or the gods. This kind of ritual emphasizes the interdependence of the human and spirit communities. As soon as the preparations are completed, the spirits are invited to come and participate. The invocation can be in the form of a prayer or a song, or even a ritual that announces the beginning of the feast. For example, in ancient Rome there were regular holy days on which to share meals with the ancestors. Food was prepared and taken to the tomb site. The ancestors were prayerfully invited to enjoy the feast. In a similar way, Christians celebrate a sacred meal in which they re-enact the last meal that Jesus had with his followers before he was arrested and crucified. In the Eucharist ("thanksgiving"), Christians repeat the words of Jesus and believe that he is present in a very real sense.

Sacrifices can be different in form, and also different in intent. Some sacrifices are cosmic in nature, that is, the gift is understood to have *a necessary role in the creation* of the world. For example, in ancient India the public fire sacrifice was part of the energy cycle of the universe. The ancient Indians believed that the gods spend energy daily in creating the world and that through the fire sacrifice, people could help to revitalize the gods, participating thus in the ongoing life of the universe.

Another reason for sacrifice is *thanksgiving*. People everywhere bring offerings to their gods to thank them for all that they have received: life, health, children, and prosperity. The God of the Israelites demanded that the people sacrifice the first fruits of the land's produce as part of a ritual in which they remembered their deliverance from slavery in Egypt: "When you come into the land which the Lord your God is giving you to occupy as your patrimony and settle in it, you shall take the first fruits of all the produce of the soil, which you gather in from the land which Lord your God is giving you, and put them in a basket." The basket is then brought to the altar in the presence of the priest, and the person offering the sacrifice retells the story of the Exodus. "Now I have brought the first fruits of the soil which thou, O Lord, hast given me."[8]

Other more specialized forms of sacrifice are intended to express expiation and supplication. *Expiation* means that the gift is given as a kind of repayment when someone has committed an offence. For example, the pre-

Greek worshipers of Meilichios, who took the form of giant snake, feared greatly the wrath of this god who punished those who killed, accidentally or otherwise, a clansman. If one were guilty of such a crime, he or she would offer a pig upon a fire altar in order to ask the god for forgiveness. Finally, *supplication* means to offer a gift to strengthen the force of a request for some future kindness from a deity: hope for healing, empowerment, or children, and so on.

Praise and Homage. In addition to gifts of sacrifice, certain religious ceremonies allow people to offer homage and praise to the spirits. In acts of homage people acknowledge the superior power and wisdom of the gods and ancestors and the creature's dependence on the Creator.

The word for worship in modern Indian tradition is puja, which is derived from the Sanskrit root meaning "honor." Both at home and in the temple, people demonstrate their reverence through ritual attention to the images of the gods. "*Puja* performed to images in both homes and temples has largely preserved its characteristics as a hospitality ritual. The ritual from start to finish is a sequence of acts of service or respect. Though the specific acts vary with the circumstances of the ritual or the ritual tradition being followed, the usual complete sequence includes invocation of the deity, offering him a seat, offering water for washing his feet, water for washing his hands, and water for sipping, bathing the image, offering a fresh garment, offering a sacred thread, anointing the image with unguents or sandalwood paste, offering flowers, offering incense, offering a lighted lamp, offering food or a gift, making obeisance to the deity, *pradakshina* ('clockwise circumambulation of the deity'), verses of praise and bidding the deity farewell."[9] In addition to bathing, dressing, and "feeding" the images, devotees may on certain occasions perform songs, recite sacred texts, or dance.

Likewise, Chinese worship takes place both in the home and in the temple. Chinese festivals, however, often take place in a fair-like atmosphere outside the temple. Temporary booths are set up and decorated for the occasion. One booth may house an altar; another may be the site for the gods and goddesses attending the festival, where their statues are lined up to observe the proceedings. Still another booth will be set up for the entertainment of the gods. Traditionally one might hear Chinese opera performed to please the spirits.

I once attended a New Year's festival in a small walled village near Hong

3. Seeking Revelation: Worship and Spiritual Discipline

Kong. The ceremonies did not take place in the temple, which was closed for the time being. Instead, colorful temporary sheds of bamboo and paper had been set up outside on a large field. Here there was the shed where a sacrificial pig and other offerings were on display; there, an outdoor altar. Facing both was a small stage where music was performed as part of the ritual proceedings. One night, instead of traditional Chinese opera, a young woman in contemporary dress was singing "rock and roll." I was curious and asked one of my Chinese colleagues,[10] a local scholar of Chinese religion, if this were really allowed. He replied that whatever humans find entertaining is enjoyed also by the gods.

This event opened my eyes to an aspect of worship that I had never before recognized: entertainment. People express their homage towards the gods by trying to please them with music, song, and dance. Even athletic competitions and theatrical productions may serve to entertain the spirits. The great king of ancient Israel, King David, loved to dance before his God. When David was first anointed king, he brought to his own city of Jerusalem the ark, a portable shrine that served the Israelites as their center for worship before the Temple of Solomon was built. As the ark was being transported, "David and all Israel danced for joy before the Lord without restraint to the sound of singing, of harps and lutes, of tambourines and castanets and cymbals."[11]

Later, the descendents of David and Solomon would enter the Temple in Jerusalem dancing and singing songs of praise:

> O praise the Lord.
> Praise the Lord out of heaven;
> Praise him in the heights.
> Praise him, all his angels;
> Praise him, all his host.
> Praise him, sun and moon;
> Praise him, all you shining stars.[12]

Praise is one way of giving thanks for life, health, family, and home. In praising the source of all that is good, people show their gratitude and at the same time celebrate the generosity of the giver.

Prayer. Prayer is perhaps the simplest form of sending a message to the spirit world. Whenever a man, woman, or child speaks to a spirit being — whether this is a family member who has died, a god or a goddess, a buddha or bodhisattva — this is prayer. Prayers can be short or long. They can be spoken in everyday language or in the sacred language of one's own religious tradition. For example, Muslims will pray in Arabic, the sacred language of the Qu'ran; and Hebrew is still used by Jews all over the world.

Prayer can be private or public. Most religions recommend that a person pray both together with others and also alone so as to develop a personal relationship with the divine. Teresa of Avila (1515–1582), Christian saint and reformer of Spanish monasticism, tells in her autobiography how as a young girl she was very easily led into frivolous and harmful activities. She relates that it was the gift of prayer that saved her, bringing her into a personal relationship with God. "It was a great thing that He [God] had given me the grace of prayer, as He had done, since this made me understand what it meant to love Him."[13] She calls her ability to pray a gift — not a personal achievement — seeing her own attraction to prayer as something like a lifeline thrown out to a person drowning in the sea.

Sometimes the community will pray together as one person. The Acts of the Apostles, a book found in the Christian New Testament, gives an account of the role of the Holy Spirit in the birth and development of the Christian Church among the followers of the resurrected Jesus. Inspired by God's very spirit, the community often prayed in unison. One day, the Christians Peter and John were on their way to the temple because it was three in the afternoon, a time for prayer. On the way they encountered a man crippled from birth, and Peter healed him. The healed man accompanied them to the temple, "leaping and praising God as he went."[14] Suspected of practicing some kind of magic, Peter and John were arrested and questioned by the religious authorities, but because they could find no evidence of wrongdoing, the officials released them again. John and Peter were discharged and returned to their friends. There they related to the followers of Jesus all that had happened, and the Christians "raised their voices as one person and called upon God." Praying spontaneously in unison, they asked God to continue to guide them.[15]

The content of prayer can be informal or formulaic. Perhaps the best way to cultivate a relationship with the spirit world is through sincere communication, sitting quietly and opening up ones heart in trust and devotion. However, there are also certain prayers that have been passed down from generation to generation and have become part of a tradition. Such prayers are particularly helpful for focusing the mind and giving the heart support in difficult times. One well-known prayer is the prayer that Jesus taught his followers[16]:

> Our Father in heaven,
> thy name be hallowed;
> thy kingdom come,
> Thy will be done,
> on earth as in heaven.
> Give us today our daily bread.
> Forgive us the wrong we have done, as have forgiven those who have wronged us.
> And do not bring us to the test,
> but save us from the evil one.

Memorized by Christians as part of their training for membership in the Church, the prayer can be then be spoken at any time and in any place, alone or with others.

Many religions have designated times of prayer. For example, extremely important in the tradition of Islam is the Salat, formal ritual prayer five times every day. Second only to the declaration of faith, Salat is one of the Five Pillars of Islam to be practiced by all Muslim adults. The morning prayer takes place between dawn and sunrise. Noon prayer is performed in the early afternoon and is followed by afternoon prayer, which ends before sunset. Evening prayer takes place as the sun goes down, and night prayer is performed when all is dark.

The words of the prayers are prescribed as well as the ritual movements that accompany them. First the person must make sure that he or she is clean and facing the Ka'bah, the shrine in Mecca. Then he or she recites the appropriate prayers, which include passages from the Qur'an. Salat may be performed alone or with others, at home or in the mosque. In some Islamic communities there is the adhan, or call to prayer, by the muezzin, a person who climbs a tall tower or any high place and chants in a loud voice. Although the words of the adhan differ slightly among the two major Islamic groups (Sunnis and Shi'ah), all agree it must be chanted in Arabic. In translation the call goes something like this[17]:

> God is the greatest.
> God is the greatest.
> God is the greatest.
> God is the greatest.

> I bear witness that there is no god except God.
> I bear witness that there is no god except God.
> I bear witness that Muhammad is the messenger of God.
> I bear witness that Muhammad is the messenger of God.
> Come to prayer.
> Come to prayer.
> Come to salvation.
> Come to salvation.
> God is the greatest.
> God is the greatest.
> There is no god except God.

Group prayers that take place in the mosque are led by an imam (leader). When women pray together without any man present, the imam may be a woman; otherwise, always a man. On Fridays the noon prayers are offered in the mosque in a special ceremony that includes two short sermons: one is a teaching sermon, and the other calls for God's blessings on the Prophet, his followers, and the congregation.

Prayer is found in all traditions and is a common part of every religious ceremony. Prayers invite the spirits to attend. In prayer, people confess their sins and give thanksgiving for blessings. Prayer is the human verbal response to revelation — it is "talking to God."

In addition to ceremonies of worship, which cultivate an on-going relationship with the spirit world, there are numerous forms of spiritual discipline that have as their goal the transformation of the individual so as to help him or her draw closer to the spirit world. Although in any given tradition, worship and spiritual discipline are related, sometimes the focus is on one, sometimes on the other.

Spiritual Discipline

Spiritual discipline, or asceticism, simply means training oneself to become closer to the spirit world. Originally, *asceticism* (from the Greek *askesis*, "training") referred to physical exercises. Borrowed by religious people to refer to those practices that lead to the realization of religious goals, the term gradually became identified with extreme austerities. For this reason,

3. Seeking Revelation: Worship and Spiritual Discipline

I prefer the term spiritual discipline, which suggests a great variety of techniques — not just austerities.

John Wesley (1703–1791), English clergyman and founder of Methodism, quotes Paul's first letter to Timothy[18] as he encourages his fellow Christians to "exercise yourself unto godliness."[19] He goes on to interpret this exhortation: "Let thy whole life be a preparation for heaven, like the preparation of wrestlers for combat." Just as athletes go into training in order to excel in their chosen sport and musicians practice and practice in order to perform well, so, too, religious people will undergo some kind of spiritual discipline in their desire to become closer to the divine.

Spiritual and Moral Law. One of the ways that people discipline themselves in all traditions is the practice of morality, or ethics. Recognition that the world is governed by universal laws of right and wrong demands that people learn this law and live their lives in accordance with it. Through this practice, they become closer to the divine source of the law.

The orderly nature of our world as the manifestation of divine law is implicit in stories about the creation. Every society has stories about how the world came into being. We sometimes call these creation myths, or cosmogonies. These sacred stories describe the precosmic situation, identify the creators, and describe the methods used in creation. For example, in the first book of Genesis the precosmic situation is depicted as darkness, water, and wind; and the creator is a God who speaks the world of time and space into being. The Scandinavian myth of creation, on the other hand, describes the precosmic situation as a giant person called Ymir. The world is constructed out of the dismembered parts of this giant by gods, who emerge out of its body.

Descriptions of primordial reality and the methods of creation appear to be unlimited in their variety. However, a survey of creation myths shows that there is always a transition from a state of chaos to one of cosmos. *Chaos* refers to a reality where human beings are unable to live and prosper: complete darkness and a world of water without land, for example. *Cosmos*, on the other hand, as "beautiful order," is a world that supports meaningful, human life.

Religious traditions generally suggest that either the gods or the ancestors, or some other positive spirits, are responsible for creating and maintaining this cosmic order. Everywhere there is the conviction also that the divine order is a moral order. In Genesis, after completing the creation of the world and all living creatures, "God saw all that he had made, and it was very good."[20] In Sanskrit the term for cosmic order is *rita*. In the *Rigveda* (c. 1200 BCE), earliest of the Sanskrit scriptures of India, common epithets for the gods are "he who possesses *rita*," "she who grows according to *rita*," and "he who is born of *rita*." The gods are intimately connected to the cosmic order, while the demons are the forces of *anrita*: the opposite dynamic, which destroys the cosmos. In later Indian tradition, which includes the origins of Buddhism as well, another word for cosmic order is *dharma*, likewise the moral and spiritual order of the universe. In Buddhism, the teachings of the Buddha are called the Dharma to suggest that his words describe the way things really are.

This notion that humans depend upon a moral order for a meaningful and worthwhile existence is the foundation of law found in all societies. Laws are tools that teach human beings how to recognize what kinds of behavior conflict with the divine order of things. Thus, ancient laws generally have some basis in revelation. For example, the Torah ("Law") is the revealed law of Judaism, derived from God's revelations to Moses. Christians acknowledge the commandments emphasized by Jesus. In response to the question, Which commandment is first of all? he answered, "The first is, 'Hear, O Israel: the Lord our God is the only Lord; love the Lord your God with all your heart, with all your soul, with all your mind, and with all your strength.' The second is this: 'Love your neighbor as yourself.' There is no other commandment greater than these."[21]

Celestial Master Daoism developed as an organized religious movement in China during the second century of the Common Era, when Zhang Dao Ling first received visions of Lao Zi. Many of the scriptures of Celestial Master Daoism instruct the faithful on how to live in accordance with the Dao, the spiritual and moral dynamic that supports the universe: "Who practices the Dao[22] and does not infringe the commandments will be profound as the Dao itself; Heaven and Earth are like the Dao, kind to the good, unkind to the wicked; therefore people must accumulate good works so that their spirit can communicate with Heaven."[23] This brief passage clearly articulates the relationship between ethical behavior and revelation. In order to communicate with the divine (Heaven), one must become as much like the divine as possible by "accumulating good works." Ethical practice transforms the individual and the society, modeling the human community on the divine order

54

that underlies all of life. In a sense, all ethical teachings belong to spiritual discipline, with the goal of sanctification.

Rites of Passage. Another category of ceremonies that share in the transformative goal of spiritual discipline is the initiation rite, or rite of passage. A great deal has been written about the religious meaning of initiation, especially by Mircea Eliade and his students.[24] Many studies are accounts of initiation in those societies that lack a written language, where scripture is absent and ritual forms an important aspect of everyday life. Indeed, research concerning such rites of passage has contributed much to our understanding of non-literary religious traditions in general. Still, initiation is not limited to small societies but is found everywhere.

Perhaps the most fundamental rite of passage is the funerary rite. Where there is a belief in an afterlife, there will be some kind of ceremony preparing the deceased for what comes next. Thus, the treatment of the dead demonstrates much about ideas concerning the spirit world. Funerary rites have as their goal the transformation of a living person into an ancestor in the spirit world.

In some small societies, for example, it is assumed that the soul (or spirit) of the deceased will make a journey to the land of the ancestors. Sometimes a local shaman, specialist in making the spirit journey, will undergo a ritual trance during which he or she will accompany the soul into the otherworld.[25] The role of the shaman in transporting the soul of the dead to the land of the ancestors is documented as part of the tradition of the Goldi, a tribe indigenous to Siberia. The funerary rites are long and complicated, but at one point the soul is taken away: "The shaman sings, dances, and daubs his face with soot. He invokes his helping spirits and begs them to guide him and the dead man in the beyond.... After shamanizing until he is exhausted, he sits down, facing the west on a board that represents a Siberian sled. The *fanya*[26] (cushion) containing the dead person's soul, and basket of food are set beside him. The shaman asks the spirits to harness the dogs to the sled and for a 'servant' to keep him company during the journey. A few moments later he 'sets off' for the land of the dead."[27]

Other common rites of passage are birth rites, puberty rites, and marriage rites. In each ceremony, the transformation of the individual person is the goal. In birth rites, the newly born child receives a name and becomes a member of the family and community. In puberty rites, boys and girls are transformed into men and women. In marriage rites, individual persons are joined together to form a new identity as a family.

Rites of passages are usually necessary components during the life of all members of a society; however there are especial rituals of initiation for the few. A community may have "secret societies," that is, associations that are limited to the initiated. In addition, ritual specialists of all kinds — from priests and priestesses to shamans and monastics — acquire their religious identity and abilities through some kind of ritual transformation.

With the goal of transformation, the initiation ceremony (regardless of type) typically consists of four phases: symbolic death, the ordeal, the acquisition of sacred knowledge, and symbolic rebirth. Often the details of the initiation are secret, but where they are public we see this pattern. For example, the very simple initiation of baptism into Christian life is an immersion in water (or symbolic sprinkling). In his letter to the Romans, the early Christian missionary Paul interprets baptism as a death of the sinful self and rebirth in union with the resurrected, and deathless, Christ: "Have you forgotten that when we were baptized into union with Christ Jesus we were baptized into his death? By baptism we were buried with him, and lay dead, in order that, as Christ was raised from the dead in the splendor of the Father, so also we might set our feet upon the new path of life."[28] In ceremonies of initiation the stage of death may be enacted by some kind of withdrawal from the community, either in the wilderness or in a special hut built for this purpose.

The ordeal — some kind of hardship imposed on the initiate — is understood by many interpreters to be linked to the powers of transformation within the human being. When it does not prove overwhelming, suffering can serve as a catalyst for personal growth. In an Australian story about the origin of the seven stars called the Pleiades, seven young girls become women by undergoing extremely painful and frightening ordeals, which include scarification, mutilation, and exposure to dangers of all kinds. Surviving the initiation, they encourage other young girls to face their rite of passage with feelings of courage and hope, "We have passed through the testing that our elders prescribed, and we have endured much pain. Now it is the desire of the Great Spirit that you should go through the same course of testing. You must know that the selfish person is not happy. This is because he thinks only of himself. Happiness comes through thinking of others and forgetting self. Greed and pain and fear are caused by thinking too much of self, and

3. Seeking Revelation: Worship and Spiritual Discipline

so it is necessary to vanquish self."²⁹ The transformation here is from a state of unhappy self-centeredness to one of benevolence and joy, and it is brought about by the experience of ordeal. The story expresses the value of this achievement by telling us that as a reward the seven maidens were turned into seven stars and placed in the sky.

The acquisition of sacred knowledge is also a part of the initiation. Often this is first-hand experience, perhaps a vision; sometimes, the sharing of secret lore. The final phase in initiation is the return to the community, but now as a person with a new identity and status.

Rebirth may be celebrated in many ways; it is usually an auspicious occasion. Karen McCarthy Brown describes the final moments of her initiation into some of the mysteries of leadership in Haitian Vodou (a form of Christianity that synthesizes French and African religious elements): "The initiates, carrying red roses and dressed in white, with strings of multicolored beads crisscrossed on their chests like bandoliers, stepped out of the initiation chamber and then turned in confusing spirals as they made their way into the *peristil* [temple]. They were at once newborn babies and gangly adolescents on a too-rapid path to adulthood. Their heads were doubly covered in scarves and straw hats, as if to protect vulnerable soft spots on the top of the skull. Their faces, not yet ready for the full light of day, were obscured with palm fringe. Cheers and applause greeted them. They had survived their trials. They had faced the fire and learned that one could choose to call it strong rather than hot. They had drunk from the mouth of death. That had tasted the sword of justice. They had been changed. They were changing. The final forms that would emerge were not yet clear. In other words, they had been reborn into the human family, this time better equipped to pit will and strength against fate."³⁰

Individual Techniques for Spiritual Discipline. Techniques that play a role in spiritual discipline can be practiced both as a group and individually. For example, silence, prayer, and the reading of sacred texts are commonly included in worship services as well as being designated as forms of spiritual training.

Another technique that is found both in the worship service and also in private devotions is chanting. Music is an important part of worship, which often includes chanting as a matter of course. But chanting is also a special category of music. In chanting, it is the repetition of particular sounds or melodies that is important. Thus, in some contexts, chanting serves as a kind of meditative technique. The goal of meditation is to quiet the body and the mind so as to create an inner silence in order to receive the divine presence. Chanting, or repeating, a mantra — the Indian word that refers to any sacred sound, such as OM or the holy name of a god or goddess — can help to focus the mind and draw its attention away from the distractions presented by the multiplicity of phenomena.

In Eastern Orthodox Christianity, one well-known chant is the Jesus Prayer, also known as the Prayer of the Heart: "Lord Jesus Christ, Son of God, have mercy on me!"[31] Repeated again and again, the prayer focuses the mind's attention and prepares the devotee for the experience of the divine light. Thus, chanting can serve as a technique to advance the experience of revelation.

Fasting — complete or partial abstinence from nourishment — can be an integral part of a collective ceremony, such as the long period of fasting during the lunar month of Ramadan, when Muslims fast from daybreak to sundown. During this month, all food, drink, and smoking are forbidden. Another form of collective fasting is the prohibition against eating meat. Found in Buddhism, certain forms of Hinduism, and elsewhere, vegetarianism for religious reasons plays an important role in training the adept. Any form of fasting can be undertaken by the individual person as part of his or her own spiritual training. For example, the first century Jewish ascetic John the Baptist is said to have been "dressed in a rough coat of camel's hair, with a leather belt round his waist, and he fed on locusts and wild honey."[32]

Charity is also a form of spiritual discipline. The word *charity* comes from the Latin word for love (*caritas*), which early Christians used to translate the New Testament term *agape*: God's love. Christians believe that receiving God's love, they are commanded to share it with others. Jesus makes this clear: "Love your enemies and pray for your persecutors; only so can you be children of your heavenly Father.... There must be no limit to your goodness, as your heavenly Father's goodness knows no bounds."[33] The practice of loving others — even those who are enemies — has as its goal drawing the Christian closer to God and also allowing him or her to attain "godliness."

Pilgrimage, too, is a technique that people employ as part of their religious training. All Muslims hope to travel once in their lifetimes to Mecca in Saudi Arabia. Buddhists will journey to Bodhgaya, India, to visit the Mahabodhi Temple, which marks the spot where the Buddha Shakyamuni experienced enlightenment. Hindu pilgrims will journey to holy fords, or crossings, located geographically on the banks of India's rivers, as, for example, Varanasi in North India. Any sacred place can become the destination for pilgrims. The journey itself is the technique for spiritual discipline, sometimes requiring austerities, such as walking on foot, wearing the simplest clothing, and fasting. Thus, the pilgrimage follows the initiatory pattern of death (leaving home), the ordeal (difficulties of the journey), the gift of new knowledge, and eventual rebirth. In his autobiography, the African American Malcolm X (Malcolm Little, 1925–1965) records the different stages of a dramatic, often angry existence. While in prison for robbery, he joined the Nation of Islam, which strongly condemned all white people because of the racism prevailing in the United States. But in 1964, Malcolm X abandoned this stance as a result of his pilgrimage to Mecca, during which he experienced an Islam that embraced people of all colors. The pilgrimage transformed him, deepening his faith and freeing him from a narrow vision based on race.[34]

The techniques that serve as components of spiritual training are both numerous and diverse. In Japan adepts will stand in the middle of winter under a cold waterfall in their desire to attain enlightenment.[35] The Mawlawiyah, an order of Islamic mystics that traces its origins back to the Sufi poet Jalal al-Din Rumi, combines music, poetry, and whirling dance. Trappist monks live in silence.[36] Daoists practice retreat, living alone in the wilderness on top of the highest mountains in China.[37] These and other techniques belong to traditions of transformation, or spiritual discipline. What is important to remember is that these are all just techniques and do not represent the goal of any tradition. Meditation is found in Christianity (where it is called contemplation) as well as in Buddhism, although the goals are different. Furthermore, meditation is used by non-religious people because it benefits the health of the body and focuses the mind. The same holds true for other techniques: retreat, for example, can be used for both religious and non-religious goals.

Traditions of Spiritual Discipline. In addition to the practice of individual techniques, several techniques may be combined to form a tradition of spiritual discipline. One example is the Lakota Hanblecheyapi, a ceremony that has the goal of developing a personal relationship with the spirits by means of visions. Translated as Crying for a Vision, the ceremony is made up of several techniques, including the steam bath, singing, prayer, retreat, and fasting. Black Elk tells us that the Hanblecheyapi was known to his people even before the appearance of White Buffalo Calf Woman. Both men and women may "cry for a vision" under the guidance of a holy man.[38]

First, the one who seeks to have a vision, or the "lamenter," builds a sweat lodge where he and his helpers will be purified. Sacred pipes are used to offer prayers and songs to Wakan Tanka and all the spirits. Prior to the ceremony a pit has been dug on a nearby mountain. Several poles with offerings, such as tobacco, tied at the top are placed in the ground there, and a bed of sage prepared for the lamenter. Carrying nothing but a pipe and a buffalo robe, the lamenter walks alone to the mountain pit. Once there he or she must slowly and carefully honor all the spirits and cry for their help. The vision quest may last two days or much longer. Neither eating nor drinking, the person waits for a vision.

At the end of the Hanblecheyapi, the helpers arrive at the pit with horses and carry the lamenter back to the sweat lodge. During this part of the ritual, the lamenter describes all that was done and seen on the mountaintop: his personal experiences of revelation. More prayers and songs then close the ceremony.

Further, a tradition of spiritual discipline may develop into a complex life style, the main focus of a person's entire life. One such tradition would be alchemy, which has both Asian and European forms. Outwardly the alchemist seeks the combined techniques that will transform common metals into gold, or simple beverages into elixirs that prolong life. However, the ultimate goal is the transmutation of the alchemists themselves — from mortal into immortal — by manipulating natural processes of transformation, such as those found in metallurgy and traditional medicines. Exceedingly complex, and often secret, the works of alchemy are nevertheless spiritual disciplines aimed at transformation.[39]

The yoga of India is another complex tradition that can become a lifelong endeavor.[40] We cannot say how old yoga is. It may even predate the arrival in India of the Indo-Europeans, as evidenced by the picture of a man seated in "lotus position" on one of the ancient seals from the Indus Valley civilization.[41] Today yoga continues to be practiced all over the world, not just in India.

Yoga is a Sanskrit word that means "union," which implies the goal of yoga: union of the human and the divine. The yogi is a male practitioner of yoga; his female counterpart is called a yogini. Yogis have as their goal union with the divine self. Over the centuries, different names are given to the self: brahman, atman, and purusha, for example.

One of the oldest forms of yoga practiced in India is Dhyana Yoga. Also known as Raja Yoga, the "royal path," it is the path that emphasizes the technique of meditation. By means of silent meditation, yogis discover a quiet place within where the divine self can be met directly and completely. This invites samadhi (Sanskrit, "to establish, or to make firm"), a state of consciousness beyond waking, dreaming, and sleeping. In Hinduism, samadhi refers to the absorption of the knowing subject (the human) into the reality of the object of meditation (the divine). Becoming one with the divine self leads to an awakening of non-dual consciousness and eternal liberation from the cycles of birth, suffering, death, and rebirth.

> The self [*atman*] is never born and never dies. Before it there was nothing, and it is one for evermore. Never-born and eternal, beyond times gone or to come, it does not die when the body dies.[42]

Thus, in union with the divine self the yogi or yogini shares in its immortal nature.

The ancient yogis would leave the family to live in the forest and follow a strict regimen that was developed over the centuries to increase the possibility of attaining samadhi. The techniques that yogis found most useful were eventually collected and preserved by Patanjali in written form as the *Yoga Sutra*. Among the many teachings of this ancient text are the "Eight Limbs of the Tree of Yoga," outlining the various techniques that together make up this tradition of spiritual discipline.[43]

1. Yamas (abstinences, or things not to do)
    Ahimsa (do no harm)
    Satya (do not lie)
    Asteya (do not steal)
    Brahmacharya (practice chastity)
    Aparigraha (take only what you need)
2. Niyamas (observances, or things to do)
    Shaucha (cultivate all forms of purity)
    Santosha (cultivate contentment)
    Tapas (accept pain)

Svadhyaya (study the scriptures)

Ishvara-pranidhana (surrender to God)

3. Asanas (physical poses to prepare the body for meditation)
4. Pranayama (breathing practices)
5. Pratyahara (withdraw attention from sense experience)
6. Dharana (concentrate on one point)
7. Dhyana (the meditative state — quiet body and quiet mind)
8. Samadhi (absorption into the divine; non-dual consciousness)

The first seven limbs are the techniques of spiritual discipline. The eighth limb is the experience of revelation, specifically mystical union, the goal of this tradition. Note that the first two limbs include ethical practice and worship. Limbs three through six are techniques for meditation, allowing the body and mind to become completely quiet. Limb seven refers to the state of inner stillness, when there is no inner dialogue and no mental images nor physical sensations. Of course, all the limbs of the tree of yoga are meant to be practiced together.

The yoga of meditation continues to flourish in the modern world. One of its most eloquent interpreters, the master yogi B. K. S. Iyengar, clarifies the interrelated development of body, mind, and soul: "In order to find out how to reveal our innermost Being, the sages explored the various sheaths of existence, starting from body and progressing through mind and intelligence, and ultimately to soul. The yogic journey guides us from our periphery, the body, to the center of our being, the soul. The aim is to integrate the various layers so that the inner divinity shines out as through clear glass."[44] This language suggests that the goal (union with the divine reality) exists already but needs to become conscious.

Dhyana Yoga is one example of a way of life that is dedicated to spiritual discipline, but it is not the only such tradition. All monastic traditions, where people withdraw from society — as hermits or together in groups of monks and nuns — belong to this category of religion. Just as in worship there are ritual specialists, such as priests and ministers, who take care of the temple or church and lead in the liturgical life of the community, so, too, in spiritual discipline there are specialists to lead others along the way. More often they are thought of as teachers and counselors. Their numbers include the holy gurus of India, the pastoral counselors of Protestant churches, and the

3. Seeking Revelation: Worship and Spiritual Discipline

spiritual directors of monastic traditions. They are the ones who have gone on before, and only for this reason are they now able to serve others as guides.

In Dhyana Yoga the ritual of meditation forms the essential component in a tradition of spiritual discipline. In a similar way, the Eucharist, which belongs to worship in all Christian communities, is for many one rite together with others that comprise a spiritual discipline of gradual sanctification, or even deification.[45]

For all Christians, the Eucharist — the Lord's Supper, or Communion — is first of all a ritual that re-enacts Jesus' own last supper, which took place during Passover.

> During supper he took bread, and having said the blessing he broke it and gave it to them, with the words: "Take this; this is my body." Then he took a cup, and having offered thanks to God he gave it to them; and they all drank from it. And he said, "This is my blood, the blood of the covenant, shed for many."[46]

By participating in the ritual meal, the members of the congregation are symbolically transported into the living presence of Christ.

The association of the Eucharist with the Jewish Passover meal adds another dimension to the symbolism. Before they were rescued out of slavery in Egypt, the Israelites (ancestors of the Jews) were commanded by God to prepare a meal of unleavened bread, in which a sacrificed lamb played an especially important role. The lamb's blood was to be smeared on the lintel and two doorposts of every Israelite home, so that when their God traveled throughout Egypt during the night and struck dead the first-born child in every household, seeing the blood, he would pass on by without entering their homes.[47]

The language of body and blood brings to mind the lamb that was sacrificed at the original Passover meal. But here, in the Eucharist, the sacrifice is Christ himself. The broken bread and the poured out wine represent the battered body and shed blood of Jesus as he died on the cross. Christ is the Lamb of God, whose crucifixion serves to protect all humankind from the power of death.

At the same time, many Christians regard the Eucharist as one of several rituals that have particular redeeming power: these are the sacraments. The English word *sacrament* derives from the Latin term *sacramentum*, which, in turn, is a third-century translation of the Greek *mysterion*. In Greek religion, the *mysterion* signaled a rite that was secret in the sense that only the initiated were allowed to participate. The rite allowed direct contact with the deity, and as a result, contributed to the salvation of the initiate. Likewise, for Christians, the sacraments are rituals that convey God's saving grace directly to the faithful. There are seven sacraments:

1. Baptism
2. Confirmation
3. Penance
4. Eucharist
5. Matrimony
6. Holy Orders
7. Extreme Unction

Baptism (ritual bathing) has as its model John the Baptism baptizing Jesus in the Jordan River.[48] "It happened at this time that Jesus came from Nazareth in Galilee and was baptized in the Jordan by John. At the moment when he came up out of the water, he saw the heavens torn open and the Spirit, like a dove, descending upon him. And a voice spoke from heaven: 'Thou art my Son my Beloved; on thee my favor rests.'"[49] For the Christian community, baptism is a ritual of rebirth: one is reborn as a member of the Church, the community of saints. By means of the water, the sinful self dies and the person is born anew in union with Christ. The Christian becomes, like Jesus, a child of God, although adopted not "begotten." Like Jesus, he or she will inherit the kingdom of God.[50]

The second sacrament may well be based on an early tradition recorded already in the Acts of the Apostles, which depicts both the sacred bath and a second rite, the laying on of hands to transmit to the new Christian the indwelling of the Holy Spirit.

> The apostles in Jerusalem now heard that Samaria had accepted the word of God. They sent Peter and John, who went down there and prayed for the converts, asking that they might receive the Holy Spirit. For until then the Spirit had not come upon any of them. They had been baptized into the name of the Lord Jesus, that and nothing more. So Peter and John laid their hands on them and they received the Holy Spirit.[51]

The inspiration of the Holy Spirit has always been central to the life of the Christian Church. The gifts of the spirit are many and include faith, wisdom, prophecy, and healing, among others.[52]

3. Seeking Revelation: Worship and Spiritual Discipline

Penance, or the ritual of reconciliation, allows the Christian to confess and take responsibility for his or her transgressions in order to experience God's forgiveness. Sometimes, confession is expressed out loud by the congregation and their leaders during worship; but individual confession with a priest as witness is also practiced.

The Eucharist can be celebrated daily, weekly, or in some churches, only on special occasions. The kind of bread (sometimes unleavened so as to recall the Passover meal) and the specific drink (sometimes grape juice instead of wine) will vary. Even more varied will be the specific rituals of the marriage ceremony, but the inclusion of matrimony into the seven sacraments underscores the role that family plays in the sanctifying life of the Christian. Thus, the wedding takes place in the presence of a priest or pastor; and in some churches, dissolution of the marriage is rarely allowed because of its sacramental quality.

The term Holy Orders refers to rituals of ordination that set apart the recipient (bishop, priest, or deacon) as a minister of the church. As for the anointing of the sick with oil, sometimes referred to as Extreme Unction (or last rites), this sacrament continues the healing ministry of Jesus, and after his ascension, that of his apostles.

In 1439 at the Council of Florence, the number of sacraments was doctrinally limited to seven.[53] Already in the mid-twelfth century the Bishop of Paris Peter Lombard (c. 1100–1160) had assumed that there were seven sacraments. Both the decisions of the council and the writings of Lombard reflect the general medieval practice. However, the Christian interest in sacraments and the religious worldview that supports the sacramental tradition begins much earlier. For example, the Latin theologian Tertullian (c. 160–220 CE) refers to the sacraments of baptism and penance as the two planks on which the sinner may be saved from the shipwreck of sin.[54]

Tertullian rejected the Platonic philosophy of his time, which he saw as a factor contributing to the development of gnostic thought and its tenet that the immortal soul leaves behind the body in order to be saved. Tertullian, in contrast, believed that the soul was not immortal but created together with the body. For him, the body was not an obstacle to knowing God — quite the opposite. Only by means of the body and the experience of the senses could God touch and transform the human being, body and soul together.

> The flesh indeed is washed in order that the soul may be cleansed.
> The flesh is anointed that the soul may be consecrated.
> The flesh is shadowed with the imposition of hands that the soul also may be illuminated by the spirit.
> The flesh feeds on the body and blood of Christ that the soul likewise may fatten on its God.[55]

Referring here to the acts of immersion, the imposition of hands, anointing, and the sacred meal that are central in the sacraments, Tertullian expresses the belief that the creation, and hence the body, is the place of God's active grace. Tertullian shares with many of his contemporaries the conviction that the body and the soul have become vulnerable to immorality, disease, and death because the two first humans, Adam and Eve, disobeyed God and were forced out of Paradise. The world that their descendents inherit is marred by this event: this is the meaning of sin. It does not refer to actual acts but rather to the corrupted state of the creation.

For Tertullian, the risen Christ lives eternally in a now incorruptible body. This is also the destiny of those who believe in him: at the end of time they too will become incorruptible and enter into the eternal life God intended for them. According to this imagery, the Eucharist contributes to this transformation process because it is to the incorruptible body and blood of the risen Christ that the sacramental body and blood (bread and wine) correspond. In the sacrament the Christian assimilates this incorruptibility and gradually draws near the ultimate goal of eternal life in the divine presence.

CHAPTER 4

Ways of Receiving Revelation

When we ask religious people why they do what they do — what, in other words, is the source of their religion — they tell us that they are simply responding to some kind of revelation: God spoke to the prophet Muhammad in order to teach the people how to live; White Buffalo Calf Woman showed us how to use the sacred pipe; Jesus of Nazareth gave us a prayer for talking to God; and so forth. So, religions begin with revelations. And these are events that happen to people; they are not "human-made." But the many different ways in which people respond to the experience of revelation leads to the creation of sacred art, the establishment of holy places, and the choreography of complex festivals. These we can see and examine. These *are* "human-made."

Because of its Gothic design, the St. Lorenz Cathedral at Nuremberg is so lofty and elegant that one feels that one has entered into a space that allows the human spirit to soar up to a God whose dwelling place, as envisioned by medieval Europeans, is in the highest heavens. However, each stone, each glass window, each wooden pew was put there by human hands. The cathedral is a human accomplishment, but the resurrection of Jesus, which is the revelation that gave birth to the Christian religion, is not "human-made." The appearance of the resurrected Jesus is something that happened to people — to his followers — in the first century of the Common Era and continues to happen to Christians still today.

The great statue of the Buddha inside the temple called Todaiji (the Eastern Great Temple) in Nara, Japan, was made by human hands, as was the temple itself. But the revelation that is being expressed in this Buddhist holy place is the enlightenment that Siddhartha Gautama experienced while sitting under the Bodhi Tree in India 2500 years ago. The temple and its sacred art are "human-made" but not the revelation.

Thus, the response to revelation results in the human traditions that we call the religions of the world. And they include not only the art, the buildings, and the rituals that we can see but also the customs, ethical teachings, and theological beliefs that further determine people's daily lives. It is possible to study and talk about all these historical phenomena that make up the world's religious traditions, and in doing so we learn much about the people of our planet, those alive today and also their ancestors. When we examine the human response to revelation, we are indeed looking at "human-made" institutions and cultures, commonly called "religion."

Whereas the word *religion* refers to concrete and historical phenomena, the term itself is rather abstract. One cannot say what a religion looks like or how big it is or how long. So, when people talk about religions in general, they sometimes use figures of speech, images that suggest the common experiences belonging to different religious traditions. One such image is the house. Referring to the human-made aspects of religion, Martin Buber (1878–1965) says that each religion is like a house, "a house of the human soul longing for God."[1] So each religion is like a dwelling place for human beings, a home.

Religion as a House

The image of a house as a symbol for a religious tradition does satisfy on many points. We live in our religions, just as we live in our homes. People often speak about "feeling at home" in their own traditions, but feeling like strangers when visiting the temples and churches to which they do not belong. Just as a house provides a context for daily life, so, too, the rituals and festivals of religion give shape and meaning to our lives as a whole.

Further, the house is a useful symbol for religion, because all humans live in some kind of house, just as they all have some kind of religious tradition. Yet, there are just as many different kinds of religions as there are houses. Some people live in portable homes, because they move from place to place, following perhaps their herds of cattle or sheep. Hunters of the buffalo in nineteenth-century United States were able to move about easily, carrying with them their tipis, tents made of wooden poles and buffalo hide. Homes can be built out of diverse materials, including stone, ice, wood, grass, or mud. They can be widely separated or close together; even one large building can contain many apartments, each one a home.

4. Ways of Receiving Revelation

In a similar way, religions look very different from the outside, because each one is affected by the historical conditions that have determined the development of the society: the environment, economic practices, relationships with other societies, and so forth. Although each religion is unique in many ways, it shares with other religions two fundamental purposes: to express the experience of revelation and to bring the people into some kind of relationship with the source of revelation.

Martin Buber goes on to say about this metaphorical house that it is "a house with windows and without a door."[2] Now the metaphor takes on a rather surprising aspect: who ever heard of a house without a door? Surely all houses have doors, so that the people who live in the house can enter and leave and so that others are able to visit them. A house without a door would be some kind of prison for a criminal or perhaps a cell for a recluse. In *The Hunchback of Notre-Dame*, Victor Hugo's novel about the confusion of religion and civil power in fifteenth-century France, a recluse by her own choice lives in a doorless cell built into the outer wall of the Tower of Roland. There is a window, so that things can be passed in and out, but no door. No one can enter, and the recluse cannot leave.

Likewise, Buber's house that represents religion does allow for communication with the outer world, but only via the window. "I need only open a window and God's light penetrates."[3] In this metaphor, God's spirit is symbolized by a light outside the house that is accessible only through the window. Light is a common image for the divine. Without light, we cannot see. More than that, without light there is no life, as our main source of light is the sun, which provides us with both warmth and energy. In this house we can open the window and let God's spirit enter into our lives, but we cannot go out and walk in the light. Why is that? It is because in this metaphor there are two lights and one of them is destructive: "if I make a hole in the wall and break out, then I have not only become houseless but a cold light surrounds me that is not the light of the living God."[4]

A second light exists also somewhere outside the house, although it is unable to enter the house through the proper window. It is not the warm light of life and God. It is cold. It is hard to imagine a cold light. Even light reflected off the snow is not actually cold. It would seem that cold light is a contradiction. Perhaps here it symbolizes an illusion — something that resembles the divine spirit but lacks God's life-giving qualities. At least we understand now that the house is constructed in such a way so as to protect people from this cold light while at the same time allowing them to experience the warm light of God.

Why would Martin Buber suggest such a metaphor for religion? Who was he and what was he trying to express?[5] Born in Vienna, Buber was educated there and in Leipzig, Zurich, and Berlin, receiving a doctorate of philosophy from Vienna after completing a dissertation on Nicholas of Cusa and Jacob Boehme, both important figures in European Christianity. Nicholas of Cusa was preoccupied with the question of how human beings can experience God, while Boehme, a mystic, wrote of his own visionary experiences. Furthermore, Boehme was influenced by both Western alchemy and Jewish mysticism, and Buber himself would later turn to the writings of Jewish mystics, specifically eastern European Hasidic Jews, as he developed his own understanding of his Jewish faith.

From 1923 to 1933, Buber was a professor at the University of Frankfurt, teaching simultaneously at the Frankfurt Jüdische Lehrhaus. In 1938 he left Germany for Palestine, where he became professor of social philosophy at the Hebrew Union in Jerusalem. His knowledge of mysticism was linked to an interest in personal religious experience. Buber always emphasized the value of personal religiosity as both spontaneous and creative, while seeing the more institutional side of religion as static but necessary.

In his writings and in his life, Martin Buber emphasized also the importance of the individual person in dialogue with others. Seeking a solution to the general sense of estrangement that he believed to be prevalent in modern society, he coined the term "inter-human relatedness," or *das Zwischenmenschliche*. In his perhaps best-known work, *I and Thou*,[6] Buber encourages people to cultivate an attitude that recognizes the unique self in each person. Much of modern alienation, he suggests, comes from a feeling that one is being treated by others as if one were a thing ("it"), not a person ("thou").

The metaphor of a house without a door certainly does express the feeling of alienation: "Each religion is an exile into which man is driven; here he is in exile more clearly than elsewhere because in his relationship to God he is separate from the men of other communities; and not sooner than in the redemption of the world can we be liberated from the exiles and brought into a common world of God. But the religions that know that are bound together in a common expectation; they can call to one another greetings from exile to exile, from house to house through the open windows."[7] Although separation is inevitable in this community of houses, still for those

4. Ways of Receiving Revelation

who can find their way to the windows of their houses and experience there the divine light, there is also the possibility of seeing and greeting each other.

Finally, Martin Buber believes that this situation of alienation — living in houses without doors — is temporary, and one day it will come to an end with the "redemption of the world." Buber clearly suggests that each religion is a temporary and limited shelter during a time when the world is in need of redemption. The existence of two lights — one, the light of the living God, and the other, a false and cold light — corresponds to this dangerous period when people must take refuge in their religions, as exiles find temporary shelter before returning home.

We can best understand Buber's imagery in terms of the traditional Jewish view of history as the period between the fall of Adam and Eve into sin and death and the hoped-for restoration of paradise at the end of time. The story of the Fall is found in the first book of the Bible.[8] God creates Adam, the first man, in a garden paradise called Eden, telling him to take care of it. In the middle of the garden are two trees: the tree of life and the tree of the knowledge of good and evil. God warns Adam: "You may eat from every tree in the garden, but not from the tree of the knowledge of good and evil; for on the day that you eat from it you will certainly die."[9] Then, feeling that Adam will be lonely, God creates numerous creatures and Adam gives each one a name. Finally, God creates a companion for Adam, a woman called Eve. Innocent and natural, they go about naked in their garden home.

Now, of all the wild creatures, the one most crafty was the serpent, who convinces Eve that God's words are not true: "Of course you will not die. God knows that as soon as you eat [the fruit of the tree of the knowledge of good and evil], your eyes will be opened and you will be like gods knowing both good and evil."[10] Trusting the serpent, Eve takes the fruit, tastes it, and gives it to Adam to eat. Immediately, they feel shame. Conscience, recognizing the difference between what is right and what is wrong, has been awakened in them. They improvise simple clothes out of fig leaves; and hearing God's approach, they hide.

God sees the change in Adam and Eve and knows that they have disregarded his warning. God then calls to Adam and asks why he is hiding; Adam admits that he was "afraid because he was naked."[11] He then tells God what has taken place. As a result of the disobedience, each one — serpent, woman, and man — is cursed: The serpent is doomed to crawl on its belly.

The woman is cursed to suffer in childbirth and to be dominated by the man. The man is cursed to hard labor and eventual death. "Dust you are, to dust you shall return."[12]

Adam and Eve are sent away from Eden into exile. History, as we know it, now begins: a time that includes both suffering and death. Banished from paradise, the descendents of Adam and Eve are dependent on their religions to provide some kind of connection to God as well as protection in a world fraught with evil. But in traditional Jewish thought, there is always the hope of a return to God's presence: redemption at the end of this age of exile. It is within this mythical framework that Martin Buber's metaphor makes sense.

Central to this metaphor is the co-existence of two very different kinds of light: the life-giving light and the cold, deathlike light. This symbolism suggests a dualistic interpretation of history.

Dualism refers to two, often-conflicting, principles of causality at work. Treating the term as a category within the history of religions (not as a philosophical concept), Ugo Bianchi distinguishes the forms of dualism that appear in myths from doctrines about dualism.[13] Thus, in the myths, radical dualism refers to those religions that recognize two causal principles, or deities, that together bring about the creation of the world. One example is Manichaeism, a religion founded by Mani in Persia during the second half of the third century. According to Mani's teaching, before the world as we know it, there existed two realms: one of light, which was above; and the darkness, below. The Father of Majesty, a good god, ruled in the light; below was the Prince of Darkness, an evil being, who invades the realm of light and initiates in this way the long struggle that results in the creation of the world.

This radical dualism, says Bianchi, contrasts to a moderate form, which is found, for example, in the monotheistic traditions of Judaism and Christianity. Monotheism, the belief that only one God exists and alone should receive worship, recognizes God as the Creator. A second being, or evil power, is not present at the time of creation but derives in some way from the first. Many myths try to account for the origins of this second, evil principle: for example, various stories about a fallen angel. In Buber's metaphor, the cold light seems to symbolize some such derivative and limited power of evil, sometimes referred to as the Devil, responsible for the evil and death that determine so much of human history. Ultimately, he is doomed to lose his power at the time of redemption. Then, there will no longer be the need for the protection of religion, because all of Adam and Eve's descendents (all humankind) will once again live together in intimacy with God, just as Adam and Eve did in Eden.

Martin Buber's metaphor for religion as a house with a window and no door suggests further that each religion has the same origin: "Every religion has its origin in revelation."[14] Religions look different because of their geographical, cultural, and historical developments, but each one is a human response to revelation. So dialogue among religions can only increase our understanding of God and of each other. It is not surprising that Martin Buber, with this interpretation of religion, was very active in seeking Arab-Jewish rapprochement in Palestine. Prior to 1948 when the modern state of Israel declared itself a Jewish nation, Buber endorsed a bi-national state, where Jews and Muslims would have equal rights and responsibilities.

Religion as a Path

Another metaphor for the term *religion* expresses an alternative interpretation of history. This is religion as a road, or a path. In the writings of Satchidananda (1914–2002), a modern teacher of Dhyana Yoga, each religion is a path that leads to the divine: "After you have decided which path is right for you, stick to that path, but do not say to others that this is the only one. Recognize all of the paths and respect them. In the spiritual life, all paths lead to the same place."[15]

As in Martin Buber's image, here, too, the members of different religions are separated. People begin the journey from different geographical places, each place with its unique history and culture. So each path is distinct and will have its own particular characteristics. One path might be steep, leading straight up a mountain; another path might consist of many switchbacks allowing for a slow but gentle climb. One path might lead beside a river, while another might pass through a forest or desert. So each path is unique, but all lead to the same place. And the pilgrims are separated from each other, not by walls, but by the natural distance that exists in-between the paths. The inability to walk on two paths at the same time is simply — in this metaphor — a matter of the limitations placed on the human body, which cannot be in two places at once. But at the journey's end, the pilgrims shall meet.

In Satchidananda's metaphor there is only one kind of light, the natural light of day. "The Light is within and without. It is in you, in everybody, in everything. Wherever we recognize that Light, we express our devotion.... It is the spirit. It is the Light that is guiding our lives. It is the awareness itself. It is in you and it is everywhere."[16] Therefore, religions do not need to provide shelter from a false light. This symbolism reflects a way of thinking that is sometimes referred to by the word *monism*: there is only one principle of causality at work in history.

In Vedanta, or the religious teachings of India that recognize the authority of the ancient scriptures known as the Vedas and the Upanishads, there is a tendency towards monistic thinking.[17] We can distinguish two major versions: absolute monism, which says that only one reality exists — the divine; and qualified monism, which argues that all existing phenomena come from one divine reality. In both forms of monism an opposing causal principle is lacking altogether.

The *advaita* (non-duality) teachings of Shankara (c. 700 CE) offer an example of absolute monism.[18] One important text in this tradition is found in the Brihadaranyaka Upanishad:

> This (self) was indeed Brahman in the beginning. It knew only itself as, "I am Brahman." Therefore, it became all. And whoever among the gods knew it also became that; and the same with sages and men.... And to this day whoever in like manner knows it as, "I am Brahman," becomes all this (universe) — even the gods cannot prevail against him, for he becomes their self. On the other hand, he who worships a god thinking, "He is one, and I am another," does not know.[19]

Building on this and similar passages, Shankara taught that liberation comes when the human being realizes his or her true identity as Brahman, the one and sole divine reality. In his view, the worship of a god or goddess will not result in this kind of knowledge. It is gained only through study of the Vedas, which awakens transcendental insight (jnana), a kind of intuitive awareness that alters consciousness.

> Stop identifying yourself with this corruptible physical body, born of the flesh of father and mother. Regard it as impure, as though it were an outcast. Attain the goal of life by realizing your unity with Brahman.[20]

Once one attains true self-knowledge, one is free from all illusion — the perception that we are separate selves and must suffer the cycles of birth, suffering, death and rebirth.

4. Ways of Receiving Revelation

In contrast, a form of qualified monism is articulated by Ramanuja (c. 1017–1137), a devotee of the god Vishnu, whom he regarded as the Supreme Self, identical with ultimate reality (Brahman).[21] In this view, individual souls exist in relation to the Supreme Self as light to fire. The souls resemble the Supreme Self in that both have consciousness and bliss as their essential characteristics. They differ, however, because the souls exist in a dependent relation to the Supreme Self, which is both all-powerful and all pervasive. According to Ramanuja, transcendental insight (jnana) by itself will not lead to liberation. What is necessary is for the soul to enter into a loving relationship with the Supreme Self, as manifest in Vishnu, whose grace alone is powerful enough to free the soul from reincarnation in the material world. For Ramanuja, devotion (bhakti), which entails worship and acts of service, is the path that leads to the goal of freedom.

With these and other related views in his tradition, Satchidananda shares a basically monistic view of reality: "There is one Cosmic Essence, all-pervading, all-knowing, all-powerful."[22] Although a teacher, like Martin Buber, Satchidananda was not trained as a systematic thinker, or academic. He was a monk. He shares with others his own spiritual discipline, which is known as Integral Yoga because it synthesizes several techniques: hatha yoga (the physical poses), chanting, breathing practices, and meditation. In addition, service and devotion as well as study of scripture, all find an important place in his yoga. Because devotion plays a significant role in Integral Yoga, we might say that his thinking is closer to the qualified monism of Ramanuja. "Treat everyone as the Lord. Feel His Presence in everyone."[23]

In 1914 he was born as C. K. Ramaswamy Gounder in Chettipalayam, South India. As a young man, Ramu, as he was called, was active in the life of his family and community. In 1945 after the death of his wife, he gave up that life and traveled to Palani to begin training as a monk. Four years later he met his primary teacher, Shivanada, who gave him the name Satchidananda.[24] In September of that same year, he experienced enlightenment at Vasishta Guha near Rishikesh.

Eventually, Shivananda sent him to serve as a monk in Sri Lanka. There Satchidananda found himself in the middle of a religious conflict between the Hindus and the Buddhists. Reaching out to both sides, he discovered his role as peacemaker, seeking to bring understanding and harmony in various interfaith settings. Satchidananda often taught his conviction that the one divine reality is experienced according to different names in different religions, but the underlying truth remains one: "This nameless, formless essence can be approached by any name, any form, any symbol that suits the individual. That is why we have all the religions. But we should never forget our essential unity."[25]

In 1966, Satchidananda was invited to the United States, where he spent the rest of his life. For many years in New York City, he and Rabbi Joseph Gelberman of the Little Synagogue participated in an annual dialogue entitled "The Swami and the Rabbi,"[26] during which they shared their traditions of Hinduism and Judaism with their audiences in order to further the goal of ecumenical understanding. Eventually Satchidananda and his followers founded an ashram, or spiritual retreat center, in Virginia. Called Yogaville, it has as its center a temple, the Lotus, within which there are numerous altars, each representing a different religion or group of religions. The temple is shaped in the form of a lotus. This flower connects all dimensions, growing in the earth and water up into the air and opening to the light of the sun. In Indian culture the lotus thus symbolizes the goal of each life, to become a reflection of the one light: alive, joyous, and awake.

Religion as a House with Windows and Doors

Both metaphors for religion — that of Martin Buber and that of Satchidananda — have their usefulness. Satchidananda's image of separate paths leading to the same goal suggests that diverse religions may have a common purpose. And Buber's suggestion that a religion is like a house reminds us of the human-made character of religion and the universality of religions that look different from the outside but serve as "homes" for the faithful.

I would like to suggest a third metaphor for religion, one very close to that of Martin Buber but serving a different purpose: Religion is like a house with windows and doors. In his metaphor involving the two lights, Buber seeks to express his theology, which emphasizes history as a time of exile. The two lights suggest the moral danger of living in this world where good and evil both exist. My metaphor has a different, non-theological purpose. We can think of religion as a house, especially a modern home, in order to conceptualize the different ways that people receive revelations.

Windows and doors are found in the modern home. Inside, there may well be a television, a telephone, a radio, a fax machine, a computer, a mail

4. Ways of Receiving Revelation

slot in the door, and so forth. If a friend who lives outside my house wants to send me a "happy birthday" message, a card or telegram could be delivered through the door slot of my home. A messenger conveying the message could be sent to knock on my door, or my friend could go on radio or television to get the message to me. E-mail, fax machines, and telephones offer other possible ways of communicating with me. This friend could also come and visit me in my house, bringing me the message in person, or invite me to a party somewhere outside my house. Although the meaning and the source of the message remain the same, there are many ways to receive the communication.

Even if I lived in a simple hut, more than one way to receive messages from the outside world would be available to me: a messenger could be sent to my home; the friend could come in person or invite me to leave home and get the message in another place. Smoke signals and drums are also useful for long-range communication.

Just as humans have multiple modes of communicating with one another, so, too, there are several ways that people receive messages from the spirit world. Regardless of the source of the message — whether it is from the ancestors, the spirits, the gods, or God — the manner according to which it comes to our attention can vary. In other words, this metaphor of religion as a house helps us to understand the types of revelation that serve as the foundations of the world's religious traditions. People see visions and hear voices, and they interpret these subjective experiences as revelations. Some travel to the spirit world; others lend their bodies as a temporary medium so that a spirit can enter the human world.

Altogether six different types of revelation can be discerned: visions and voices; divination; spirit journey; spirit mediation; mystical union, and divine incarnation. Learning to identify each type and understand how it operates deepens and enriches our appreciation for all forms of religious experience.

By visions and voices we are referring to revelations that are experienced by means of the bodily senses or the imagination, which draws its imagery from physical sensations. Something seen, heard, or felt is interpreted as a message from the gods. The vision can be personal or collective. For example, Black Elk tells us of the bird that spoke to him in the forest, saying "Listen. A voice is calling you." Already as a child, he saw and heard messages from the spirits. On the other hand, the visit of White Buffalo Calf Woman to the ancestors of Black Elk would be a group vision, something like a waking dream experienced by many people at the same time.

The second type of revelation is divination, a fairly widespread phenomenon. Divination is based on the conviction that the spirits, ancestors, or gods can communicate to human beings by means of omens and signs, that is, symbolic patterns that appear in the natural world. These events are often interpreted by individual specialists, such as the astrologer, palm reader, or geomancer. Divination has played an important role in ancient Chinese culture, for example, where the king was understood to receive his authority from divine Heaven. If the ruler failed in his responsibility to be a just and good king, he would lose the Mandate of Heaven. How was this communicated to the people? Heaven would inform them by causing a natural disaster, such as a flood, earthquake, or drought. Each catastrophe could be interpreted as a message from the gods that it was time to find a new king.

Spirit travel is the third type of revelation. The spirit (mind, or soul) of the person leaves the body to travel, both in the natural world and also in the spirit world. Then it returns to the body, at which time it can report to others what it has seen and heard during the spirit journey. This is the most important form of revelation in certain small hunting societies, especially in areas close to the Arctic Circle. The one who makes the spirit journey often serves as the healer and spiritual guide of the community as well, because it is he or she who maintains on-going contact with the spirits in the otherworld. Through this contact, vital knowledge and power is gained for healing and hunting.

Perhaps the opposite type of revelation is spirit mediation. Here a spirit temporarily enters the human world through a medium. The possession can be total or partial; the medium can be conscious or unconscious. Even inspiration — where the human being is completely conscious and in control of his or her own actions but aware of a guiding spiritual presence — belongs to this category of revelation. One example comes from ancient Greece. By visiting Apollo's medium at Delphi, kings desiring divine guidance would consult with this god of clarity and order, who was the special patron of kings. At Delphi, the female medium, or Pythia, served the god, who took control of her body in order to answer the questions of mortals.

Mystical union must also be seen as a type of revelation. Here the boundaries that limit human consciousness collapse. Sometimes mystical union is felt to be a union with God or with the divine self. At other times,

4. Ways of Receiving Revelation

it feels like an expansion of consciousness so as to embrace all of reality. Many practices are cultivated in order to facilitate the revelation, which all mystics agree lies beyond human control: it happens to them.

Last, divine incarnation is also a form of revelation. Here the spirit does more than briefly visit the human world by means of a medium. The incarnating spirit is born as a baby, grows up as a boy or girl, and lives the life of a human being in order to help people. Tibetans, for example, believe that certain great spirits called tulkus freely choose to have a human life in this world in order to guide others on their way to enlightenment. Indeed, the Dalai Lama is believed to be the incarnation of the Bodhisattva of Compassion, whose sole aim is to bring others to their own spiritual fulfillment.

These six types of revelation are found alone and in combinations throughout human history. Sometimes, one type will be more central to the traditions of a people: for example, visions and voices are primary in the prophetic traditions of Judaism and Islam, whereas mystical union lies at the heart of Hinduism and Buddhism, both of which emerge from the soil of India. Often, however, people will recognize many or all of these types of revelation as ways that the spirit world can communicate with human beings.

Part Two.
A Typology of
Revelation

CHAPTER 5

Visions and Voices

"Seeing visions" and "hearing voices" both refer to the most common type of revelation, one that is found in all religions and in every part of the world. In defining this category of revelation we might say that visions and voices are messages from the spirit world that are received by means of the senses or the imagination (drawing on the memories of sense experience). Something seen, heard, felt, smelled, or tasted is interpreted as a revelation. Thus, visions and voices resemble ordinary bodily awareness, except that one is convinced that what one perceives is somehow under the influence of the spirit reality. For example, both the beauty of White Buffalo Calf Woman and her wisdom suggested to the Lakota that she was a wakan woman ("spirit" woman, or goddess). Her transformation into a buffalo calf was even more convincing. No ordinary woman could do such a thing!

Although people more commonly see a vision or hear the voices of the spirits, yet all senses may facilitate the reception of revelation. Early Christian writer and bishop Augustine of Hippo (354–430) describes the body's role in knowing God:

> Late have I loved thee, beauty so ancient and so new!
> Late have I loved thee!
> Thou wast within me, and I stood without.
> I sought thee here,
>   hurling my ugly self on the beauty of thy creatures.
> Thou wast with me, but I was not with thee.
> Thou hast called me, thy cry has vanquished my deafness.
> Thou hast broadcast thy perfume,
>   and I have breathed it: now I sigh for thee.
> I have tasted thee, and now I hunger for thee.
> Thou hast touched me, and now I burn with desire for thy peace.[1]

In his poem, Augustine relates how while he was seeking God somewhere outside in the world around him, God was already present within. He hears God's voice. He smells the fragrance of the divine. He tastes God and feels the touch of God. Augustine's entire physical being is able to perceive that God is reaching out to him.

Among the five senses, that of smell is perhaps least often associated with revelation. Sometimes people underestimate the power of fragrance, but in fact, smell is closely linked with the autonomic nervous system and with memory. This nonverbal communication affects humans on a deep, even unconscious, level. In many religious ceremonies incense of one kind or another evokes in the worshippers a connection to holiness. Incense is frequently offered to the gods as a gift of sacrifice, and fragrance can serve as a medium for revelation.

One example of the role of smell in the experience of holy revelation is found in the *Vimalakirti Sutra*, an important Mahayana Buddhist text of particular influence in both Chinese and Japanese schools of meditation (Chan and Zen). Probably written in the first century of the Common Era, the text relates a story believed to have taken place during the lifetime of Siddhartha Gautama, the historical Buddha, more than four hundred years earlier. Vimalakirti is not a monk but rather a wealthy townsman. Still, the Buddha sends some of his close disciples to visit him and so to learn from him. Vimalakirti speaks with authority and wisdom, demonstrating that even a layperson can attain enlightenment.

On the day of the visit, noon arrived and the monks began to worry about their midday meal. Realizing this, Vimalakirti entered into the mystical state (samadhi) and "employing his transcendental powers, showed the great assembly a country called Many Fragrances, situated in a region high above, beyond Buddha lands as numerous as the sands of forty-two Ganges."[2] This was the dwelling place of the buddha named Fragrance Accumulated, where even the halls and towers were built out of fragrances. Vimalakirti then invoked the spirit of a bodhisattva and sent him to this land to obtain a bowl of rice from the Fragrance Accumulated Buddha. Returning to the home of Vimalakirti and his guests, "the bodhisattva then presented the bowl filled with fragrant rice to Vimalakirti. The fragrance of the rice perfumed the entire city of Vaishali and the whole thousand-millionfold world.... Various earth deities, sky deities, and heavenly beings of the world of desire and the world of form, smelling the fragrant aroma, all likewise came to Vimalkirti's house."[3]

5. Visions and Voices

The host invited his guests to eat freely of the rice, but they were skeptical. How could such a small portion of rice feed the entire assembly? To this, Vimalakirti replied, "Though the four seas run dry, this rice will never come to an end."[4] He then proceeded to feed them all, and yet the bowl of rice remained full.

As soon as they had eaten, the visiting monks wanted to know how the Fragrance Accumulated Buddha preached the Dharma, that is, the way to attain enlightenment. "He just uses various fragrances to induce heavenly and human beings to undertake the observance of the precepts."[5] Indeed, certain fragrances are said even to induce the state of samadhi itself.

Another example where it is fragrance that conveys to the sense of smell a message from the spirit world is found in thirteenth-century Jewish mysticism. Ein Sof,[6] the absolute reality that is the source of all and transcends both being and nonbeing, can be known only through its sweet fragrance: "Ein Sof does not abide being known." When the mystics are able to ascend into the presence of Ein Sof, "they know only the aroma, as one inhaling an aroma is sweetened."[7] Here the "image" of God is not a person, not an animal, not even a voice, but a fragrance.

Perhaps more common, the sense of taste may serve in the reception of a revelation. One example is found in an interesting Taiwanese text entitled *Journey to the Underworld*. The book describes the sixty-two visionary journeys (usually at night) taken by the soul of one Yang Sheng between 9 September 1976 and 30 July 1978. According to the text, the journeys were authorized by the Jade Emperor and facilitated by Ji Gong, who served as guide. Both are Daoist deities. The purpose of the numerous journeys was to provide a human witness who could persuade others of the reality of the underworld both as a place of judgment and punishment as well as the location where individual reincarnation is determined. This knowledge, shared freely in Chinese and various other languages by means of translation, will benefit all of humankind: "so that everyone can try to do more good than evil; then only, will this world of ours be a better place to live in — Hell will then be less crowded and Paradise will receive the virtuous, like readers of this Book, with doors wide open."[8]

On the thirty-sixth journey (18 September 1977), Ji Gong brings Yang Sheng before the Sixth Tribunal. The chief judge, Bian Cheng Wang, greets them and calls for "heavenly tea." Yang Sheng is grateful, and after tasting the tea he exclaims that "the taste is sweet and pleasant and moistens the throat."⁹ Judge Bian explains that heavenly tea is the reward for those who are virtuous. "It is all left to human beings to choose what kind of reception they wish to get after their death — [to] drink Heavenly Tea or to get suffering through punishment."¹⁰

An example of touch playing an important role in a revelation comes from the mystics of Islam and is found in the dream of a Sufi woman, Umm 'Abdallah. The dream was recorded in the ninth century by her husband, Abu 'Abdallah Muhammad ibn 'Ali al-Hakim al-Tirmidhi. Al-Tirmidhi gives a personal account of his own spiritual life in his book called *The Way of the Friends of God*. There he claims that "the dream of the faithful is God's word spoken to him in his sleep."¹¹ In one dream, Umm 'Abdallah "sees the prophet [Muhammad] enter their house. She wants to kiss his feet, but he does not allow it. 'He gave me his hand,' she told her husband, 'and I kissed it.'"¹² The dream of the kiss proved to be instrumental in awakening in her the urgent desire to know and experience union with God.

The Imagination as a Vehicle for Revelation

Visions and voices can resemble ordinary physical events, or they can feel slightly less real, as in a dream or fantasy, both of which arise spontaneously as products of the imagination. When we use the word *imagination* we again emphasize visual experience: "the act or power of forming a mental image of something not present to the senses or never before wholly perceived in reality."¹³ But here the expression *mental image* actually refers to impressions on all the senses. The dreamed kiss differs in degree from the actual, physical kiss: it is a "mental touch," an imaginary kiss. Thus it is that for religious people all over the world visions may include both physical and imagined events.

Thus, we can speak of both waking and sleeping visions. As in Islam, other Western religions include the tradition of receiving visions in both states: for example, in his *God, Dreams, and Revelation: A Christian Interpretation of Dreams*, Morton T. Kelsey examines the history of dream interpretation in Judaism and Christianity. In the Hebrew Bible "we find the belief that [God] is concerned with human beings and makes direct contact with them in order to give them direction and guidance. Dream and vision experiences were one medium of this communication. Through this means, which was not subject to ego control, God brought people special knowledge of the world around them and also knowledge of the divine reality and will."[14]

Present also in the Bible is the idea that some people might manufacture dreams or visions in order to influence others. Therefore, the Israelites developed a variety of ways to discern the true messages of God as opposed to false reports. This critical attitude, however, did not discriminate between waking and sleeping visions: "there is no clear-cut distinction between the dream and the vision in the Hebrew language; where moderns see a great gulf of separation, the Hebrews did not."[15] Sometimes, as in Job 20:8, the dream experience is simply referred to as a vision of the night: "He will fly away like a dream and be lost, driven off like a vision of the night."[16]

Kelsey goes on to point out the same absence of distinction in the Greek language of the Christian New Testament. There the most common term for vision is *horama*, which refers both to waking visions and visions of the night, dreams. "*Horama* is used to translate the Hebrew words for both dream and vision, and since it can refer to the state in which one receives a vision, it may also refer to the dreaming state. Significantly enough, this word does not make the distinction we so carefully make either between dreams and visions or between physical and nonphysical [imaginary] perceptions."[17]

Whereas modern people tend to see dreams as normal, they may refer to visions as hallucinations, symptomatic of an abnormal psychology or a drug-induced state. For people in most traditional societies, however, visions are rarely confused with hallucinations. The vision gives knowledge about the spirit world and "only indirectly of the physical one." In hallucinations people have "lost their ability to distinguish between these two kinds of experience, so they project their inner images directly upon the outer world. Because they cannot distinguish between the two, they are not able to deal adequately with either the outer world or the inner one. Their actions become inappropriate, and they are seen as sick."[18] Whether one is awake or asleep does not seem to be significant; what identifies the vision is the personal belief that the event is a message from the spirits.

Visions Give Rise to Sacred Stories

The experience of a vision is easy to remember and relate to others, since it shares in the imagery of ordinary experience. Many sacred stories and holy images are expressions of the experience of visions and voices. These then become part of a tradition that is handed down from generation to generation. Small societies, literary religious traditions, and world religions — all are profoundly affected by revelations received as visions and voices.

Lame Deer. Among the Lakota, the Hanblecheyapi, or Crying for a Vision, has as its goal the experience of visions and voices. After several days alone in a wilderness pit, the "lamenter" returns to the community and shares his or her encounter with the spirit world. The main purpose of this spiritual discipline is to have direct contact with the spirits, which can help people in all aspects of life. The North American holy man Lame Deer (1903?–1976?) has written in detail about his first Crying for a Vision.[19]

When Lame Deer was sixteen years old, he made his first Hanblecheyapi. After a ritual sweat bath, old man Chest, the medicine man, brought him to a pit that had been dug out of the earth at the top of a hill and left him there for four days and nights. At this time, the boy still had his childhood name; he was not yet called Lame Deer.

He had nothing with him except a star blanket for warmth, a gourd rattle, and a pipe with tobacco made of red willow bark. His grandmother had made the blanket herself. It was white, with a large morning star of many colors in the center. A ritual blanket, it was intended for use by a medicine man. She had also prepared the gourd rattle, cutting forty pieces of her own skin and, after drying them, placing them in the gourd[20] along with several tiny fossil "stones of power" that had been found in an ant hill. The pipe was, of course, sacred to his people, the Lakota. The first pipe was the gift brought by White Buffalo Calf Woman, who taught his people how to live in harmony with each other and with the spirit world.

For the first time in his life, the boy was alone. After darkness fell, he sensed the presence of a huge bird flying around him inside the pit. Terrified, he reached for the rattle and began to shake it. Grasping the pipe with his other hand, he began to sing and pray. Nothing seemed to allay the fear; weeping, he wrapped himself up in the blanket.

The boy could hear the cries of the bird. He felt the touch of its wings, and understood its speech: "You are sacrificing yourself here to be a medicine man. In time you will be one. You will teach other medicine men. We are the fowl people, the winged ones, the eagles and the owls. We are a nation and you shall be our brother. You will never kill or harm any one of us. You are going to understand us whenever you come to seek a vision here on his hill. You will learn about herbs and roots, and you will heal people. You will ask them for nothing in return. A man's life is short. Make yours a worthy one."[21]

The boy's fear finally vanished. He lost all sense of time. He had other visions, including one of his great-grandfather, who had the name Lame Deer. This ancestor had been killed by a white soldier. The boy felt for the first time an inner power being released within himself: he knew with conviction that the visions were true and that he would become a medicine man. Again he wept; this time, for joy.

Finally, old man Chest returned to the pit, bringing food and water. Together they returned to the community, where the visions were shared and interpreted. The old medicine man told the boy that he had been changed in ways that only the future would make clear. No longer was he a boy. From that day on, he was to be called Lame Deer after his great-grandfather.

This vision gave direction for a life of healing and spiritual leadership. Spirit guides appeared to Lame Deer in the form of birds and taught him the path of the medicine man. Lame Deer had sought a vision by undergoing the ordeal of Hanblecheyapi, but visions also come to those not seeking them.

Lu Dong Bin. In Daoist tradition the title Immortal[22] refers to certain humans who have attained such close harmony with the Dao, the underlying mystery of the universe, that they become like the gods. However, unlike the gods and the ancestors in Chinese culture, the Immortals are completely free from being identified with any specific location. Nor are they worshipped. Instead, they are held up as models of what is possible for every human being. During the early Han period (c. 100 BCE), the Immortal was often depicted as a winged human who lived either on a sacred mountain or on an island paradise in the east, ingested jade, and knew the secrets of deathlessness. Many techniques of spiritual discipline were practiced to attain this state: meditation, visualization, breathing practices, and so forth.[23]

In popular tradition, eight Immortals are particularly well known. Among them is Lu Dong Bin, whose exploits are often the subject of Chinese art and literature. One story describes Lu Dong Bin as an official in the Chinese imperial government who was destined for great success and honor. A religious man, he spent a great deal of time studying the writings that contained ancient wisdom. However, he sometimes neglected his spiritual life because he was so busy with his work-related duties.

One day Lu Dong Bin was making an official journey and stopped for the night at an inn.[24] Another visitor at the inn was the Immortal Han Zhong Li. Recognizing Lu Dong Bin as a future Immortal who was distracted from his course by the dazzling seduction of worldly success, Han Zhong Li decided to come to his aid. He invited the traveling official to join him for a cup of wine.

"Han Zhong Li[25] drew the little heater to him and began to warm the wine. Lu Dong Bin found that the fumes of the warming wine and the effects of the journey made him sleepy. Before he knew what was happening he was fast asleep.

"As he slept, he had a most convincing dream. He saw himself returning from his journey and being promoted to a very senior office. From there he rose within a few years to the most senior post in the Emperor's court. For fifty years he was favoured and blessed by fortune. Emperors listened to his every word, governments quaked at his anger and favours were bestowed at his command. But it was not to last. One day he offended the new Emperor, who, tired of this powerful man, was delighted to have an excuse to dismiss him. Immediately his enemies closed in. The Emperor was told alarming tales of Lu Dong Bin's plans and ambitions. Soon the Emperor was convinced that Lu Dong Bin was an enemy of the state. Summoning Lu Dong Bin, he ordered him into exile. But worse was to come. Shortly afterwards, the Emperor ordered that the whole of Lu Dong Bin's family be executed. Not a single one was spared.

"Alone, exiled and mourning for his murdered family, Lu Dong Bin sat sighing bitterly in a faraway country, when suddenly he woke up. He was still in the inn and the wine was not even hot yet!"

The dream carried a powerful message. It convinced Lu Dong Bin that the ways of the world are unpredictable. He gave up his official post and joined Han Zhong Li. Together they went to dwell in the mountains as hermits and practice the way of immortality, especially the secrets of alchemy and the arts of swordsmanship. Lu Dong Bin eventually transformed the external arts of alchemy into an internal form of visualization and meditation. Because he emphasized the value of compassion in attaining immortality, many Daoist adepts often sought him out to be their spiritual teacher.

5. Visions and Voices

Paul the Apostle. Whereas Lame Deer and Lu Dong Bin were both drawn to the religious life, Saul of Tarsus (c. 5 BCE–c. 67 CE)[26] was an enemy of Christianity when he first received a vision of Christ. His job was to track down the followers of Jesus of Nazareth and bring them to the city of Jerusalem for trial.

One day on his way to Damascus in pursuit of some Christians, Saul had the following experience: "Suddenly a light flashed from the sky all around him. He fell to the ground and heard a voice saying, 'Saul, Saul, why do you persecute me?' 'Tell me, Lord,' he said, 'who you are.' The voice answered, 'I am Jesus, whom you are persecuting. But get up and go into the city, and you will be told what you have to do.'"[27] When the voice ceased speaking, Saul got up from the ground and opened his eyes, but he could not see. For three days he was blind. He ate and drank nothing. Then a follower of Jesus, a man called Ananias, had a sleeping vision in which Jesus told him to go and find Saul and heal him. When Ananias came to where Saul was staying, he placed his hands on the blind man and said: "Saul, my brother, the Lord Jesus, who appeared to you on your way here, has sent me to you so that you may recover your sight and be filled with the Holy Spirit." At once, Saul's sight returned. He was baptized as a Christian, took a meal, and his strength returned to him. He was given a new name, Paul, and he became the apostle who was perhaps most responsible for the survival of the Christian Church.

The earliest Christian fellowship was located in Jerusalem. It was a Jewish group led by James, a brother of Jesus. Sent out as an apostle, or missionary, by this group, Paul founded Christian churches all over the Roman Empire and invited all kinds of people — Jews and Gentiles (non-Jews), men and women, slaves and free — to be baptized.

Later, during a conflict between the Roman government and the Jews of Palestine, the Jewish Christian community was destroyed. This was the first Jewish-Roman War (66–73), known also as the Great Revolt. The Jews of Judaea rebelled against their rulers, with the result that the Roman emperor Titus destroyed Jerusalem and burned down the Temple. The inhabitants were either killed outright or sold into slavery. Only the mission churches outside of Palestine survived; and with them, the teachings of Paul and other apostles. Survival resulted, ultimately, in unimagined success: In 381 after centuries of persecution alternating with indifference, the Roman government declared Christianity the official religion of the empire. Wedded to the imperial organization, Christianity flourished in all the lands then under Roman rule.

Lame Deer experienced a waking vision; Lu Dong Bin, a vision while asleep; and Saul, blinded by a light, heard the voice of Jesus. All three men experienced revelations that were conveyed to them through the senses of the body or the imagination. Furthermore, each revelation contained a message, a meaningful communication that changed the life of the one who received it. Lame Deer became a Lakota healer and holy man, Lu Dong Bin became a Chinese Immortal, and Paul stopped persecuting the followers of Jesus and began instead to spread Christian teachings throughout the Roman Empire.

Visions and voices are found in all cultures. Sometimes the vision is very personal and affects only the life of the individual; at other times, the revelation contains a message that will change the destiny of an entire people. Among the latter are two prophets found in Judaism and Islam: Moses and Muhammad.

The Prophet as Visionary

The word *prophet* is commonly used in to refer to certain religious specialists found in the Western monotheistic traditions. There the prophet is primarily one who has been personally commission by God to bring a message to the people. The term goes back to the Greek word *prophetes*, one who speaks for a god and interprets the divine will. It appears in the Greek translation of the Hebrew Bible as well as in the Greek New Testament. What lies behind the word, however, belongs not to Greek religion but to Hebrew tradition.

The biblical prophet was primarily a visionary: on the one hand, he heard the voice of God and then reported God's will to others; at other times, the prophet shares his visions.[28] The messages were given orally; later they were written down, usually by others, and collected so as to be preserved as sacred prophecy. Not all prophets were happy about their commissioning, but they were usually compelled to obey sooner or later. The prophet Jeremiah, for example, claimed that God's message was like a "fire blazing" in his heart and allowing him no peace until it was delivered.[29]

However, the prophet was not exclusively a visionary: very often he

5. Visions and Voices

served also as a medium for God's spirit in the world. In the story about Saul, the first king of a united Kingdom of Israel, we learn that the prophet Samuel anointed him with oil and then kissed him. Samuel then prophecies about the signs to come that will make it clear that Saul is chosen by God to govern his people. Above all, the new king will resemble the prophets: "The spirit of the Lord will suddenly take possession of you, and you too will be rapt like a prophet and become another man."[30] The text goes on to say that as King Saul departed from Samuel, God gave him a new heart. Later in the day, when the people saw the new king filled with prophetic rapture, they exclaimed: "Is Saul also among the prophets?"[31]

Again and again, the biblical account recounts how "the hand of the Lord" fell upon the prophets, guiding their words and actions.[32] Similar expressions include the following: the spirit of God "rested on them" (Numbers 11:25 f.) and the spirit of God "clothed itself" with them (Judges 6:34).

Imbued with the divine spirit, a prophet is capable of miraculous actions. King Ahab (mid-ninth century BCE) killed all of the prophets of God except for Elijah and introduced the worship of a foreign god into the Northern Kingdom of Israel. The foreign god is referred to simply as "lord" (Baal). Thereupon, Elijah challenged Ahab to a contest on top of Mount Carmel. Both sides prepared an altar and placed upon it a sacrificial bull; then each invoked his god to send fire down so as to consume the bull.

Ahab had in his company 450 prophets in service to Baal; Elijah stood alone. Whereas nothing that Ahab and his companions did brought about the desired result; Elijah's prayer to God was instantly answered: "'Lord, God of Abraham, of Isaac, and of Israel, let it be known today that thou art God in Israel and that I am thy servant and have done all these things at thy command....' Then the fire of the Lord fell. It consumed the whole-offering, the wood, the stones, and the earth."[33] Elijah caused the prophets of Baal to be seized and killed. Ahab he spared. Then, aware of an approaching storm, Elijah orders the king to mount his chariot and ride fast to safety. Meanwhile, "the power of the Lord had come upon Elijah," so he "tucked up his robe and ran before Ahab all the way to Jezreel [fifteen miles]." Running faster than the swift horses of King Ahab, Elijah demonstrates the presence of God's spirit within him.

Among the Israelites, the word for prophet was *navi'*. It was a word originally used in the northern kingdom for one who had "heard" God's voice. In addition, the *navi'* was dedicated to the preservation of religious tradition in general. In the southern kingdom, the preferred term was *hozeh*, or "visionary." But eventually, after the Babylonian Exile (586–537 BCE), *navi'* became the sole term for prophet among all the Israelites. Other terms that are less common include the seer (*ro'eh*), who also practiced divination; the man of God (*ish ha-Elohim*), capable of amazing feats; and sons of the prophets (*benei ha-nevi'im*), which referred to members of prophetic groups.

Because the prophet is a religious leader with numerous abilities and ways of knowing God's will, we cannot say that every visionary is also a prophet. Yet, it is clear that seeing visions and hearing the voice of God is fundamental to the role of the biblical prophet. Further, both in Judaism and later in Islam, it is prophecy that gives tradition its shape. Especially, it is prophecy that gives these religions their sacred books: the Torah and the Qur'an. To understand the significance of these prophetic books, we need to examine the revelatory experiences of two important prophets: Moses in Judaism; and Muhammad in Islam.

Moses. One is born into Judaism[34]; it is an ancient religion and there have been many Jewish prophets. The lives and teachings of the prophets are recorded in the Hebrew Bible, or *Tanakh*,[35] along with books of history, religious poetry, and wisdom literature. Hebrew is the language of the Jewish Bible; the ancestors of the Jews, the Israelites, were also sometimes called the Hebrews.

The Israelites saw themselves as descendents of the twelve sons of Israel, another name for the visionary Jacob, a name that he had received directly from God in a vision.[36] At one point in their history, the Israelites lived in two separate kingdoms in what is modern Palestine: Judah in the south and Israel in the north. Israel was destroyed by the Assyrians, a northern neighbor who had developed an empire in competition with Egypt to the south. The kingdom of Judah survived and became the source of the name that today still identifies this ancient tradition: Judaism, the religion of the people of Judah.

The first five books of the Jewish Bible[37] are often referred to as the Books of Moses. Tradition says that the prophet Moses wrote down the content of these books following divine instruction given to him on Mount Sinai.[38] Moses is certainly a founding prophet of Judaism: he is central in the story of the liberation of the Israelites from Egypt, where they lived as slaves, and their formation as a people living in a sacred relationship with the god Yahveh.[39] We find this story in the biblical book called Exodus.

5. Visions and Voices

The descendents of Jacob sought refuge in Egypt during a time of drought and famine. Because of the Nile River, Egypt possessed a reliable source of water, and the Egyptians had developed further a method for storing food in case of need. After they arrived in Egypt, the Israelites were forced gradually into slavery. However, as their numbers grew they became a source of concern for the Pharaoh, or king of Egypt. He was afraid that the Hebrew men might join forces with his enemies and overthrow his rule. Thus, around 1300 BCE the Egyptian king ordered his people to kill every infant boy born to a Hebrew mother.[40]

One Hebrew woman was able to hide her newborn son in safety for about three months. Then she built a watertight basket, lay the child within, and placed it in the Nile among the reeds at the side of the river. The infant's older sister was sent to watch over him. The daughter of the king came with her handmaidens to bathe in the river. Hearing the child crying, she took pity on him and decided to raise him as her own son. She lifted the baby up out of the basket and saw that it was a Hebrew child. His sister then came forward and offered to find a Hebrew woman as nursemaid for the baby. The princess agreed, and so the baby's mother raised him until he was weaned and then brought him to the palace where the princess adopted him. The princess gave him an Egyptian name, Moses.

Although he was raised as an Egyptian prince, Moses knew that he was Hebrew, and it disturbed him to see Egyptians mistreating his countrymen. One day he saw an Egyptian strike a Hebrew slave; in anger, he killed the Egyptian and tossed the body into the sand. Already by the next day, news of the murder was widespread; as soon as the king heard of the crime, he ordered the execution of Moses.

Moses fled. He traveled into a neighboring land called Midian, where he married the daughter of a priest who had both a large family and a great flock of sheep. As son-in-law, it was one of his duties to help care for the sheep. One day, after many years, Moses was minding the flock when he came to the foot of a mountain. On the mountain was a bush that was filled with flame but did not seem to be burning. Curious, Moses went closer to have a better look, and he heard a voice from within the bush calling his name. "'Come no nearer,' said the voice. 'Take off your sandals; the place where you are standing is holy ground.... I am the God of your forefathers, the God of Abraham, the God of Isaac, the God of Jacob.' Moses covered his face, for he was afraid to gaze on God."[41]

The vision continued as God commanded Moses to return to Egypt and rescue the Israelites, to bring them out of Egypt — out of slavery. Moses protested. He argued with God that surely Pharaoh would not listen to him. But God had a plan. First of all, Moses would not go alone. His brother Aaron would accompany him and speak for him. But more importantly, God himself would force the Egyptian ruler to release the slaves by displays of his power.

Moses with his wife and children returned to Egypt, and with the help of Aaron confronted the king, arguing that the Israelites were called by their God to hold a pilgrim-feast in the wilderness. Of course, the king only laughed. In ancient Egyptian thought, it was Pharaoh himself who was divine; as a child of the gods, he was invulnerable to the power of any alien deity.

And so began the contest between Pharaoh and the God of the Israelites. Moses and Aaron would command the release of the Israelites; Pharaoh would refuse. Then Moses, as an agent of his God, would inflict upon the Egyptians some catastrophe until finally Pharaoh would relent and promise to let the Israelites leave Egypt. But, as soon as everything was restored to normalcy, Pharaoh would change his mind and stand firm again in his opposition to Moses and his God.

This back-and-forth struggle continued through the succession of nine catastrophes, or divine signs, perpetuated upon the Egyptian people: (1) The Nile River was turned to blood for seven days. (2) Then came a plague of frogs; (3) a plague of maggots; and (4) a plague of flies. (5) Next, the sheep, horses, cattle, camels, and donkeys of the Egyptians died of a terrible disease. (6) This was followed by an illness that attacked the Egyptians themselves, causing open wounds on their bodies, (7) a hailstorm, (8) a plague of locusts, and (9) a time of total darkness covering the land. Still Pharaoh refused to release the Israelites. The tenth plague, however, would be the last.

> Moses then said, "These are the words of the Lord: At midnight I will go out among the Egyptians. Every first-born creature in the land of Egypt shall die: the first-born of Pharaoh who sits on his throne, the first-born of the slave-girl at the hand-mill, and the first-born of the cattle."[42]

Meanwhile, Moses and Aaron had learned from God how to prepare the Israelites in order to be protected during the night of this terrible sign: On the fourteenth day of the month each family was to sacrifice a lamb at sundown. The blood of the lamb was to be smeared on the two doorposts and on the lintel of every Hebrew house. The lamb was to be roasted and eaten together with unleavened cake and bitter herbs. Anything uneaten must then be destroyed. The people must prepare for the feast fully dressed for travel. During the night of the feast, they must all remain inside their homes and not pass out through the doors marked with lamb's blood.

On the fourteenth day of the month the Israelites did as God commanded. The next morning there was a cry and lamentation throughout Egypt. Everywhere — in the palace and in the lowliest hut — the firstborn child was found dead.

In rage and fear, Pharaoh commanded the Israelites to leave his kingdom. Prepared already for the journey, they fled, crossing the Red Sea,[43] the waters of which miraculously parted to allow passage. Then, Pharaoh changed his mind again and sent his armies after the slaves. But as the army rushed into the sea, the waters once more merged, drowning the soldiers and ending the pursuit.

The deliverance of the Israelites is certainly one of the most sacred revelations in Jewish tradition. With the help of the prophet Moses, God saves his people from slavery and oppression in a foreign land. Eventually they will return to the country where their ancestors had tended their flocks. In English the rescue mission is called the Exodus, which derives from the Greek words meaning "the road out" and refers to the road out of Egypt, out of oppression, out of powerlessness and suffering.

Once the Israelites were delivered out of Egypt, Moses continued to receive instructions from God. First of all, they were to remember the Exodus and teach their children how God had saved them. This was to be achieved by celebrating for one week every year a holy festival called the Passover. During Passover, Jews reenact the history of the Exodus and tell the story to their children. They eat a meal that recalls the feast of the lamb on their last night in Egypt. The festival is called the Passover, because in the night when God went throughout Egypt, killing in each home the firstborn, God *passed over* the homes of those who had smeared the blood of a sacrificed lamb on the doorposts.

In addition to establishing the festival of Passover, Moses helped the people renew their Covenant with the God of their ancestors. A covenant is a mutual contract, an agreement between two parties where each has a responsibility and each receives some benefit. The Covenant between God and the Jews has a long history going back before Moses even to Abraham, who is considered their first ancestor. The Covenant is one whereby the Jews promise to worship and obey the God of Abraham and no other god.[44] In return, God promises to protect them and allow the people to flourish. With the prophetic leadership of Moses, the Covenant was further supported by the gift of the Torah (God's "Law"). Torah is the Hebrew name for the Five Books of Moses.[45] The purpose of these written texts is to guide the Israelites in their fulfillment of the Covenant: the text makes it clear how the Jews are to worship and how they are to live in order to please God. Among other things (such as sacred stories and history) the Torah is thus a handbook for both worship and spiritual discipline.

Muhammad, also called the Prophet, is the founder of Islam. Simultaneously a religious and a political leader, he effected significant and lasting changes in both the religion and the government of his society.

The Islamic concept of prophecy is based on the Biblical view of the prophet.[46] In both Judaism and Islam, the prophet is one whom God commissions to bring a message to the people. Islamic tradition insists that God's messengers are numerous, as many as 124,000 prophets whom God has instructed to guide each and every human community. According to this view, Muhammad was not meant to cancel earlier revelations but to bring knowledge of God to the Arabs.[47] Other important prophets include Abraham, Moses, and Jesus, whose prophecies culminate in those of Muhammad. Thus, one of his titles is the Seal of the Prophets.[48] This title probably had the original meaning of "one who confirms previous prophets," but eventually it came to signify the belief that Muhammad's message was universal; and as a result, after him there would be no more prophets.[49]

Orphaned rather early, Muhammad grew up in the family of one of his paternal uncles as a member of the Quraysh tribe. Originally nomads, shortly before the birth of Muhammad, the Quraysh had come into possession of the valley called Mecca, an urban environment dotted with holy shrines and plentiful water from wells. They settled there and lived a life of commerce. Still, the ancient relationship of the Quraysh with the surrounding desert was strong, and so they sent their children to live from time to time with nomads in the wilderness. Thus, Muhammad grew up primarily in the city, but he was at home also in the desert.

The religion of the Arabs, Muhammad's people, was polytheistic: they worshipped many gods and goddesses. Their most sacred shrine was the

5. Visions and Voices

Ka'bah in Mecca, which housed the black stone, a meteorite. When the Quraysh settled there they brought numerous images of their tribal deities and set them up in the shrine. A common destination for pilgrims, Mecca likewise became a center for trading among the tribes of the area. Indeed, because of the shrine, "all violence was forbidden in Mecca and the surrounding countryside at all times. This had been a key factor in the commercial success of the Quraysh, since it enabled Arabs to trade there without fearing the reprisals of vendetta warfare."[50]

When Muhammad was twenty-five years old, he acquired the position of steward on a trading journey to Syria. His employer was Khadijah, a wealthy widow who was so impressed with him that she asked him to marry her. Together they had two sons (who died in infancy) and four daughters. Muhammad lived this life of trade and family concerns until the time of his call.

Every year he spent the month of Ramadan praying and fasting in a cave situated on the summit of Mount Hira near Mecca. In 610, during his annual retreat, Muhammad experienced the vision of the angel Gabriel, who called him God's Messenger and commanded him to "recite."[51] Muhammad interpreted the vision as coming from the Allah, the Arabic name for God. One of the most important consequences of Muhammad's religious transformation is that he became a strict monotheist, believing that only one God exists and that this God was Allah, the Creator. He identified Allah with the God of his neighbors, the Jews and the Christians. From this time forth, Muhammad consciously joined the tradition of prophets that for him included both Moses of Judaism and Jesus of Christianity.

In addition to strict monotheism, Muhammad's prophecy contains two essential teachings: one describes his eschatology, or doctrines about the afterlife; the other makes clear the implications of this eschatology.[52] "When [Muhammad] attempts to state the content of his faith in the briefest possible form he refers to it as 'belief in Allah and the last day.'"[53] The resurrection of the dead and divine judgment, followed by a terrifying punishment or eternal bliss — this is the religious vision that lends urgency to his preaching. According to Muhammad, when the body dies, the soul remains unconscious until the day when all the dead will be bodily resurrected. Since the soul is incapable of consciousness without the body, the resurrected person will think that they have been dead for only a brief time. Then comes the judgment.

The implications of this eschatology led the Prophet to emphasize the importance of surrendering to God's will before it is too late. Hence the word *islam*, which mean "submission" to God.

How does one submit and thus become a Muslim? The answer is found in a sacred book, which is the collection of Muhammad's prophecies. When the angel Gabriel commanded Muhammad to "recite," he was asking him to make known to others his own experience of what God was saying to him. Thus, whenever Muhammad heard God speaking to him, he would recite aloud. His companions would memorize the recitations and eventually write them down. The collection of these written recitations is what we call the Qur'an.

Muslims believe that the sacred book consists of the very words of Allah as heard by the Prophet. Even the language of the book, Arabic, is believed to be holy, the language of Allah. The Qur'an is the highest authority in all matters of Islamic religion and also social law. Muslims read, memorize, and study this sacred book in order to live as God wants them to live. Like the Torah, the Qur'an is a book that helps people get closer to their God. The Five Pillars of Islam, the most clear-cut practices of the faith, are found in the sacred book revealed to Muhammad.

By surrendering to God, one becomes sanctified, holy. How does one do this? The Five Pillars of Islam provide the instructions:

1. The Confession of Faith. Once in the life of every Muslim, he or she must sincerely speak aloud the creed of Islam: "There is no god but Allah and Muhammad is His Prophet."

2. Prayer. Adult Muslims are to pray daily. Five times a day, facing the Ka'bah in Mecca, Muslims draw close to God in prayer.

3. Charity. Muslims are to practice some kind of formal alms giving.

4. The Fast. Every year the lunar month of Ramadan is set aside as a time of fasting. During the hours of daylight, eating, drinking, and smoking are forbidden. During this month one is to focus ones mind more firmly on God.

5. Pilgrimage. Once in the life of every Muslim, a pilgrimage to the sacred Ka'bah in Mecca is undertaken. The entire journey, from beginning to end, is marked by numerous rituals that strengthen the pilgrim's connection to the entire Islamic community and its history.[54]

5. Visions and Voices

The teachings of Muhammad are not meant solely for individual salvation but also for the creation of a just society, specifically the *ummah*, or community of Muslims. This was a new social entity, one that was open to people from different tribes. In pre–Islamic Arabia, the tribe and its powerful leader provided the only reliable source of security for the individual person. "Without a protector who would avenge his death, according to the harsh vendetta lore of Arabia, a man could be killed with impunity."[55]

Under the guidance of the new religion, the tribal warfare that dominated Arabia at the time would eventually give way to co-operation, as Arabs began to identify with a social reality larger than the tribal unit. "When Muhammad died in 632, ... almost all the tribes of Arabia had joined the *ummah* as Confederates or as converted Muslims. Since members of the *ummah* could not, of course, attack one another, the ghastly cycle of tribal warfare, of vendetta and counter-vendetta, had ended. Single-handedly, Muhammad had brought peace to war-torn Arabia."[56]

The prophets of Judaism and Islam, especially Moses and Muhammad, served as messengers for their God. Hearing the words of God — sometimes seeing visions as well — they provided their peoples with sacred writings, the Bible and the Qur'an, which even today continue to guide people in their everyday lives.

Chapter 6

Divination

Many people believe that spirits can manipulate at will objects and events in the natural world in order to communicate. This conviction makes possible the type of revelation that we call divination. In divination, natural events and random patterns are interpreted as messages from the spirit world. Widespread, the practice of divination can be very uncomplicated, as when someone interprets personal misfortune as divine punishment. On the other hand, some forms of divination can be quite complex, as in astrology, where a specialist interprets the position of celestial bodies — sun, moon, planets and stars — at the time of birth in order to predict a child's destiny.

In other words, in this view, the natural world itself can reflect specific divine meanings. The diviner is the specialist who is trained to "read" these messages, sometimes called "signs" or "omens." In astrology, for example, we call the diviner an astrologer. Some diviners specialize in one form of divination, perhaps palm reading or interpreting the pattern formed by a random display of Tarot cards. Other diviners may practice a wide variety of techniques.

Signs and Omens

Many extraordinary events that occur in the natural world can be interpreted as messages from the spirit world. For example, we all experience the sun's daily round as it moves across the sky from east to west. During a solar eclipse, however, the sun vanishes from sight and darkness covers the earth in the middle of the day. In numerous societies, this phenomenon has been interpreted as resulting from the activity of spirit beings. For example, among some indigenous peoples of South America there is a commonly held view that an eclipse occurs when a giant jaguar living in the heavens hunts both the sun and moon, causing temporary darkness on earth.¹ The Tatars of Europe and Asia feared a vampire spirit being who lived in a star and sometimes attacked the sun, causing darkness on earth. On a more positive note, the early inhabitants of Tahiti taught that the darkness of the eclipse was a sign that the sun and the moon, two celestial beings, were busy making love.² In each case, the natural event of the eclipse has been incorporated into a mythical framework and interpreted accordingly.

The birth of twins is another example of an extraordinary phenomenon that is often believed to have some kind of religious meaning. Among the Yoruba of western Africa, the birth of twins expresses the will of Olorun, the Supreme Being, who assigns a new life and destiny to each soul as it is about to be reborn. The doubleness of the twins brings with it a concentration of spiritual power that can benefit those who honor the twins and harm those who neglect them.³ In contrast, among the Igbo (also of western Africa) as soon as they were born, twins were traditionally cast outside the boundaries of the village into a sort of no-man's land called the Evil Forest.⁴ This was the place for anything that might be considered an "abomination," or offense to the goddess of the land, Ani. The bodies of those who died of certain illnesses (such as leprosy and smallpox) were thrown into the Evil Forest, as were the bodies of those who died during the Week of Peace. When great healers died, their powerful medicines were cast there, too. It was "alive with sinister forces and powers of darkness."⁵ Casting the infant twins into the Evil Forest signified that they were considered unlucky, even potentially dangerous to the inhabitants of the village.

Miracles are signs of divine intervention. During the time of the Roman Empire, there was a widespread religious belief in so-called god-men, or wonder workers. The god-man (Greek, *theos-aner*) was half divine and half human, because as it was generally thought, his father was a god and his mother, human. The wonders and miracles that these holy men were able to perform were evidence that they were half divine. One example is Apollonios of Tyana, a wandering miracle worker who lived in the first century of the Common Era. He was a healer and a teacher, who on one occasion even brought someone back from the dead. As Apollonios entered Rome one day, he happened to come across the funeral procession for a young maiden who had died in the very hour of her wedding. Weeping, the bridegroom followed the bier that carried her corpse. Seeing this, Apollonios approached the procession and touched the girl, speaking softly to her. Immediately, she came back to life and returned to her home.[6] Although Apollonios made no such claim, because of this and similar feats, most people thought that he must be a son of the Greek god Zeus.[7]

This tradition of the god-man who revealed his relationship to the gods by producing miracles is reflected in the New Testament accounts of Jesus of Nazareth, who lived in Palestine during this same period. In addition to preaching, Jesus worked miracles of many kinds. Perhaps most important was his ability to heal those who were sick, either in body or mind. On one occasion, when Jesus had healed a man who was both blind and dumb, some bystanders expressed their amazement while others accused him of being an agent of Satan, prince of devils. Jesus replied by saying that since illness comes from the Devil, if healing should also be the Devil's work, then "Satan is divided against himself." His own ability to heal the sick, Jesus argues, is better understood as evidence of God's healing power, and "if it is by the Spirit of God that I drive out the devils, then be sure the kingdom of God has already come upon you."[8] In Christian theology, the miracles of Jesus are a sign that he is the Son of God, who initiates an end to the Devil's reign on earth.

Arts of Divination

In addition to interpreting natural events as supernatural messages, diviners will employ various techniques to invoke such a message. The diviner will have his or her divining tools, everything from divination blocks and tealeaves to dice and Tarot cards. Just as there are many techniques used by diviners, so, too, there are many so-called arts of divination. As in any other art (dance, calligraphy, music), the diviner must be trained in the techniques and interpretive skills of the tradition. A few examples typical of the arts of divination are as follows:

- Casting lots: using some kind of object (dice, stones, seeds, sticks) to determine random patterns.
- Palmistry, also called chiromancy: reading the lines and other configurations found on the hands of human beings.
- Hepatoscopy: interpreting the shape of an animal's liver.

- Haruspicy: interpreting the state of the entrails of an animal.
- Phrenology: interpreting the shape of a person's head.
- Astrology: reading the movements of the planets and stars.
- Geomancy: reading the patterns found in earth formations.
- Ornithomancy: observing and interpreting the flight patterns of birds.

Each divination art—and this is only a partial list—is based on the interpretation of seemingly random events that are thought to be manipulated by supernatural forces to convey messages from the spirit world.

Casting Lots. In the temples of Taiwan, the devout often use divination blocks in order to receive messages from the sea goddess and maternal ancestor Mazu.[9] Also called moon blocks because of their crescent shape, the blocks are made of wood that has been painted red. They are identical: one side is flat (representing yang, the power of heat) and the other is rounded (representing yin, the power of the cold moisture). The blocks are thrown upon the ground after a question has been addressed to the goddess. Basic to this form of divination is the understanding that Mazu knows how to influence the position of the blocks after they fall, so that her devotees will be able to perceive the answers to their questions: if two flat sides face up, this means "rephrase the question"; if two rounded sides face up, this means "no"; if one rounded and one flat side face up, this means "yes."

Not only are the arts of divination quite varied—from reading the stars to interpreting the entrails of a sacrificial animal—this type of revelation is widespread. No longer important in modern Judaism, divination was a normal practice in the religion of the Israelites, the ancestors of the Jews. For example, in the Jewish Bible there is reference to the Urim and Thummin, sacred objects that were found in the temple in Jerusalem where they were used to cast lots.[10] In I Samuel 28, King Saul goes to the temple to seek God's guidance as he wages a war with his neighbors. Each time he asks a question of God, the Urim and Thummin are used to determine God's answer.

The Book of Jonah in the Bible provides another example of divination. In this story, Jonah is a prophet, but an unwilling one. God speaks to him directly, commanding him to go to Nineveh, the capital of Assyria, and bring a message calling for the repentance of the people in that city. But Jonah does not want to go, because the people of Nineveh are not his people, not

Israelites. He believes that God should not have anything to do with these foreigners. So Jonah tries to run away from God. He boards a ship sailing in the opposite direction. However, a hurricane arises in the sea, endangering both the boat and its passengers. The sailors' reaction to the storm is religious: they believe that it conveys a message from some god who wants to get the attention of one of the passengers. To decide who is the object of divine wrath, they cast lots. "Come and let us cast lots to find out who is to blame for this bad luck."[11] And when they had drawn lots, the lot fell to Jonah, indicating him as the guilty person.

The sailors then ask Jonah to explain how he has offended his God. Jonah tells his story and suggests that if they will cast him overboard, the storm will surely abate. The sailors follow Jonah's advice, and as the winds cease blowing, the sea becomes calm once again. The sailors on the ship immediately bow down in worship to Jonah's God, offering gifts of thanksgiving. As for Jonah, he is swallowed whole by a giant fish, which carries him back to land and deposits him there safe and sound. Eventually, Jonah obeys God and takes God's message to the people of Nineveh.

The tradition of casting lots continued in Judaism certainly up to the time of the Hellenistic age, as evidence of the practice appears in the writings of the earliest followers of Jesus. It was Judas, one of the twelve disciples, who betrayed Jesus by leading the local authorities to him so that they could arrest, imprison, and eventually kill him. But after this betrayal, Judas felt such remorse that he went out and hanged himself. In Judaism, the number twelve is a sacred number: it refers to the ancestors, the twelve tribes of Israel, whom God through Moses rescued out of slavery in Egypt. Thus, the number twelve becomes a symbol for the whole community. This symbolism continued to have meaning for the early Christians, who lived in Jerusalem and identified themselves as traditional Jews. So with Judas dead, the eleven remaining disciples felt the need to complete their number by recruiting a new disciple. Since they had all been chosen by Jesus, who was no longer with them, they wanted God to determine the identity of the new disciple. They put forward two suitable candidates: Joseph Justus, also known as Barsabbas, and Matthias. They prayed asking God to indicate which of the two should assume what had been Judas's role of "ministry and apostleship." The two men then drew lots. The lot that indicated the new disciple fell to Matthias.[12]

Tossing a coin, throwing dice, drawing straws — these are some of the ways that people cast lots. The role of the diviner is quite easy in this form of divination. Yet, many of the arts of divination are complex, and the diviner must undergo a long period of training in order to know how to interpret the messages correctly.

The Mouse Oracle. One interesting example of a more specialized art of divination is the mouse oracle found among the Baule, who live on the Ivory Coast of Africa.[13] The Baule tell the story of how their first ruler, Queen Aura Poku, left her home in Ghana in order to establish her realm in a new land. The journey brought the queen and her followers to a river that was so deep and rapid that they were unable to cross. A mouse oracle was consulted, and the diviners — the mouse oracle specialists — learned thereby the proper sacrifices to offer in order to placate certain angry water spirits. Once the sacrifices were made, the river grew calm and the journey continued.

The mouse oracle consists of a wooden or terracotta basket with two chambers, one below the other. A plank resting on the lower floor leads to a hole in the upper floor large enough for a mouse to pass through. A wild field mouse is placed in the lower chamber; bones mixed with rice, in the upper.[14] As the mouse eats the rice, it scatters the bones in a random pattern. This pattern is then interpreted as a message from the spirits. The Baule believe that mice, because they move easily back and forth above and below the surface of the earth, have access to the ancestors and other spirits of the underworld. Therefore, they can be employed as messengers in this way.

Astrology. One art of divination has a long history in Western civilization, moving from one society to the next and surviving still today in modern popular culture. This is the astrology that was developed by the Egyptians and the Greeks but has its origins in the astral religion of ancient Sumer (c. 3500 to 2000 BCE). Astral religion refers to the worship of celestial bodies — the sun, the moon, the planets and the stars — as visible manifestations of the gods and goddesses. We have extensive knowledge about Sumerian astral religion because the Sumerians had a system of writing and also because their culture survived for thousands of years. Even after they were conquered by other peoples, their civilization continued. The Akkadians and Babylonians simply assimilated Sumerian civilization, with some modifications.[15] Today the site of ancient Sumer is modern-day Iraq.

The Sumerians believed in a pantheon of personal gods and goddesses. These deities lived in the heavens and their immortal bodies gave off light. The most important deities were the Sun, the Moon, and the so-called Morning and Evening Star, known as the goddess Inanna. Today we call her the planet Venus (after the sun and the moon, the brightest celestial body). Because they believed that the heavenly lights were divine beings, the diviners of ancient Sumer sought to discern messages from the gods in the movements of the stars. Thus, every night they carefully observed the position of all the lights in the sky. They wrote down their observations, and these records exist still today.

The Sumerians interpreted the meanings associated with specific movements and star patterns. For example, one ancient omen reads, "If Inanna appears in the East in the month of Airu, and the Great and Small Twins surround her, all four of them, and she is dark, then will the King of Elam fall sick and not remain alive."[16] Clearly, the astrologer believed that the goddess Inanna knows the future and wants to communicate it to the rulers of Sumer in order to help her people in their day-to-day lives.

Over time, Inanna became one of the deities most connected with government in ancient Sumer. Because of her astral nature — as a heavenly light being — she was called Queen of Heaven. Initially, only in her city of Uruk, but then later, in other cities as well, tradition stated that it was Inanna who decided what man was qualified to be king. Therefore, any ambitious man wanting to rule would require both her approval and support. Indeed, he became king through celebrating a ritual marriage with the divine Queen of Heaven.[17] Once chosen, the man to be king of Uruk would participate in two important rituals: the coronation and the sacred marriage ceremony. There is evidence that the sacred marriage rite may have taken place both during the original coronation and annually as part of the New Year festival during which the king's authority was renewed.

According to the Sumerian text called the "Blessing of Shulgi," the second king of the Third Dynasty of Ur journeyed to Inanna's temple in Uruk, bringing in his boat sacrificial animals as gifts to the goddess: bulls, sheep, goats, and kids. Dressed in ritual garments, his head covered by a crown-like wig, he learns from the goddess Inanna that he will acquire the powers of kingship as a result of their lovemaking.

When on the bed he shall have caressed me,
Then shall I caress my lord, a sweet fate I shall decree for him.

> I shall caress Shulgi, the faithful shepherd, a sweet fate I shall fate I shall decree for him.
> I shall caress his loins,
> The shepherdship of all the lands I shall decree as his fate.[18]

In a later, Babylonian account of the sacred marriage ritual, the people beseech the goddess to fulfill all her promises:

> May the lord whom you have called to your heart, the king, your beloved husband, enjoy long days at your holy lap, the sweet.
> Give him a reign godly and glorious,
> Give him the throne of kingship on enduring foundation,
> Give him the people-directing scepter, the staff and the crook,
> Give him an enduring crown, a radiant diadem on his head."[19]

The Sumerian practice of kingship founded on an intimacy with a goddess who lived in the sky as the brightest of stars gradually spread throughout the Western world. Here and there, a local goddess was identified as a manifestation of the Queen of Heaven. In every instance, the goddess had a special relationship with the living king. The Romans, for example, believed that the Greek sea goddess Aphrodite (whom they also called Venus) was the Queen of Heaven and the ancestress of a lineage of kings that included Julius Caesar. Today many Christians call Mary — mother of their "king," Jesus — Queen of Heaven.

Not only the idea of the Queen of Heaven but the Sumerian attention to the movements of the stars had a great influence on neighboring cultures, especially the Egyptians and the Greeks. It is the Greek form of astrology that has survived in the West, because of the widespread influence of Greek culture during the Hellenistic period. However, this is not clear at first to the English reader. This is because English developed under the influence of Latin during the long history of western European Christianity, and so it tends to use the Latin names for the Greek gods. Thus, modern astrologers (along with their scientific cousins, the astronomers) use the Roman names of the Greek gods for the planets and stars: Jupiter (Zeus), Venus (Aphrodite), Mercury (Hermes), and so on. Astrologers will study the traditions surrounding the Greek gods in order to better interpret the symbolism of the stars and planets associated with them. For example, the influence of Mars — the Greek martial deity Ares — is thought to inspire courage and military skill.

In astrology, the sky is likened to a great map in the shape of a revolving wheel, the zodiac. When viewed over successive nights from one spot on earth, the sky appears slightly different each night; it also varies when viewed in the same moment from different places on earth. Thus, a particular configuration of stars and planets can be associated with each place at any given time. The correlation that exists between the heavens and the earth is the basis of astrology, which regards any specific pattern of stars and planets as having a particular correspondence to earthly events.

The zodiac is divided into twelve sections, or constellations (more or less arbitrary grouping of stars). Each constellation is assigned an individual identity, such as the Bull (Taurus) or the Waterbearer (Aquarius). Constellations are further divided into four categories that are governed by certain natural elements: earth, air, water, and fire. Thus a multitude of qualities becomes part of the meaning of each constellation. For example, the Crab (Cancer) is a water sign and its meaning combines both the symbolism of water and the characteristics of the animal.

Astrologers examine the configuration of the sky at the time of birth to "read" the infant's destiny; or they examine the configuration of the sky in the present moment to foretell the immediate future. Learning the detailed movements of heavenly bodies, along with a highly developed system of symbolism, takes much time and training.[20]

The Ifa Oracle. From the Yoruba of western Africa comes yet another complex art of divination. The Yoruba appeared in their present home of Nigeria around 500 CE. Over the centuries to follow, they developed into a highly complex society with many cities and numerous cultural institutions. Between 900 and 1500, the people in the kingdoms of Yorubaland experienced a golden age. Yoruba culture survives today, not only in Africa but also in the African diaspora found in the Americas. The religion of the Yoruba is thus well known to us. One of the important figures in the religion of the Yoruba is the specialist in the art of divination known as the Ifa oracle.

The Ifa diviner (or babalawo, literally "father of secrets"[21]) undergoes a long period of religious training,[22] which includes the memorization of 256 poems (*odu*). Each poem refers to a story drawn from Yoruba sacred lore; and along with the story is the recommended attitude for dealing with the suppliant's situation, such as "go ahead, you will succeed" or "wait, the time is not right for action." The collection of 256 poems, or Odu Ifa, is thus a vast system of symbolic signs, each one representing a message from the god Orunmila (sometimes called Ifa), who because he was present at the time of creation has knowledge about the past and the future. Originally, Orunmila lived on the newly created earth, and he raised there several sons. But eventually he chose to return to the spirit world, leaving his sons behind to help the people in their daily lives. So that they could continue to communicate with him, Orunmila created and left behind the Odu Ifa and the techniques of divining. A Yoruba diviner has a very high status in the society because he is considered to belong to a lineage that begins with the god Orunmila.

Young boys are chosen for training as a babalawo in different ways: sometimes because of their natural imaginative abilities, but also through the divination ritual called Imori ("knowing the head"), which determines who is a "child of Ifa." Training means living with a practicing diviner as his apprentice and later on, working with several diviners until one is experienced enough to divine independently. In addition to memorizing the Odu Ifa, the diviner must cultivate a relationship with each of the gods.

The actual practice of divination begins with an invocation, inviting Orunmila and the ancient diviners to serve as witnesses. This is done by tapping the divination tray with a beautifully carved stick, usually made of ivory. Both the outer edges of the tray and the tapper are decorated with figures from Yoruba mythology.

The center of the tray is a flat surface, which the diviner covers with a fine white powder. With one quick movement of his right hand, he scoops up a handful of nuts from among the pile of sixteen palm nuts resting at his side. Counting the nuts that remain on the ground, the diviner determines whether they represent a single or a double line: if one nut remains, he marks down a double line on the tray; if two nuts remain, a single line. If zero or three nuts remain on the ground, he starts over. This action is repeated sixteen times until there are two columns consisting of single and double lines in a random pattern.

The supplicant has whispered his or her life concern to the diviner at the beginning of the divination. Now the diviner recites the message from the god of destiny, Orunmila. For example, *odu* 175 relates how a man was able to sacrifice correctly in order for his wife to bear children:

Oladipupo was divined for Aroko (Okro),
who was crying because his wife had no children.
He was told to sacrifice a she-goat and sixteen thousand cowries so that his
      wishes might be granted.
He heard and sacrificed.[23]

Each verse instructs the supplicant how to make the proper sacrifice: should it be a prayer, a kola nut, or a slaughtered animal; should the gift be a present to a deity, to the ancestors, to ones own personal god, or to a malevolent spirit? In closing, the god Elegba (or Esu), the divine messenger and guardian of the ritual, will also receive a gift of thanks.

For hundreds of years the verses of the Ifa tradition have been part of an oral tradition, memorized by each diviner and passed on to diviners in the next generation. In 1995 Afolabi A. Epega, a fifth-generation babalawo and scholar, together with American babalawo Philip John Neimark recorded the 256 verses of the Odu Ifa in the original language of the Yoruba[24] and then translated them into English. In this way, what was once a purely oral tradition has become a written tradition.

It is to be noted further that in the Ifa tradition, the diviner usually knows his client personally. So when someone asks the babalawo for a reading, the understanding of the verse will be affected by their relationship and shared history. Thus, the act of divination is something more than the discernment of divine will. It becomes also an experience of therapeutic counseling. The one seeking a message brings his or her concerns to a specialist, who demonstrates both caring and wisdom while seeking the advice of the god.

Divination and Ancient Chinese Culture

Divination is a widespread practice in Chinese communities today. A visit to any Chinese temple, whether Buddhist or Daoist, will typically include the opportunity to cast lots. In addition to the use of moon blocks, one can also employ the so-called lots barrel to receive messages from the ancestors and the gods. The lots barrel is a cylinder filled with long bamboo strips, each one marked with a different number. After offering reverent prayers and gifts to the spirits, one kneels before the altar and gently shakes the cylinder until, at last, one bamboo strip falls out onto the temple floor. The number of the strip will correspond to the number of a specific text, found on a slip of paper hanging on a rack to the side. In some temples, the texts correspond to those found in the *Book of Changes*, a Chinese divination manual.

There are also various methods used to examine the burning of incense sticks in order to receive revelations. This is called "Forecasting bad and good fortune by burning incense."[25] One method interprets the speed at which three separate incense sticks burn. For example, when the stick on the right burns much faster, this means that someone will die within the next year, or else someone will be injured within the next six months. If it burns only slightly faster than the other two, then a family member will have to wear the clothes of mourning within the next seven days. On a more positive note, if the incense stick in the middle burns slightly faster, then someone will arrive within three days bringing news of good fortune. These and other interpretations are available in the temples, which often publish their own divination handbooks.

The importance of divination in Chinese history cannot be overstated. In the past, even the kings — or especially the kings — had diviners who counseled them in matters of royal concern. One example, the oracle bones, provides modern scholars with the earliest Chinese written records as well as knowledge of early Chinese history.

Oracle Bones. The earliest evidence of Chinese writing is found in the inscriptions on fragments of tortoise shell and animal bone used during the Shang Dynasty (c. 1200–1059 BCE) for divination. These are the so-called oracle bones: *jia-gu*, literally "shell bone." Typically, the word *shell* refers to the underbody shell of a tortoise, and *bone* refers to the shoulder blade of cattle. These were used by Shang royalty to communicate by means of divination with their ancestors. Later, the practice was abandoned and the actual significance of the fragments of bone and shell forgotten. Certainly, in the nineteenth century oracle bones were not recognized as tools for divination. Called "dragon bones," they were ground into powder and used as medicine.[26]

Scapulomancy, divination using the shoulder bone of animals, was practiced already by the ancestors of the Shang. Scapula from cattle, sheep, pigs, and deer with surface traces of drilling, boring, and burning have been found at many Neolithic sites in China. But only with the Shang were inscriptions included for the first time as part of the divinatory process.

Each oracle bone poses in writing a question for the ancestors. The divination ritual involved drilling holes in the shell or bone and placing it in fire. The resulting cracks were understood to be coded messages from the spirit world. It was then the task of the diviner to interpret the cracks. The complete oracle shell or bone could include the following sequence of inscriptions[27]:

1. Preface: Date of divination and the name of the person executing the divination.
2. Charge: The question asked in the divination.
3. Prognostication: The interpretation of the cracks as response to the inscribed questions.
4. Historical verification: What actually happened.

Unfortunately, both the prognostication and the verification of the revelation are frequently missing. So what exist in most cases are questions that express the concerns of Shang royalty. These are quite wide-ranging and include queries about the weather; what sacrifices should be offered to the gods and ancestors; matters of warfare or illness; and the interpretation of dreams. Some of the oracle bones also contain reports to the ancestors about important activities, such as success in the hunt. Even the question concerning the gender of a newborn child can be the subject of divination, as in the following illustration.[28]

1. Preface: Divination on the day of *Jia-shen* for "X."[29]
2. Charge: "Fu Hao[30] will soon give birth; will it be fine?"
3. Prognostication: On the basis of the divined omens, the king predicted, "If she gives birth on a *Ding* day, it will be very good; if she gives birth on a *Geng* day, it will be auspicious."
4. Verification: After thirty-one days, Fu Hao gave birth on the *Jia-yin* day. It was not good: she gave birth to a girl.

It is rare to find all four parts of the divination process recorded as in this case, which comes from the collection of oracle bones at the Institute of History and Philology in Taiwan.

Oracle bones are not limited to Shang relics. Recently a small number of oracle bones have been found that date back to a later period, that of the Zhou Dynasty (1059–221 BCE). Furthermore, up to the present day, minority ethnic groups in the southwest regions of China, such as the Yi Nationality (Yizu), the Moxie, and the Nasi, retain the custom of using animal bone for divination.[31]

The Book of Changes. One well-known art of divination from ancient China is the casting of lots using the milfoil stalks of the yarrow plant (*Achillea millefolium*).[32] The technique was used to determine one out of sixty-four possible patterns, each one assigned a specific meaning. "Out of a total of fifty stalks, forty-nine are divided and subdivided into groups, and depending on the random way in which this is accomplished, the diviner forms one of sixty-four written patterns of six lines, or hexagrams." Each hexagram consists of two trigrams (each having three lines) and represents one possible answer relevant to the question that has been put forward.

The technique is similar to that of the Ifa oracle in that both are based on determining which one of numerous more-or-less fixed signs expresses the view of the gods. Similar to the Odu Ifa, which offers 256 possible readings, Chinese diviners compiled various collections of instructions on how to interpret the sixty-four hexagrams. Eventually these were written down to form divination manuals. One such divination manual, dating to the early Zhou period, is the *Book of Changes*.

In addition to the hexagrams, together with their original interpretations (the "image" and the "judgment"), the *Book of Changes* includes extensive commentaries. The older texts are written as poetry; the commentaries are in prose. Already by the time of the Han Dynasty, the original meanings of the poems assigned to each hexagram had become somewhat obscure, so the diviners of that period tried to explain them by referring to contemporaneous views. In doing so, they introduced their own newly developed ideas about yin and yang as complementary forces that together determine the constantly changing nature of the universe. Thus the *Book of Changes* reflects both Zhou and Han cosmologies.

Yin and yang designate the two polar energies that underlie all cosmic processes. Originally the characters stood for the shady and sunny sides of the mountain. Over time, as they came to represent two universal categories, each one became a symbol for a complex of related meanings. Yin is associated with the dark, the wet, the cold, the female, and stasis. Its opposite, yang is the light, the dry, the hot, the male, and movement. Thus, all things and all times are determined by the interaction of yin and yang: yin conserves; yang radiates. Both are necessary for existence, where the two energies are constantly seeking to balance each other.

In Chinese thought, human beings can make their lives easier if they, too, seek to balance the forces of yin and yang. For example, Chinese New

Year celebrations take place at the coldest time of the year and so emphasize the yang quality during a season that is dominated by yin. Even Chinese medicine interprets the various physical and emotional states of the human being according to the relationship of these principles. For example, the activity of the heart is seen as a resting stage (yin) alternating with a working stage (yang). If there is too much heat in the body, cooling agents are introduced, and vice-versa.

The two trigrams that make up each hexagram are understood to indicate the present situation in terms of the relationship between yin and yang. Yin is represented by a broken line; yang, by an unbroken line. In addition, there are the changing lines: extreme yin must be followed by a movement in the opposite direction. The same goes for extreme yang. Altogether four lines are possible: yin; yin becoming yang; yang; and yang becoming yin.

The first trigram has three unbroken yang lines and its name is Heaven. A trigram of three broken lines — completely yin — is called Earth. Other trigrams combine broken and unbroken lines. There are six additional possible combinations, each represented by an image: Water, Fire, Mountain, Lake, Wind, and Thunder. In divination, two separate trigrams are determined through the casting of lots. There are sixty-four possible combinations of the eight trigrams. Thus, the final reading is suggested symbolically by the relationship of the two trigrams. For example, when both trigrams are made up of unbroken lines, they represent the doubling of Heaven. The hexagram is called the Creative. Both the image and the judgment describe a situation dominated by yang qualities[33] and recommend the appropriate attitude for such a time.

> Image
> The movement of heaven is full of power.
> Thus the superior person makes himself strong and untiring.
>
> Judgment
> The creative works sublime success,
> Furthering through perseverance.

The prose commentary describes the philosophical basis of the image and the judgment as well as their ramifications for the individual person, especially the ruler. In comparison, the commentary can be quite lengthy. An excerpt will serve to suggest the style of the commentator:

6. Divination

Since there is only one heaven, the doubling of the trigram, of which heaven is the image, indicates the movement of heaven. One complete revolution of heaven makes a day, and the repetition of the trigram means that each day is followed by another. This creates the idea of time. Since it is the same heaven moving with untiring power, there is also created the idea of duration both in and beyond time, a movement that never stops nor slackens, just as one day follows another in an unending course. This duration in time is the image of the power inherent in the Creative. With this image as a model, the sage learns how best to develop himself so that his influence may endure. He must make himself strong in every way, by consciously casting out all that is inferior and degrading. Thus he attains that tirelessness which depends upon consciously limiting the fields of his activity.[34]

Other hexagrams include the doubling of Earth to form the hexagram called the Receptive, as well as all possible combinations of the eight trigrams. The symbolic names of the hexagrams vary considerably: Difficulty at the Beginning, Waiting, Youthful Folly, Conflict, Peace, Work on What Has Been Spoiled, and so forth.

Today the *Book of Changes* has been translated into many languages. In addition to serving as a divination manual, it provides scholars with a valuable resource for the study of early Chinese language, symbolism, and thought.

The popularity of divination in Chinese cultures is reflected in ideas about the role of the ruler. The interpretation of natural events as signs or omens sent by the gods has played a significant role in the political life of the Chinese people. The ruler is constantly under divine surveillance; and the gods have many ways to reveal their will concerning him.

The Mandate of Heaven. Kingship in China was long based on the conviction that the ruler was a steward of the gods. According to the principles of divination, it was believed that the gods could express approval or disapproval of the king by manipulating natural events. Evidence of this view is found already in writings from the Zhou Dynasty.

The oldest surviving Chinese book dates back to the first half of the Zhou Dynasty. This is the *Book of Songs*, comprising some three hundred hymns that were chanted during the ceremonies of worship attended by the royal family. The hymns are of many kinds and include prayers, confessions of offences committed by the king, and reports of his great deeds. All are addressed to the ancestors of the royal family, especially Shang Di (Emperor on High), ancestor of the ruler. Gradually Shang Di was identified also as Heaven, and so the sovereign acquires the title Son of Heaven. As such, he represents the authority of Heaven; and his role as priest-king is to show the people how to live according to divine will.

> O prince, let your practice of virtue
> Be entirely good and admirable.
> Watch well over your behavior,
> And allow nothing wrong in your demeanor.
> Committing no excess, doing nothing injurious —
> There are few who will not in such a case take you for their pattern.[35]

When the ruler fails to serve as a model for virtue, Heaven will send messages to the people so that they know that it is time to replace him. In the next passage, advice is given to a wayward sovereign:

> Heaven is now inflicting calamities
> And is destroying the State.
> My illustrations are not taken from things remote.
> Great Heaven makes no mistakes.
> If you go on to deteriorate in your virtue,
> You will bring the people to great distress.[36]

It is a common theme: "Heaven is sending down death and disorder, and has put an end to our king."[37]

The Chinese expression that identifies the source of the sovereign's authority is Tian Ming, or the Mandate of Heaven: "The prince's right to rule comes from the gods." His authority was never absolute.[38] The ruler received his power to govern from the gods, and so he must live up to their standards or else calamities would occur.

The scholarly tradition that begins with Confucius (at the end of the sixth century) looks back to the rulers of the Zhou Dynasty and their royal traditions as the ideal for all time. Thus, Confucian thought emphasizes the importance of the ruler as a model for all the people: Heaven "chooses the sovereigns to bring civilization to the people and to instruct them in the correct human relationships. The rulers' charisma is sanctioned by the mandate they receive from Heaven…, and it is by this sanction that they exercise their power and ensure a ritual order in the symbiosis of gods, ancestors, and men, in which each has his proper station."[39]

The identity of the "true" Son of Heaven could be made known through dreams and other omens. During the first century of the Common Era, two men were vying for the role as emperor of the Han Dynasty: Guang Wu Di and Gong Sun Shu. Both pointed to various signs and omens that they believed would support their claims. They even interpreted the same dream from opposite perspectives: Gong Sun Shu dreamed that a man appeared to him and said, "Gong Sun, twelve is the limit." According to his interpretation, the number twelve refers to the twelve previous Han rulers, so the dream indicates the end of a dynasty, which he, Gong Sun, was to supplant. Later, however, the diviners of Guang Wu Di would offer an alternative interpretation when during the twelfth year of his reign, Gong Sun was overthrown. According to the second interpretation, the dream meant that twelve years would be limit of his, that is to say Gong Sun's, reign.[40]

How was the emperor to keep the authority given by Heaven? In two ways: by maintaining a good relationship with his ancestors, especially Heaven, that is, Shang Di, through the regular ceremonies of worship; and by leading a virtuous life. As long as he fulfilled his role, Heaven would be pleased and the realm would flourish. In fact, if a dynasty was overthrown by military means, this was evidence that the ruler no longer pleased Heaven. According to one Chinese proverb, "He who succeeds becomes emperor; he who fails is a bandit."[41]

In other words, the prosperity of the kingdom is both the outcome of successful leadership and a sign from Heaven that the ruler is fulfilling his responsibility. This way of thinking, which clearly argues the dependence of the ruler on divine will, has served in China as the basis for regarding natural events as messages from the gods. If peace and prosperity is a sign that Heaven is pleased with the king, then natural disasters must have the opposite meaning. Terrible events, such as flood, defeat in war, drought, and earthquake, have been interpreted as expressions of divine displeasure with the ruler. More than once in Chinese history a successful revolution began with the confidence that the sovereign had lost his mandate to rule.

Employing techniques of divination so as to further human communication with the ancestors and the gods is certainly widespread, affecting people living in traditional societies on a very deep level. The practice of divination thus expresses the human conviction that the world as a whole is ultimately under the control of transcendent realities.

Chapter 7

Spirit Travel

So far, we have discussed two types of revelation: visions and voices, where the message from the spirit world appears to the person by means of the physical senses or the imagination; and divination, which may require a specialist (or diviner) to interpret the spiritual messages conveyed by symbolic patterns that appear in the natural world. Like divination, spirit travel may involve a specialist, one who has learned how to contact the spirits by entering their realm.

During the spirit journey the human spirit (mind, soul) moves without the aid of the body: as it travels around the natural world it may scout for animals to hunt or search for someone who is lost. Or the traveler may enter the realm of the spirits in order to communicate directly with spirit beings of all kinds. Thus, destinations of the journey may lie in the heavens, under the earth, or below the surface of the sea, depending on where the spirits are known to dwell.

What happens to the body while the spirit soars? According to many accounts, it enters into a death-like state. While the conscious center of personality experiences spirit travel, the body resembles a corpse, but one that will revive as soon as the spirit returns.

Spirit travel is not a religion but a type of revelation found in many different religions. Sometimes spirit travel is part of communal ritual life, as, for example, a journey to the Kingdom of Shadows taken by the spirit traveler Nelbosh and recorded by ethnologists Waldermar and Dina Brodsky Jochelson in the Siberian village of Kamenskoye during the winter of 1900/1901: "Then the shaman [spirit traveler] stopped beating the drum, put it down near by, and remained motionless, lying on his stomach on the reindeer skin. This meant that the soul of the shaman had left his body and through the drum as through a lake, had descended into the Kingdom of

7. Spirit Travel

Shadows." After the ceremony was completed, Nelbosh explained what had happened while his soul was out of the body and how he had been able to recover the soul of a sick man that had sought refuge among the souls of the ancestors.[1]

But spirit travel is not exclusively connected with ritual: it can also appear as the theme of individual visions. For example, in his Second Letter to the Corinthians, Paul of Tarsus says that he will "tell of visions" granted by God. He then relates how "a Christian man" was carried up first into the third heaven and then later into paradise, where he heard words so sacred and so secret that human lips could not utter them.[2]

Rituals of Spirit Travel

The spirit journey as an important source of revelation is found most commonly among people who live in small societies and depend on hunting or fishing to survive. Often there is the related belief that the soul, or spirit, will leave the body at death in order to join the ancestors in some kind of paradise. In these communities, the one who is able to make the journey to the spirit world and return to life in the body without dying or going insane is the ritual specialist of the spirit journey, or spirit traveler.

A ceremony is performed to aid the spirit traveler in making his or her journey. Drumming, chanting, singing, dancing, and other activities take place. The clothing of the traveler may be symbolic in some way, so as to represent the spirits who will guide and protect the traveler. When the spirit travelers return to ordinary consciousness, they usually report to others their experience. Thus, the journey is undertaken for the good of the whole community.

The spirit traveler can be a man or a woman, one who receives specialized training in order to connect the people with their spirits through the spirit journey. Often those who make the spirit journey will serve as healers and spiritual leaders for the community as a whole. They will practice spirit travel along with other forms of revelation, such as divination and spirit mediation.

Spirit travel is found in various religions as one part of a complex tradition that is passed on from generation to generation. Its origins, its methods, and the goals of spirit travel become part of sacred lore. For example, there may be a myth about a primordial being that was first to make the spirit journey. For example, among the Krahó of South America, contemporary spirit travelers recognize the mythical model for their work in stories about Tir'kre, the first spirit traveler.

One day an ant crawled into Tir'kre's ear as he lay sleeping. As a result he became disoriented; his spirit wandered, lost and isolated from human contact. Eventually, Tir'kre was rescued by the spirits of various birds: after the smallest birds were able to remove the ant, the vultures then transported Tir'kre high up into the heavens. There, a hawk brought him food: birds of diverse kinds, which he had to eat raw. In the spirit world, Tir'kre learned how to shape-shift, taking on the forms of birds, ants, and the otter. When he finally was able to return to earth, he brought with him new knowledge of how to heal those who were sick, in mind or body. So it is among the Krahó that the spirit travelers usually undergo a period of retreat during which they, too, are fed uncooked birds. Guided by spirits in the form of animals, they follow in the footsteps of Tir'kre. One visitor reports that "since we showed our surprise when the curer Zezeinho told us that a hawk taught him to cure, he queried: 'And was it not the hawk who taught Tir'kre?' as if to say: If Tir'kre, in whose existence, and the truthfulness of whose story, we all believe, received instruction from a hawk, so why cannot the same happen to me?"[3]

Our knowledge of spirit travel has been greatly influenced by the research concerning certain ritual specialists in Siberian small societies. A look at the life and religious work of a Siberian spirit traveler thus provides a good introduction to the more general phenomenon of ritual spirit travel.

Siberian Shamans. The spirit journey has played an important role in the traditions of the hunting peoples of northern Siberia. Until recently, these peoples lived in small clans and sustained themselves by herding reindeer and hunting. The shaman — one who could make the spirit journey as well as practice other forms of revelation — served both as healer-protector and as one of the leaders of the clan. Many scholars have borrowed the term *shaman* from the Tungus language to refer to the spirit traveler found more generally.[4] Still, it must be remembered that, each culture will have its own term for the spirit traveler, and rituals of spirit travel take on different forms within the overall symbolic context of each tradition.

The shaman (or shamanka, if a woman) is a member of the clan: "it

7. Spirit Travel

was ... his job to maintain contact between the living and the dead members of the clan and to arrange the shamanizing connected with the calendrical hunting rites. It was during these rites that the shaman would retrieve the souls of the animals to be hunted from the keeper of the species in the otherworld store. The shaman helped individual members of the clan by curing diseases and infertility, by prophesying, and by preventing misfortune threatened by the spirits."[5] Strengthening the spiritual, emotional, and physical well-being of the clan, the shaman must employ a variety of techniques, of which spirit travel is only one. Some shamans are primarily mediums, but "in the western and northern parts of Siberia — among the Samoyeds and the Ob-Ugrians, for example ... the shaman is imagined as traveling to the otherworld with his spirit helpers."[6]

The shaman is one who has developed a long-term relationship with the spirits that are willing to teach and guide him in his work. He is able to contact them at will. Through their instruction, he has come to know the spirit realm as well as the natural world. In the religious life of the shaman we can thus distinguish several important stages: the call; training; initiation; and ritual spirit travel.

Siberian shamans can inherit their religious role from a relative or experience a spontaneous vocation — the call — that is, undergo certain events that lead him or her into the work of shamanic leadership. For example, often the shaman undergoes an illness while he or she is a teenager, something like what modern people call a psychological breakdown or period of madness. With the help of an older, experienced shaman the young person heals himself. This self-healing is the foundation of the shaman's life-long work as one who can heal others. In these societies, illness is as much a spiritual as physical crisis, and so the healer is one who is at home in the spirit world.

The training of the shaman can take quite a long time. In addition to undergoing a self-cure, the shaman must learn all about the geography of the spirit world and come to know the spirits that inhabit it. The identity, role, and nature of each spirit must become familiar. Then the pathways that lead from the world of the living to the land of the dead must be learned. Sometimes there is a tree (among the Abakan Tatars, it is a white birch) that connects the different realms, and the shaman learns how to move up and down the tree. He may even use the wood of the tree to construct his drum. Then, too, it is believed that the spirit world is full of dangers and numerous difficulties. These must be faced and successfully overcome before one is truly a shaman.

Often the shaman will have a spirit helper that he first encounters during the period of training. The spirit helper is something like a teacher or a guide. It might appear as an animal spirit with whom the shaman has a special relationship; at other times, the helper takes on human form, a spirit husband or spirit wife who is committed to the education of the shaman. The Nanai shamans, for example, inherit an *ajami*, a spirit that "marries" the novice shaman, instructing him or her in all that concerns the spirit world.[7]

Initiation refers to the experience by means of which a novice is transformed into a practicing shaman. It usually takes place in the dreams or visions of the novice, after which the members of the community can recognize the transformation by accepting him or her as their healer. Sometimes a public ceremony of consecration will follow to confirm the shaman in this new role.

One major theme found in the visions that mark the final step in becoming a shaman is dismemberment followed by the creation of a "new" body — one that has magical powers. The new body may be one that can travel in all realms of reality or one that can understand the languages of animals and spirits. For example, in a vision the future shaman may see his own body as it is being torn apart and boiled in a large cauldron; eventually, the body parts are reassembled and the apprentice is reborn.

> Then the candidate came to a desert and saw a distant mountain. After three days' travel he reached it, entered an opening, and came upon a naked man working a bellows. On the fire was a cauldron "as big as half the earth." The naked man saw him and caught him with a huge pair of tongs. The novice had time to think, "I am dead!" The man cut off his head, chopped his body into bits, and put everything in the cauldron. There he boiled his body for three years.

After a lengthy process, the blacksmith puts the bones back together and covers them with flesh. The head and the eyes have been altered so that the shaman can see what is invisible to others, and his ears have been pierced so that he can understand the language of birds. The novice then "woke in the yurt, among his family. Now he can sing and shamanize indefinitely, without ever growing tired."[8]

When the shaman wants to make a spirit journey, he will first prepare himself in seclusion, fasting and meditating. The ceremony to contact the spirits must take place after dark, since spirits fear the light. Common aids that help the Siberian shaman make the spirit journey include the beating of drums, the singing of songs and chants, and dancing. The spirit traveler may put on a special set of clothes for the journey, fur or leather decorated with the images of sacred animals and other symbolic emblems. The feathers of birds may be important props in the ceremony, since it may be expected that the spirit will be flying to the otherworld. A mirror is often worn, hanging perhaps from a belt. The meaning of the mirror varies from place to place: sometimes it is treated as a window through which the shaman can look directly into the spirit world. Spirit travel itself is experienced only by the shaman's spirit, while his body lies still. Regaining full consciousness, he then shares what he has learned during the journey.

The goals of the spirit journey are numerous: (1) The shaman will sometimes go to the spirit world to find a lost spirit and bring it home. This happens when a member of the community manifests some kind of mental illness. The interpretation is that the person's soul has left the body and because disoriented, is unable to return on its own. (2) When someone dies, the shaman will make a spirit journey in order to guide the soul of the deceased person to the land of the ancestors. (3) The shaman may also journey to the spirit world to gain knowledge that can serve the community, for in the spirit world the shaman can communicate directly with and learn from the gods, the ancestors, and the spirits of animals.

(4) Another goal of the journey is to gain success in hunting. The shaman may visit the spirits that care for the animals and ask for help. One Siberian shaman describes a visit to the Owner of the Earth that began with a respectful request: "Earth-Owner! Your children [that is, the reindeer] send to me for some food for the future." If the god loves him, he will receive the soul of a reindeer, which he can later give to the hunters, telling them where the reindeer can be found to hunt.[9]

The Ancient Scandinavian Seidr. Ritual spirit travel is documented also in the records of the ancient Germanic peoples who lived in the far northern lands of Scandinavia, in Iceland, and in Greenland. Here the evidence points to women as specialists of the spirit journey. Called seidkona, the female spirit traveler rode in a cart from farm to farm, conducting a ceremony of spirit travel known as the seidr. The legend of the hero Norna-Gest includes a reference to this practice: "at that time wise women used to go about the land. They were called 'spae-wives'[10] and they foretold people's futures. For this reason folk used to invite them to their houses and give them hospitality, and bestow gifts on them at parting."[11]

The ancient Scandinavians believed that the seidkona was under the tutelage of Freyja, a beautiful goddess. It is she who taught the arts of soul flight, not only to women but also to the gods, to Odin, for example.[12] As symbol of her own role as spirit traveler, Freyja possessed a feathered garment, or falcon form, enabling her to fly easily from one realm to another. More commonly, she was known to travel about in a carriage drawn by cats.

Perhaps the most interesting description of a seidr to survive is the one recorded in *The Saga of Eric the Red*.[13] Originally, Eric the Red came from Iceland, an island colonized by the Norwegians. During the tenth century he discovered and settled in faraway Greenland. The religious traditions of the pre-Christian Scandinavians survived longer in Greenland because of its distance from Norway, which was Christianized already in the tenth century under King Olaf Tryggvason. In this account, the seidkona wears a blue cloak and jewels, along with a headdress made out of black lamb's wool and the fur of white cats. She carries a staff, and during the ceremony she sits on a rather high platform. Her cushion is filled with the feathers of chickens. Her boots are made of the skin of a calf; and her gloves, cat's skin. Her companions include fifteen girls and fifteen boys, whose role it is to provide a singing chorus for the seidr.

After the ceremony, the seidkona reports that the singing has been quite effective, having attracted many spirits. This made it easier for her to contact them. The purpose of the seidr was to serve as a link between the human community and the spirit world. Once her spirit returned to the body, the seidkona was able to prophesy about the future or heal the sick.

Knowledge about the spirit world gained through the spirit journey is the special gift of the seidkona: this knowledge spans the past and the future as well as the different realms in the present. In the most sacred of ancient Scandinavian poems, the *Voluspa* (Prophecy of the Seeress), a seidkona, or seeress, tells how the gods created the world out of the body of the primordial giant, Ymir. She then describes the cosmology: "Nine worlds I know, the nine abodes / of the glorious world-tree the ground beneath." She describes the various realms of the gods, other spirit beings, the living and the dead. All are connected by Yggdrasill, a gigantic ash tree whose roots lead into the underworld and whose branches reach the heavens.

As for the future, the spirit traveler goes on to predict a war between the gods and the monsters that will destroy the world. But this is not the end.

> On unsown acres the ears will grow,
> all ill grow better; ....
> I see a hall than the sun more fair,
> thatched with red gold, which is Gimlé hight.
> There will the gods all guiltless throne,
> and live forever in ease and bliss.[14]

Destruction is to be followed by a new creation. The spirit traveler brings a mixed message, but one ultimately of hope, to her people.

Aids for the Spirit Journey. Spirit travel as a theme found in ritual activity occurs also among many of the indigenous peoples of South America. In *Icanchu's Drum: An Orientation to Meaning in South American Religions*, Lawrence E. Sullivan presents detailed information about two aspects of ritual spirit travel: the use of sound and medicinal plants to help the spirit leave the body and enter the spirit realm.

The ceremony of the spirit journey typically includes sound: drumming, chanting, music, and song. Sound journeys forth from its source — the drum, the gourd rattle, the human voice — into the surrounding space. It moves invisibly, a model for the human spirit that likewise leaves the body behind. The symbolic parallelism that exists between sound and the journeying soul augments the sacredness of music in the ritual life of these peoples, for whom the gourd rattle is the spirit traveler's single, most important instrument.[15] Widely used is the bottle gourd (Lagenaria), which must be cultivated, yet is never served as food. Nevertheless, the gourd is found throughout the continent as well as in the grave sites of Bolivia and Peru. Among the Guarani, the sound of the gourd rattle (*mbaraká*) has the power to induce the beginning of the spirit journey. "As soon as the *mbaraká* sounds, serious and solemn, it seems to invite one to present oneself before the divinity; at times it sounds strongly and wildly, transporting the dancers toward ecstasy."[16] Here, the word *ecstasy* refers to the out-of-body experience. It is used in its original sense of the mind outside the body, deriving from the Greek word *ekstasis*, which literally means "standing outside (the body)" or "(psychological) displacement."

In addition to the gourd rattle, sacred songs aid the spirit traveler. Usually the songs are first acquired during a vision, and because of this, they are believed to have a power that has nothing to do with the beauty of the melody or even the meaning of the words. Indeed, the songs of the spirit traveler are often composed in strange or esoteric languages. Sometimes the "secret" language of the song is believed to belong to the animals or spirits. Singing such a song, the spirit traveler assumes his out-of-body spirit-form:

> Ededee edee, ededee edee
> I am the same as you, I am spirit now spirit
> A bird am I, a white heron
> Just as I am a spirit…

The songs are directed at the spirits that empower the journey: he invites them to draw close and entreats them for aid. Further, the songs have a transformative power of their own, giving the traveler a spirit-form.

The song might be addressed to the spirit of a hallucinogenic vine from which is concocted a potent drink that will serve as a spirit guide:

> Phantom revealing spirit of the vine
> we seek your guidance now
> to translate the past into the future
> to understand every detail of our milieu
> to improve our life
> reveal the secrets that we need.[18]

The spirit travelers of South America are experts in the practical use of plants of all kinds: healing herbs, tobacco, and consciousness-altering plants. "South American cultures, perhaps more than those in any other region of the world, make religious use of plants that spark luminous visions.… The power of these sacred plants rearranges the [spirit traveler's] entire sensible being and lifts him or her to another plane of unearthly light."[19]

Of course, the ingestion of hallucinogenic plants can be dangerous. In 1902 at the age of fifteen, Manuel Córdova-Rios was kidnapped by Amahuaca Indians, who then continued to care for him deep in the jungle of the Amazon basin. He later describes how the tribe's elderly chief and healer, Xumu, was training him to become his successor. This instruction included the ritual use of a drink made from an hallucinogenic plant called *nixi honi xuma* (Banisteriopsis caapi). The substance increased the young man's ability to travel about and perceive everything in the jungle around him, even in the middle of the darkest night or with his eyes closed. But the mental changes that he experienced during the time when he was being trained by Xumu frightened him: "At times during all this, which went on for months, I became nervous, high-strung and afraid of going insane. The chief and the old women noticed this. They took pains to explain and reassure me that as long as I followed the diets and instructions everything would come out well."[20]

Indeed, the difficulty and dangers inherent in the spirit journey is emphasized everywhere in the accounts of spirit travelers, who point out that only the exceptional individual — disciplined, intelligent, and emotionally balanced — can survive the training and demands of this religious role. Further, they stress the importance of an experienced guide to protect the novice during his or her initial training. It is well to remember that above all, the practicing spirit traveler is a healer, restoring health to the individual person and protecting the community from harm. Health, physical and spiritual, is his or her domain. It is no wonder that spirit travelers often report long and active lives.

At the age of twenty-one, Córdova-Rios managed to escape and return to his family in Peru. Living in the midst of Western society, he practiced the healing knowledge that he had learned from Xumu. At the age of ninety-five, Cordova-Rios was still seeing twenty to thirty patients every day.

Visions of the Spirit Journey

In addition to rituals of spirit travel, the spirit journey appears as a common theme in the visionary experiences of people all over the world. In dreams and visions people see themselves leave the body and travel to faraway places, other lands and spirit worlds of all kinds.[21] Interesting examples of the vision of the spirit journey appear in two heterodox forms of Christianity: the heavenly journey of the soul in early gnostic Christianity and the celestial meeting with God and Jesus experienced by Hong Xiu Quan, leader of the Taiping rebellion that took place in nineteenth-century China.

A Gnostic Vision. The details of a journey to the spirit world reflect the cosmology of the traveler. If the spirits live under the earth, the journey will be subterranean; if they live in the sky, the traveler will ascend. For centuries, Western conceptions of the world were based on what is called the Ptolemaic cosmology, combining Sumerian and Babylonian star worship with Egyptian and Greek astronomy. The final synthesis was written down by Claudius Ptolemaeus of Alexandria (second century CE) in his book called the *Almagest*.

According to Ptolemaic cosmology, the earth lies at the center of the world. It is encircled by seven spheres, arranged something like the layers of an onion. Dominating each sphere and serving as its mover is a celestial being: the moon, the sun, or one of the five visible planets (the "wandering" stars), identified either with the gods or with angels (in the case of monotheists). For example, the English terms Mercury, Venus, Mars, Jupiter, and Saturn derive from the Roman names for the gods that were identified with these five planets that can be seen with the naked eye.

Closest to the earth is the sphere of the changeable moon, which governs the cycles of transformation that determine earthly existence: birth, growth, decay, and death. Above the moon is an eternal realm, where neither change nor death exist. Higher than the planets, in this view, is the Ogdoas, or eighth sphere, that of the so-called fixed stars. Beyond the Ogdoas is a realm of pure divinity. The Ptolemaic model of the universe was generally accepted in the West until the scientific revolution in the seventeenth century, which resulted in the discovery that the earth is merely one of many planets circling the sun.

However, at the time of the Roman Empire — when the Ptolemaic cosmology was generally accepted — the theme of heavenly ascent was quite common. For example, Philo of Alexandria (c. 20 BCE to 50 CE), the scholarly commentator on the Jewish Bible, describes the ultimate religious goal as a journey of the mind,[22] which leaves behind the material realm in order to ascend through the planetary spheres to the highest heavens, a place of pure thought beyond which is the presence of God, the Great King: "Again, when soaring upward the mind has spied the atmosphere and its changes, it is borne yet higher to the ether and the celestial revolution, and is carried around with the dances of the planets and fixed stars, in accordance with the laws of perfect music, following the love of wisdom that guides it. When it has transcended all sensible substance, at that point it longs for the intelligible, and on beholding in that realm beauties beyond measure, the patterns and originals of the sensible things in the world below, it is possessed by a sober intoxication ... and is inspired, filled by another sort of longing and more fitting desire. Escorted by this to the uppermost vault of things intelligible, it seems to be on its way to the to the Great King himself; but while it keenly strives to see him, pure and untempered rays of concentrated light stream forth like a flood, so that through its flashing bursts, the eye of the understanding spins with dizziness."[23]

The *Poimandres of Hermes Trismegistos*, a polytheistic text from the same period, presents the same basic pattern of the soul's ascent: "And thereafter, man thrusts upward through the Harmony" of the spheres, where he surrenders the qualities that are governed by each planet. "And then denuded of the effects of the Harmony, he enters the nature of the Ogdoas, now in the possession of his own power, and with those already there, he exalts the Father." Those who reach the Ogdoas, or level of the fixed stars, are able to hear sweet voices coming from beyond the cosmos. "And then in procession they rise up towards the Father and give themselves up to the Powers, and having become Powers, themselves, enter the Godhead."[24]

Later, even in Islam there developed a narrative about how Muhammad ascended into the heavens so as to talk with God. "Then Jibrîl [Gabriel] takes the Prophet on a tour of the heavens: in the first he meets Adam, in the second Jesus and John the Evangelist, in the third Joseph, in the fourth Idris-Enoch, in the fifth Aaron, in the sixth Moses, and in the seventh Abraham. They subsequently come to the lotus of the border line (*sidrat al-muntahâ*), where Muhammad contemplates God's glory and talks to Him."[25] Known as "the night journey," this tradition is commemorated by the Dome of the Rock, a beautiful mosque in Jerusalem that is built on the rock from which Muhammad's heavenly journey began.[26]

It is against this cultural background depicting the eternal and divine world as high above the stars in heaven that the early Christian debate about the nature of the resurrection played out. For at the same time, a commonly held philosophical belief suggested that the human being was actually composed of three parts, the so-called tripartite anthropology of Middle Platonism. In addition to the body, the human possesses both a soul[27] and a spirit.[28] The spirit is both eternal and divine. But what about the soul and the body? Some gnostic Christians claimed that with the help of the spirit, the soul would be resurrected. But other gnostic Christians doubted even the salvation of the soul, arguing that the eternal realm is limited to pure spirit. Opposed to both views, those who came to be called orthodox Christians insisted that both the body and soul will be resurrected together with the spirit.[29]

At issue is the relationship between the material creation and the God revealed through Jesus of Nazareth. Orthodox Christianity is rooted in the Jewish conviction that the God of salvation is also the creator of the earth and its creatures. This view emphasizes the value of God's creation, which includes, of course, the human body. Gnostic Christians, however, felt that the creation — the earth, the body, and all sensible experience — was either a mistake or the workings of an inferior power, the Demiurge, for instance. Gnostic Christians, as for example the author of the *Gospel of Thomas*, sought to be delivered from all material existence, seeing the world as nothing more than a corpse: "Jesus said, 'He who has known the world has found a corpse.'"[30] The world is a corpse[31] because, for the gnostic Christian, it is empty of true life, the life that comes from the spirit, which exists apart from the world. The gnostic Christian is one for whom sensible existence has no meaning; he or she strives to live in union with the divine in a purely spiritual realm.

Thus, one gnostic Christian text, *The Exegesis on the Soul* describes a vision of the soul leaving the material world in order to return to its purely spiritual home with God. Written during the Roman period and translated from the original Greek text into Coptic (the Egyptian language written with the Greek alphabet), the text is found in the Nag Hammadi library,[32] which lay hidden for centuries in an Egyptian cave. It tells the story of the soul: her fall into the world of the body, her reunion with her heavenly counterpart, and her ultimate return to the highest heaven.

In the beginning the soul exists in complete freedom together with the Father in the highest heaven. The soul is androgynous, half male and half female, but it is only the female half that is attracted to the sensible realm governed by the power of the goddess Aphrodite (the planet Venus) and the other rulers of creation (the planetary spheres). Leaving behind her masculine half, the feminine aspect of the soul, called Psyche, descends into the sublunary realm of the body, change, suffering, and death.

Once she has descended into the creation, she begins to miss her masculine counterpart. She seeks him everywhere. Again and again she feels that she has found him, but the text tells us that these "husbands" are nothing but robbers who seduce Psyche, only to abandon her again. The author then informs us that, in fact, the word *husband* is a symbol for each enticement found in the sensible realm: attachments such as pleasure, love, knowledge, fame, and so forth. Ultimately, these attachments prove to be temporary and imperfect. In despair, Psyche begins to weep. She calls out to the Father to deliver her.

Hearing her lament, God is moved by pity for Psyche, and so he restores to her the inner capacity to receive the spirit, her true husband. This "baptism" is followed by a reunion with her masculine counterpart in the bridal chamber: there, Psyche receives her heavenly bridegroom. However, unlike physical marriage, where two come together and a third is created, this union results in the restoration of the original, androgynous soul, able to move on its own.

> And it was right for Psyche to give birth to herself and become again as she had been in the beginning. Now the soul moved on its own and received divinity from the Father, enabling its rejuvenation so that it might be received again in its original home. This is the resurrection from the dead. This is the ransom from captivity. This is the ascent to heaven. This is the way to the Father.[33]

The author believes that only the spirit has the ability to ascend to God. So, in union with the body, poor Psyche is stuck in the "land of the dead." Her resurrection is possible only when she is reunited with the spirit. In this text, the spirit is identified with the masculine half of the soul, also called both her brother and her savior.[34]

The Visions of Hong Xiu Quan. The theme of spirit travel is common also in the religious literature of traditional Chinese culture. For example, a collection of poems compiled in the second century, the *Songs of the South* is filled with such imagery. One poem called "The River Earl" describes the poet's flight in a chariot drawn by dragons:

> With you I roam the nine rivers,
> Balanced on the rising winds and poised above the waves;
> Riding a water chariot canopied with lotus,
> Drawn by a brace of dragons, sea-serpents at their sides.
> Ascending K'un-lun Mountains I gaze into the
> four directions.
> My mind soaring out into the vast expanse.[35]

As the sun begins to set, the poet and her companion join hands and travel together towards the southeast. The spirit traveler appears to be a woman; and the journey's destination, a spiritual wedding. She comments that the fishes of various kinds will serve as her "bridesmaids."

Found also in the *Songs of the South*, but perhaps from a somewhat later period, the "Far-Off Journey"[36] begins as a lament: the poet feels frustrated with everyday life and looks longingly at the heavens. Suddenly, his "spirit flashes forth and does not return, and [his] physical frame withers and is left behind"; the spirit journey begins. The vision describes all the spirits that he meets and the vast dimensions of the universe that he crosses. In the end, the poet goes beyond heaven and earth and enters into the soundless, invisible source of all, "the Great Beginning."

A more recent example of the theme of the spirit journey appears in visions of Hong Huo Xiu (1813–1864), founder of the Heavenly Kingdom of Great Peace in nineteenth-century China.[37] Hong grew up in the southern China's Guangdong Province, known in the West as Canton. He belonged to the Hakka ("guest"), a Chinese people with their own language and customs who over time had wandered south and settled among various other Chinese communities. In 1836 while residing in the provincial capital to take the imperial examinations by means of which the officials of the government were recruited, Hong encountered some Christians disseminating the *Good Words for Exhorting the Age*, compiled by the convert Liang Fa[38] (1789–1855). Liang's book consists of stories taken from the Christian Bible, both Old and New Testaments. Beginning with the creation of Adam and Eve, it tells the story of the Flood, cites the warnings of the great prophets, records Jesus' Sermon on the Mount, and ends with the last chapter of the Revelation of John. Young Hong failed the examination, but he kept the book.

The next year Hong again returned to the capital to try his luck taking the examinations. Failing once more, he returned home, where he fell deathly ill. While his body lay inert in bed, he began to have dreams of a compelling nature.

In the first sleeping vision, Hong is carried in a sedan chair towards the rising sun. His bearer and attendants are dressed in dragon robes. In imagery that recalls the initiatory visions of Siberian shamans, he envisions a transformation of his own body: "Though they slit him open, like the fiends in hell, it is not to torment him but only to remove the soiled mass within, which they at once replace with new organs, sealing the wound as though it had never been."[39] He is then greeted by a woman who calls herself his mother. She takes him to bathe in a nearby river in order to purify him of the contamination from his "descent into the world." After this baptism, Hong enters into the presence of the one who claims to be his heavenly father.

The father welcomes him back to heaven and explains why it is that he has brought Hong there. His help is urgently needed. Led astray by demons, the people on earth have lost their "original nature." Even worse, the forces of evil have begun to invade heaven itself. Hong has been brought to heaven in order to lead a battle against those demons that fight under the command of the Dragon Demon of the Eastern Sea. For the battle, Hong's father gives him a golden seal and a great sword called Snow-in-the-Clouds. As Hong fights with the sword, his older brother stands behind him holding aloft the golden seal. Its reflected light blinds the enemy. Driven out of heaven, the demon king is allowed to flee. Hong rests and learns more about his celestial family.

Both Hong and his elder brother are married and have children. Living in a palace with his wife, First Chief Moon, and their son, Hong is daily tutored by his father and elder brother. They prepare him for his return to earth, where the war with the demons must continue. They give him a new name, Hong Xiu Quan, and a formal title: Heavenly King, Lord of the Kingly Way, Quan.

Having returned to earth, Hong awakens from his long sleep shouting strange slogans of battle and running around the house like a madman. His family is terribly concerned and continues to watch over him day and night. Gradually, his mental state returns to normal, and he takes up his studies once more. Later, Hong will interpret the vision of his journey to heaven. Identifying the demons with the Manchu rulers of China's Qing Dynasty, he begins to assemble an army to overthrow the emperor and to found God's Kingdom of Great Peace (Taiping).

In 1853, after many years of successful fighting together with the support of thousands of followers, Hong established his government in the city of Nanjing. He called it the New Jerusalem. By now, Hong understood his vision in terms of Christian symbolism: his father is God and his elder brother, Jesus. The Christian Bible supplants the Confucian classics as the text to be studied by leaders of the new kingdom. During the 1840s Jesus begins to communicate through a medium — Xiao Chao Gui — lending his guidance and encouragement to the growing community of "God-worshipers."

The history of the rise and fall (in 1864) of the Taiping is complex.[40] The Chinese imperial government collaborated with foreign armies to destroy the fledgling society in Nanjing. The cost on both sides was great: approximately 20 million people lost their lives in battle or to starvation.[41] Nor did the Heavenly King live to see this tragic end. Hong Xiu Quan died quietly in Nanjing in June of 1864. Wrapped in yellow silk, the body was buried underground without a coffin. "Hong indeed has long before ordered that coffins be abandoned and that the word for 'death' be tabooed amongst his followers, who should use instead the phrase 'ascend to Heaven' or 'find one's happiness.'"[42] Hong Xiu Quan never lost faith in his vision.

The spirit journey lies at the heart of ritual life in certain small societies both past and present; it appears also as a major theme in the visions of religious traditions as different as early gnostic Christianity and the Taiping revolt of nineteenth-century China. The conviction shared by all these traditions is that more than one world exists. There is the material world of the body, and there is also a separate, purely spiritual world, where the body cannot enter. In death, in visions, in the ritual of spirit travel — the human spirit may leave the body to enter this otherworld. The journey facilitates both the acquisition of sacred knowledge and a strengthened relationship with spirit beings, be they animal spirits, ancestors, or gods.

CHAPTER 8

Spirit Mediation

We come now to the fourth type of revelation: in spirit mediation the message from the spirit world takes place by means of a medium. In other words, a non-human spirit "borrows" a body in order to come into the human community and express itself by speaking (sometimes using the language of the person but at other times, esoteric language), through dramatic action, or simply by participating in a communal meal.

Many apparently bizarre actions, such as walking through fire or placing one's hands in boiling oil, are intended to reveal the presence of a powerful spirit. For example, in 1989 as in every year the people of Hong Kong celebrated the birthday of Monkey King, the hero of *The Journey to the West*, a Buddhist tale of adventure and enlightenment.[1] Monkey King had appeared to a local man in a dream, asking him to be his medium. During the birthday celebrations, the medium climbed barefoot up a ladder of swords, cut his tongue with a sword, placed his hands in boiling oil, and walked back and forth across a pit of burning coals. This demonstrated to the believers that Monkey King was actually occupying the medium's body and making it invulnerable. A similar phenomenon is found among the snake handlers of southern Appalachia in the United States. These Christians believe that a power inspired by Christ protects them as they dance with poisonous snakes in their hands. They seek to be witnesses to the scripture that declares, "I have given you the power to tread underfoot snakes and scorpions and all the forces of the enemy and nothing will ever harm you."[2]

The word designating the person whom the spirit uses in order to enter into the natural world so that it can communicate in some way is *medium*. This suggests something in the middle, a meeting place between two worlds. Related words are *mediation* and *intermediary*, both of which give us the sense of a reconciling role. We also talk of the media (radio, television, newspapers, etc.) that serve to connect people and enable them to communicate when they are physically apart. The medium connects what is separated. In a religious context, the medium serves to connect the human and the spiritual realms.

The religious phenomenon that we are calling spirit mediation (also known as "spirit possession") is quite common and found all over the world. Anthropologist Ericka Bourguignon[3] has studied 488 different societies for the prevalence of spirit mediation and has discovered that in 74% of these societies people recognize some form of this kind of revelation. Further, spirit mediums are more frequently active in societies where farming is the chief economic activity. Cultures around the Pacific Ocean show the highest incidence of spirit mediation, whereas the indigenous peoples of North, Central, and South America are least likely to have mediums.

The mediation of a non–human spirit can be interpreted as either a positive or negative event, depending on the identity of the spirit. For many, both helpful and harmful spirits exist. Different kinds of spirits evoke very different human responses. Demons will be exorcised, whereas ancestors and deities may be entertained, consulted, and venerated by means of spirit mediation.

It is the belief that harmful spirits can take over the body of a victim that has led to the expression *demonic possession*. In such cases, the most common response is exorcism: ritual expulsion of the spirit. In her fascinating account of Japanese religious activities and beliefs, Carmen Blacker describes several "witch animals" (snake spirits and fox spirits) that are believed to possess humans in order to torment them.[4] Those "witch animals" that resemble snakes are found only on the island of Shikoku and in the Chugoku district on the main island of Honshu, whereas fox spirits — depicted as "long and thin with reddish-brown fur, short legs and sharp claws"[5] — are feared everywhere in Japan. The Japanese believe that possession by such witch animals, as well as by unhappy ghosts, can cause physical pain and illness, mental imbalance, bizarre behavior, and so on. One form of exorcism in Japan combines a variety of sacred techniques to force the evil spirit into the body of another person, one who is ritually prepared and thus immune. Prayers, the reading of sacred texts, the chanting of sacred spells, and drumming can compel the spirit to leave the body of the afflicted person and enter the body of the trained medium, who has the power to control it.[6] Once the spirit has been forced into the medium, it is able to communicate verbally both its identity and its reasons for maltreating the victim.

Techniques of exorcism are complex and vary from culture to culture,

8. Spirit Mediation

as well as within a given society. The relationship between exorcism and healing is quite close, since oftentimes disease is attributed to the presence of malevolent spirits. However, while harmful spirits are banished through ritual exorcism, beneficial spirits, in contrast, are invited to come and be present by means of a medium.

In ancient China, spirit mediation played a valuable role in ancestor veneration. For example, as reported in *The Book of Rites* a medium was provided so that an important ancestor might join a banquet in his honor. Compiled before 200 CE, this collection of miscellaneous writings is a good resource for examining the ritual life of early Chinese people. The section entitled "The Principles of Sacrifice"[7] teaches that the care of ones parents should be freely offered without thought of receiving anything in return. Through ritual sacrifice one is able to continue this caring relationship after the parent has died and the period of mourning is completed. In this text sacrifice refers to a great banquet in which the living honor and entertain their ancestor.

For several days, those who will take part in the banquet prepare themselves: no music is allowed and they focus their attention on the meaning of sacred teachings. Then, by means of divination one of the young men in the family is determined to act as the ancestor's medium, the "personator of the dead." The banquet commences with libations of wine presented to the ancestor-medium. The animal to be sacrificed is led forth and slaughtered, after which the head of the family offers certain choice organs from its body to the "personator of the dead." In addition to the meal, entertainment is extremely important and consists of music, singing, and dancing. Bearing martial attire, the head of the family "takes up his shield and battle-ax" to lead in the dance. Thus through spirit mediation the young man who lends his body to the ancestor for a brief period enables the reunion of the family divided by death.

In addition to harmful spirits and ancestors, spirit mediation may facilitate the temporary visitation of a god or goddess. In ancient Greece, one might travel to the temple of a deity in order to consult with the god or goddess about concerns as diverse as health and war. Kings and other rulers, for example, would travel to the temple of the Apollo at Delphi in order to get his advice on matters of state.

Apollo was a powerful Greek god who loved order, in society as well as in nature. The sun was associated with Apollo because it gives us the order of day and night as well as the four seasons. Apollo loved music, which the ancient Greeks saw as bringing order to the emotions. Medicine was also in Apollo's domain, because through healing, the order of the body is restored. The social order of the early Greeks was patriarchal and hierarchical: the father ruled in the family and local kings governed each realm. So, too, Apollo was friend and defender of both fathers and rulers. Kings especially were likely to seek his advice.

The temple at Delphi was only one place where Apollo was worshipped, but it was the most important one during the period from approximately 750 to 330 BCE. Located on Mount Parnassos situated among the hills of central Greece, the temple at Delphi lay outside the boundaries of the various Greek kingdoms. Therefore, individual kings and other powerful men could freely approach the site during times of conflict or crisis. This was before the reign of Alexander the Great, who expanded the Greek world eastward and created an empire, making it more difficult for Greek rulers to return to their homeland in order to consult with Apollo. The oracle did continue to be active on a lesser scale until 392 CE, at which time Emperor Theodosius I ordered all non–Christian temples to close.

The method of consultation was relatively simple. Bringing gifts to the god, the petitioner would write down his question. This was presented to the priests. The medium was an older woman called the Pythia. Dressed in the clothes of a young woman, she was often considered to be the bride of Apollo. According to the Homeric Hymn to Pythian Apollo, the medium's title was based on Pytho, an ancient name for Delphi. Pytho is related to the verb *pythein*, which means "to rot," for it was here that Apollo is said to have killed and left to rot "the bloated, great-she-dragon, a fierce monster wont to do great mischief to men upon earth, to men themselves and to their thin-shanked sheep; for she was a very bloody plague."[8]

During the spirit mediation, the Pythia would sit in her chamber on a tripod, a stool with three legs, holding in her hand a branch of laurel, the tree sacred to the god. It was believed that during a state of trance, she was possessed by the spirit of Apollo and that her words were actually his speech. The priests then wrote down the messages and kept them in their temple annals. Thus, we have records of these ancient Greek rites.[9]

Not only the kings would appeal to Apollo for guidance. One interesting story[10] relates how through the Pythia the god Apollo declared that Socrates, the philosopher and mentor of Plato, was the "wisest man in the world."

8. Spirit Mediation

Upon hearing this, thoughtful Socrates went about questioning all who claimed to be wise. And he discovered that he was wisest only in the sense that he alone seemed to recognize his own ignorance.

Spirit mediation is often accompanied by a change in the medium's quality of consciousness. From their own accounts, we learn that mediums can experience different kinds of trance, or altered mental states. The medium is never truly unconscious: the body can act and respond to external stimuli. However, both ego-awareness and personal will can be affected, to different degrees.

In a total trance the medium is both unaware of what is happening and unable to control his or her actions. A non–human spirit has taken over the body, using it in whatever way it wants. When the possession is over, the medium has no memory of the experience. What was said, what was done, cannot be remembered.

On the other hand, the medium may remain aware while being overwhelmed and controlled by an outside power. In a lucid trance such as this, there is the sense that another being is present, providing the person with information or even supernatural powers beyond what he or she ordinarily knows. The medium experiences a split of personal will from awareness. Witnessing the event, the medium is nevertheless unable to act on his or her own volition. The spirit is in control.

Finally, there is inspiration. The person feels completely aware and also in control of what she or he is doing; yet sensing the presence of a spirit, the medium yields to its influence. For example, sacred texts are often called inspired, and it is believed that the author has consciously allowed some spirit to guide him or her in composing them. Today, people often use the word *inspired* without any religious intent. What they mean is that something — a book, a musical performance, a poem — is so special or unusual that it seems as if it could not have been the work of a human being. We see the religious meaning of the term lurking in the background, even in the secular use of the word.

Sometimes one form of spirit mediation will dominate in a given religious tradition, but often there is a fluid movement among the many states of awareness: moving back and forth quite freely among total trance, lucid trance, and inspiration. At the heart of all three forms of spirit mediation lies the conviction that non–human spirits have the desire and the power to communicate through humans in this way.

Spirits and Mediums in Vodou

One example of spirit mediation involving a total trance is described in Karen McCarthy Brown's study of Alourdes Kowalski, or Mama Lola, a *manbo* (female medium)[11] in Haitian Vodou. During a ritual designed for the mediation of one of the saints (*lwa*),[12] Mama Lola is overcome by the power of its spirit.

> Her body shuddered and jerked, went lax for a moment, and then jerked again rapidly. These movements mark the struggle between the *lwa* and Alourdes's *gwo bònanj* (big guardian angel), who ordinarily presides "in her head." When the spirit wins the contest (it almost always does), the *gwo bònanj* is sent from the body to wander, as it does routinely during sleep, and Alourdes becomes the *chwal* (horse) of the spirit.[13]

Here the trance state begins with a struggle between Alourdes' personal awareness (her "big guardian angel") and the powerful *lwa*. If the spirit succeeds in occupying her body and using her as a medium, it will control the body so as to interact with other people and the environment, but when the spirit leaves and Mama Lola's self-awareness returns, she will not remember what happened. The trance might last for an hour or more, during what Brown calls the "possession performance," but it is by no means a permanent condition.

The possession performance plays an important role in Vodou. This is a time when the family—comprised of humans, their ancestors, and their protective spirits (or saints)—gather for a meal, festivities, and the transaction of family business. Today, Haitians may live far away from their blood relatives, so friends can become a substitute family.

Vodou is an African American form of Christianity.[14] The word *vodou* comes from the language of the Fon peoples of present-day Benin and is related to *vodu*, which means "spirit" or "deity." Vodou (or Voodoo) as the name for the religious customs of the people of Haiti was the invention of outsiders. Haitians, on the other hand, see themselves as Roman Catholic Christians and refer to the ongoing practice of these ancient African traditions as "serving the spirits."

The culture of Haiti grew out of a meeting of French and African peoples during the eighteenth century, when French settlers imported African slaves to work their highly profitable plantations of sugar cane.[15] At that time Haiti supplied a large percentage of the sugar consumed in western Europe. The slaves belonged primarily to three of the peoples of western Africa: the

Yoruba, the Fon, and the Kongo. The French plantation owners forced their slaves to convert to Christianity; baptism was mandatory. As a result, the Christianity of France was brought into relationship with the beliefs and traditions of west African religions. Haitians worship Bondye, the "Good God," their name for the Christian God. At the same time, they continue to rely on intermediary spirits (comparable perhaps to the angels and saints found in many Christian communities) for day-to-day guidance.

> Bondye is remote and unknowable. Although evoked daily in ordinary speech (almost all plans are made with the disclaimer "if God wills"), Bondye's intervention is not sought for most of life's problems. That is the work of the spirits.[16]

This way of thinking reflects a pattern known among the religions of Africa that combines monotheism and polytheism. A supreme being is recognized as the ultimate principle of the cosmos, but he stands above the reciprocal relationships that mark the commerce between lesser gods and ordinary people. Indeed, these lesser gods and also ancestor spirits have the role of being intermediaries between the supreme being and humans.[17]

In spite of the religious origins of Vodou, in the popular culture of the United States and elsewhere it has been mistaken for some kind of devil worship or so-called black magic. This negative evaluation of the Haitians' religion by their neighbors most likely has its origins in political conflict. The country of Haiti is unique in that it is the oldest African American free state. Already between 1791 and 1804, the African slaves in Haiti rebelled and forced out their French overlords. This successful rebellion led to decades of freedom accompanied by isolation. Slaves in the southern United States just north of Haiti were not freed until the end of the Civil War in 1865. Thus it was that slave owners in the United States and in other countries in the western hemisphere feared and denigrated the free citizens of Haiti, perhaps because they worried that their own slaves might follow suit and rebel as well. It is hard to imagine slavery not based on fear — for the slave owner as well as the slave.

Although Haitian Christianity has been demonized as "black magic" and "devil worship," it resembles indigenous traditions the world over, where an intimate relationship between the human community and the spirits is cultivated and maintained. In Haiti the spirits are identified primarily as ancestors and saints.[18] Officially Christian, these descendents of former slaves have reinterpreted their African traditions by identifying their African gods with Christian saints.[19] For example, Danbala Wedo is a Fon god whose main concern is to help the living stay in contact with their ancestors, who dwell under the water. Able to move easily between the water and the surface of the earth, he sometimes takes the form of a serpent. Thus, he is identified with the Christian saint most commonly associated with snakes, Saint Patrick.

> [Danbala Wedo] is the ancient, the venerable father; so ancient, so venerable, as of a world before the troubles began; and his children would keep him so: image of the benevolent, paternal innocence, the great father of whom one asks nothing save his blessing. He comes as a snake, plunging at once into the [basin] of water which is built for him, and then writhes, dripping and inarticulate, upon the ground, or mounts a tree, where he lies in the high branches, the primordial source of all life wisdom.[20]

Images of Saint Patrick found in Haitian homes usually show the saint surrounded by snakes and close to some form of water.

Likewise, three of the saints important in Vodou — Ezili Freda, Ezili Danto, and Ezili Lasyrenn — represent different manifestations of the Virgin Mary, mother of Jesus.[21] Ezili Freda appears as a white woman who loves beauty and romance. Ezili Danto is black, the strong mother of a female child; she is both comforter and protector. Ezili Lasyrenn takes the form of a mermaid, sometimes black and white, her long hair reaching down to her feet. She is at home in the sea, which for Haitians represents the realm of the ancestors. Those who follow her will either die or return to the world blessed with profound spiritual power.[22]

Today, if someone of Haitian descent wants to make contact with a saint, he or she goes to a medium. The medium can be a man or a woman. The meeting with the spirit is quite a long and complex ritual, but one full of fun and music. The favorite foods of the spirit must be prepared. Many guests arrive, as if to a party. They invite the spirit with prayers of invocation, songs, and dance. Meanwhile, the medium dresses in clothes that are believed to resemble what the spirit would wear. Eventually, the medium is possessed by the spirit: in the language of Vodou, the medium becomes the horse (a living vehicle) for the spirit. At this time, dialogue (as well as numerous other activities) between the spirit and the participants of the ritual can take place. At the end of the session, the spirit departs. The medium comes out of the trance and the party breaks up.

The saints of Haitian tradition are respected as powerful members of the extended family. Along with the ancestors, they give advice, offer help in economic matters, and guide the people in all that is important. In spite of all its complexity, Haitian Vodou remains very intimate, centered primarily in the family.

Inspiration in Early Christianity

The lucid trance and the experience of inspiration are both described in the records of early Christians.[23] According to Christian tradition, the birth of the Church occurred when the followers of Jesus received the gift of the Holy Spirit, sent by God to sanctify them and guide them from within. This event, celebrated as the Christian Pentecost, is recounted in the Acts of the Apostles, which is included in the Christian Bible.

Jesus of Nazareth lived in Palestine during the first century of the Common Era. Preacher, healer, and miracle worker, he was a friend to the powerless and marginalized, especially the sick and the poor. According to the Gospel of John,[24] Jesus had even raised back to life a man named Lazarus of Bethany, who had been entombed for four days.

Steeped in the religious heritage of his Jewish ancestors, Jesus left the simple life as son of a carpenter in order to wander among his neighbors announcing the imminent arrival of the God's kingdom: "The time has come; the kingdom of God is upon you; repent, and believe the good news."[25] The symbolism of God's kingdom had powerful resonance for the Jews living at that time in a country that was part of an empire under Roman rule.

For six centuries, ever since the Neo-Babylonians had conquered the Kingdom of Judah and destroyed the Temple of God (in 586 BCE), the Jews had been governed by foreign powers: after the Neo-Babylonians were overthrown, Judaea became a part of the Persian empire and later the Greek empire. Now the Romans were in power. Nonetheless, the Jews remembered a time of independence, when they were ruled by God through his chosen kings. The announcement of the arrival of God's kingdom was a message of hope for the Jews, but a threat to those in power — the Romans.

Meanwhile, the Jewish leaders were caught in the middle. Trying to keep the peace, they became nervous in the face of local rebellions that might lead to outright war with Rome. As history demonstrates, this fear was not unfounded: conflict with Rome did eventually lead to war, the first Jewish-Roman War (66–73), sometimes called the Great Revolt. In 70 the military commander Titus (later emperor) led his Roman legions as they besieged and eventually destroyed the city of Jerusalem, burning down the Temple. The people who survived the killing were sold as slaves.

But was this Jesus, who proclaimed a new kingdom, really a revolutionary? The answer must be "no." From what we know about his life and teachings, Jesus envisioned the kingdom of God as a spiritual not a political reality. According to his teachings and example, the kingdom of God refers to the human life that is lived as if ruled by God's loving spirit. It is not a geographical or political place in the present or in the future. It refers to the relationship between God and those who submit to God's will.

So it is that repentance and faith, not personal power or achievement, usher in the new age. For example, in the Gospel of Mark Jesus tells his followers that the rich will have a difficult time entering the kingdom of God.[26] Indeed, it is impossible for any human being to enter on his or her own initiative, because experiencing God's ruling presence is a divine gift.[27] Indeed, to become an inhabitant in the kingdom one must first become like a little child, trusting and depending on God's care.[28]

Nevertheless, the expression that Jesus used — "the kingdom of God is upon you" — could easily be misinterpreted as a call to revolt. And although he did not surround himself with soldiers and revolutionaries, it is not surprising that he was accused of treason against the Roman Empire. At his execution he was mocked as "King of the Jews."[29]

What is important for Christians is their conviction that Jesus' death was not the end, that his resurrection from the dead is very real. The disciples of Jesus were convinced that he died and then returned to life. For them, this was proof that Jesus was the king (Hebrew, *masiah*; Greek, *christos*)[30] that they longed for — and even more, that he was the Son of God with the power to overcome death. They believed that his kingdom lay in the future, at a time when he would return to rule. At the time of the Second Coming of Christ, all the dead would be raised, and those who had put their trust in Jesus would, like him, enter into eternal life as God's children. The arrival of God's kingdom and the end to death's absolute power — this was the good news that Jesus commanded his disciples to share with all humankind, so that everyone would have the opportunity to know him, believe in him, and thus gain eternal life in his company. Christianity began, thus, as a Jewish movement with a new message and mission.

The Gift of the Holy Spirit. Just how was this good news (or Gospel)[31] going to reach the people throughout the Roman Empire and beyond? Before Jesus departed by ascending into the heavens, he urged his followers to remain

8. Spirit Mediation

in Jerusalem in order to receive the help that he would send them. Thus, they were gathered together on Pentecost (Hebrew, *Shavu'ot*),[32] the day when Jews celebrate the gift of the Torah, which God gave their ancestors in order to help them fulfill their part of the Covenant. All of a sudden, the friends of Jesus felt the presence of God's spirit.

> While the day of Pentecost was running its course they were all together in one place, when suddenly there came from the sky a noise like that of a strong driving wind, which filled the whole house where they were sitting. And then there appeared to them tongues like flames of fire, dispersed among them and resting on each one. And they were each filled with the Holy Spirit and began to talk in other languages, as the Spirit gave them power.[33]

The followers of Jesus who were present at Pentecost were partially possessed by God's spirit: experiencing a lucid trance, they were aware of what they were saying and doing and able to remember the event afterwards, but at the same time, they found themselves speaking in foreign languages that they had never learned. As a result, they were able to share the good news about Jesus, his resurrection, and God's kingdom to all the people gathered in Jerusalem, regardless of nationality.

The gift of the spirit was not restricted to those who were present at Pentecost. Early Christians believed that they could receive the Holy Spirit during baptism (as in the example of Jesus)[34] or in the ritual known as the laying on of hands[35] and that this divine power guided them and sanctified their lives. The apostle Paul reminds his fellow Christians in Rome of the miracle of divine inspiration: "For all who are moved by the Spirit of God are children of God."[36]

From Paul's passage it is clear that the term *Holy Spirit* refers to God's spirit and not to a separate deity. God acts in many ways, creating the world as well as interacting with the creation and its creatures. This notion is expressed in the Christian doctrine of the Trinity,[37] which was first formulated during the fourth century by three Cappadocian[38] theologians: Basil of Caesarea (c. 329–c. 379), Gregory of Nyssa (c. 335–c. 395), and Gregory of Nazianzos (c. 329–c. 391). God is one in essence but has three manifestations: "*mia ousia, treis hupostaseis.*"

Karen Armstrong, author of *A History of God: The 4000-Year Quest of Judaism, Christianity, and Islam*, reminds her readers that the doctrine of the Trinity is a symbolic way for Christians to convey their experience of God. The doctrine should not be mistaken for an objective statement or theory about God; it is rather an "imaginative paradigm," one that confounds reason.[39] God is the ineffable mystery that confronts human beings in the world, not an object or thing that can be counted. The very paradox of referring to God as "one essence, three manifestations" points to the divine mystery. "Thus the Trinity must not be interpreted in a literal manner.... [The doctrinal formula] reminded Christians that the reality that we called 'God' could not be grasped by the human intellect."[40]

Greek-speaking Christians and Latin-speaking Christians tended to have different understandings of the Trinity because the two languages reflect different cultural contexts. The Greek term that is translated here as "essence" refers to God's unity as divinity. What then are the three manifestations? Here "manifestation" translates *hupostasis*, which can mean "a particular reality." Something is real if it can affect other phenomena. So perhaps one way to understand the idea of the Trinity is that although one divinity, God affects the world in three ways. In Greek Orthodox Christian theology, the doctrine of the Trinity is often used to delineate salvation history: God the Father is the creator of the world; God the Son is the redeemer; and the Holy Spirit refers to God's ongoing presence transforming (sanctifying or divinizing) the human being and indeed all of creation.

Latin-speaking Christians have translated the Greek formula to mean "one substance, three persons," which seems to suggest three personal gods. In order to retain the unity of God, Latin Christians sought ways to relate the three "persons" so as to avoid tri-theism (the worship of three deities). For example, Augustine of Hippo suggested that the three "persons" of God might be understood as something similar to three components of human psychology: memory, intellect, and will. While memory, intellect, and will are three distinct human activities, they are in no way separate beings.

Today, Christians continue to use the doctrine of the Trinity as a symbolic tool for contemplating the ineffable mystery of divinity. Perhaps yet another way to understand the meaning of the Trinity would begin with a focus on the three ways that humans experience God.

Above all, God is experienced as beyond human knowledge. As source of all, the Creator cannot be completely known by the limited creature. The symbol for the divine mystery is God the Father.

At the same time, God can be known to some degree, both by observing the creation and through specific revelations. Christians believe that the world itself makes known the nature and purposes of God. In addition, one can know God by learning about his revelations in history, as recorded in the Bible and in other sacred writings. But most important is the revelation in Jesus. Christians say, if you want to know what God is like, look at Jesus. Thus, they use the symbolism of God the Son to refer to the reality of God that we can know.

Finally, Christians use the term *Holy Spirit* to refer to God's ongoing and sanctifying activity in the creation and in human life, God's presence here and now. Today, baptism is believed by many to be the way that a Christian receives the inspiration of the Holy Spirit:

> The gift of God is the Divine Indwelling. It comes quietly into your frailty at baptism. You become a tabernacle for the Source of Life.[41]

Inspired Tradition. The author of the Acts of the Apostles reports the many ways in which the Holy Spirit guided the early followers of Jesus as they created a new religious community. Preaching the Gospel, healing the sick, worshipping God, and even group decision-making — all were evidence of the Holy Spirit's presence, or inspiration.

Like Jesus, his followers were empowered by the Holy Spirit to heal the sick and raise the dead. Peter not only cured Aeneas, who had been bed-ridden with paralysis for eight years, he also restored to life the seamstress Tabitha. A Christian woman of kindness and charity, Tabitha (known also by her Greek name, Dorcas) fell ill and died. Her family washed the body and laid it in an upstairs room. Her friends sent for Peter. Alone in the room, he kneeled beside the bed and prayed. Then, turning towards the body, Peter simply commanded the woman, "Get up, Tabitha," and she opened her eyes.[42]

Preaching and healing were ways in which the Holy Spirit was able to spread the Gospel by means of the followers of Jesus. In addition, by inspiring acts of worship, it served to strengthen the bonds of the fledgling community. Many early Christians lived together in a simple form of communism. Indeed, all possessions were held in common. In addition to daily worship in the Temple, they met privately to listen to the teachings of the apostles and share their food and drink. In Acts 4:24–31, we read how the Holy Spirit inspired the followers of Jesus to pray in unison: "all were filled with the Holy Spirit and spoke the word of God with boldness."

Finally, early Christians believed that they were guided by the Holy Spirit to make important decisions determining the beliefs and customs of the Church. Very early on, a conflict arose between certain Christians who were Jewish and the new converts from other ethnic groups. Throughout the Roman Empire, many non–Jewish people, or Gentiles, were attracted to the new faith, but at the same time they had no desire to become culturally Jewish. Especially the Jewish custom of male circumcision was regarded as an obstacle to joining the new religion. Still, the original community of Christians in Jerusalem was made up of devout Jews, who followed the Torah and expected other Christians to do likewise: "Now certain persons who had come down from Judaea began to teach the brotherhood that those who were not circumcised in accordance with Mosaic practice could not be saved. That brought them into a fierce dissension and controversy with Paul and Barnabas."[43] To make matters worse, according to the Torah, Jews were forbidden to dine together with Gentiles at the same table. This created a problem, because the central ritual in Christian worship was the shared bread and wine of the Eucharist. How could Jewish Christians partake of this sacred meal together with their Gentile neighbors and still remain faithful to their own traditions?

So the question arose: Can a person become a Christian without first becoming a Jew? The apostles gathered in Jerusalem, where James, a brother of Jesus, was the leader. They held a meeting, their first council, the Council of Jerusalem. Peter argued in favor of allowing Gentiles to become Christians without having first to convert to Judaism. He claimed that God had already shown his consent by bestowing the gift of the Holy Spirit on Gentile believers: "God showed his approval of them by giving the Holy Spirit to them, as he did to us."[44] Moreover, Peter reminded the members of the council that it was "by the grace of the Lord Jesus that we are saved," not be obeying the Torah, that is, the laws given to Moses. Then, fellow Christians Paul and Barnabas supported him by telling various stories about divine signs and miracles that had happened among the Gentiles.

Peter's interpretation of the situation prevailed. The resulting letter sent by James to the young churches throughout the Roman Empire began thus: "It is *the decision of the Holy Spirit*,[45] and our decision, to lay no further burden upon you...."[46] Gentile Christians were asked to abide by the Jewish laws governing sexuality and to avoid eating blood or any food sacrificed to other gods. Otherwise, they were not required to follow Jewish customs.

Most important, this decision was attributed to the will of God, as made known by his spirit influencing the members of the council. This

8. Spirit Mediation

precedence has been at the heart of Christian councils throughout the centuries, gradually building up what is known as Christian Tradition, customs and beliefs believed to be inspired by God. Even the decision to include certain books in the Christian Bible — that is, compiling a New Testament as supplement to the Jewish Bible — was understood in this way, as inspired by the Holy Spirit.

During the first century, Christians continued to read and study the Jewish Bible in its Greek translation (the Septuagint). Religious authority was attributed to this book together with the sayings of Jesus, which the apostles and those who knew Jesus shared with others. Oral tradition continued to be authoritative because it consisted of eyewitness accounts about the Christ. It was not until the middle of the second century, with the passing of early witnesses, that Christians began to feel the need for a collection of writings to supplement the Jewish Bible. And as in many instances of Christian development, this felt need emerged in the midst of conflict.

Marcion (d. 160?), a Christian from Asia Minor living in Rome, accepted a gnostic understanding of the Gospel. Gnostic Christians believed that the creator of this flawed world was not the father of Christ, whom they believed to be a purely spiritual being, one who never suffered and only appeared to die. According to this view, the redeemer was sent into the material world to rescue those who harbored by nature fragments of the divine spirit, which exists wholly apart from the creation. By 144, Marcion had successfully established his own Christian organization, complete with bishops, elders, liturgy, and a canon of holy scripture. Arguing that the God of the Jews (that is, the Creator) was not the Christian God, he excluded the Jewish Bible from his canon. Christian scriptures that were circulating at the time he modified so as to reflect his theology. His canon included his own edited version of the Gospel of Luke together with ten letters of Paul (also modified). Indeed, Marcion believed that Paul was the actual author of the gospel attributed to Luke.

The "orthodox" Christians were thus spurred on to respond to Marcion. Calling on the Holy Spirit for inspiration, they eventually confirmed that the God of the Jewish Bible (their "Old Testament") was also the father of Jesus; and so the Old Testament was authoritative. To this they added a collection of Christian writings, the New Testament, as we know it today. So it is that the Christian Bible belongs to inspired tradition. It is not the source of tradition; the Holy Spirit is the source.

Indeed, when Christians disagree it is most often about what beliefs and customs belong to inspired tradition. Some find it easier to simply ignore tradition altogether and see the Bible alone as authoritative. Others try to balance Bible, tradition, reason, and personal experience (or any combination of these) as sources of religious knowledge.

Today, divine inspiration continues to play a central role in Christian teaching, as is clear from this well-known hymn.

> Spirit divine, attend our prayers and make this house thy home;
> Descend with all thy gracious powers, O come, great Spirit come!
> Come as the fire and purge our hearts like sacrificial flame;
> Let our whole soul an offering be to our Redeemer's name.
> Come as the dove and spread thy wings, the wings of peaceful love,
> And let thy Church on earth become blest as the Church above.[47]

Not only do Christians see the Holy Spirit as the guiding force in the Church, for individual men and women it is God's presence ("make this house thy home") that molds them and sanctifies their individual lives.

Spirit Mediation in Tenrikyo, a Japanese New Religion

Another example of spirit mediation comes to us from modern-day Japan. There we find that the medium can also be the founder of a world religion. Tenrikyo ("the teaching of heavenly reason") is a basically monotheistic religion that was founded in 1838 by Nakayama Miki (1798–1887), a woman who spent nearly fifty years of her adult life experiencing varying degrees of trance and inspiration.

As a girl, Nakayama Miki was a devout follower of Pure Land Buddhism. This form of Mahayana Buddhism teaches that through devotion to Amitabha Buddha and recitation of his name, one can be reborn in his paradise. Amitabha is the Buddha of Boundless Light. In Japanese, he is known as Amida. He rules over Sukhavati, which means "The Blissful" and is also referred to as Western Paradise. Dwelling in this state of blissful awareness, the devotee can prepare for a final birth in the world and the attainment of enlightenment. At this time, Miki's desire to become a Buddhist nun was countered by her parent's wish for her to marry. She fulfilled their hopes and became a wife and mother. During this next period of her life, her religious devotion was redirected towards various deities of Shinto, the indigenous faith of Japan.[48]

In 1838 Nakayama Miki was possessed by the god who gave his identity as Tenri O no Mikoto ("lord of heavenly reason").[49] Her eldest son, Shuji, had been afflicted with severe pain in his left leg for many months. The only relief was found in the performance of a healing ritual in which the healer, Ichibei, forced the pain out of the boy's body with the help of a medium, a woman by the name of Soyo. But relief was not permanent and the ritual was performed over and over again. On 23 October 1838, Soyo was not available and so Ichibei asked Miki to substitute for her. She held the two *gohei*, sacred staffs decorated with paper streamers, and assisted the healer.

Suddenly, in the midst of the prayers, an unknown spirit spoke through her mouth: "I wish to receive Miki as the Shrine of God."[50] Miki's husband entreated the spirit to withdraw, saying that because of her family duties as the mother of many children, his wife was too busy for this role. Ichibei also urged the spirit to depart. In the meantime, Miki was in a state of total trance, unable to eat, drink, or sleep for three days. Her body was agitated, and the voice of the spirit continued its demand: "You shall do as the God of Origin wills and comply with My demand. I shall save all mankind if you will listen to Me; but if you should object to it, I shall destroy this house so completely that not a trace of it will remain."[51]

Finally, her husband declared his willingness to obey the spirit, saying, "'I offer Miki to you.' At this, Miki's agitated behavior became quiet for the first time in many hours, and at that instant Miki Nakayama was settled as the Shrine of God. The mind of God the Parent entered into Her, and She, revealing the divine will, began the ultimate teaching for saving all mankind."[52] In future revelations, the god explained that it was the one true god, Tsukihi ("sun-moon," or "time"). Creator of all, Tsukihi was the divine parent, who had descended into the body of Miki in order to save its offspring, humankind. Out of compassion, God chose to reveal the way to salvation through the one called a living Shrine (medium): "What I, Tsukihi, think now is spoken through Her mouth. Human is the mouth that speaks, but divine is the mind that thinks within."[53] Until the end of her life, Nakayama Miki served as the voice of Tsukihi.[54]

Sometimes Nakayama Miki would enter into a state of total trance in order to allow the god to speak directly; at other times, she allowed the god's influence to guide her as one inspired. She gave away all her possessions and even tore down the family home. As a healer, she introduced a ritual that allowed for painless childbirth. Through her were revealed instructions for the foundation of a new religion, including two books: *Songs for the Sacred Dance* (Mikagurauta) and *Tip of the Divine Writing Brush* (Ofudesaki). Further, she taught her disciples a form of worship called the Salvation Dance Service (Kagura Zutome).

The deity who communicated through Nakayama Miki taught that human beings were created to live a joyous existence. All the doctrines of Tenrikyo are meant to lead people into a life of blessed communion with God.[55] The only obstacle to salvation is alienation from God, which manifests as thoughts in the mind opposing the divine will. These are called "dust," and it is the sweeping away of such thoughts that frees the natural mind to open again to God's presence. The techniques for cleansing the mind are two-fold: the incorporation of worship into daily life and the protection of health through rituals of compassion. Thus, it is no surprise that the community life of the followers of Tenrikyo centers in beautiful temples where worship is held on a regular basis as well as in schools and hospitals that benefit all.

In spite of the persecution directed at Nakayama Miki and her disciples during the early years of the movement, Tenrikyo eventually spread quite rapidly throughout Japan. In 1888, the Japanese government recognized the religion as an official sect within Shinto. Moreover, its success has not been limited to Japanese society. With its message of salvation for all humankind, Tenrikyo has established missions in over thirty countries around the world.

Spirit mediation is based on the belief that human beings can serve as mediums for spirits of all kinds — ancestors, saints, gods, and even demons. Sometimes the non–human spirit completely overwhelms the medium in order to use the body as a vehicle for revelation; at other times, the medium is conscious and more or less under the influence of the spirit presence. Spirit mediation is a form of revelation that allows for communion between humans and the spirit world, and it allows people to receive both knowledge and power from their gods.

CHAPTER 9

Mystical Union

The next type of revelation that we are going to discuss is mystical union. Though not uncommon — mystics are found in numerous contemporary religions, such as Judaism,[1] Christianity, Islam, and Buddhism, as well as in the indigenous traditions of India and China[2] — for many, it is perhaps the type of revelation least understood. In fact, some people use the word *mysticism* for any religious phenomenon that they do not understand: confusing *mystical* with *mystifying* ("perplexing" or "bewildering")!

The confusion probably has its origins in the Greek word that is translated as mysticism: *mysterion*. This ancient term referred originally to the early Greek mysteries, as for example, those of the goddess Demeter at Eleusis. The mysteries were rituals leading to salvation through an acquired relationship with a god or goddess. They were practiced in highest secrecy by members of a religious society; initiation into the society was required in order to participate in the saving rites. The person who was initiated was the *mystes*, and central to the meaning of these and related words is the acquisition of secret, sacred knowledge. Mystical union, however, is secret (or "mysterious") only in the sense that it is an ineffable experience, impossible to describe.

Drawing, however, on the writings of the mystics themselves as well as the studies of scholars interested in the phenomenon, we can find ways to distinguish mystical union from other forms of revelation. The first definition given for *mysticism* in *Webster's Ninth New Collegiate Dictionary* is as follows: "the experience of mystical union or direct communion with ultimate reality reported by mystics." This definition points only to the goal of mysticism: "communion with ultimate reality," however that ultimate reality is envisioned. Perhaps a more useful definition for mysticism itself would comprehend also the life oriented towards the mystical experience: Mysticism is any religious tradition that seeks as its ultimate goal union with ultimate reality. Thus, we can speak of mystics who have experienced mystical union; but we can also include in our discussion the many people all over the world who practice some kind of spiritual discipline that has mystical union as its goal.

Such a goal lies at the heart of numerous traditions that have their origins in India. The Upanishads, scriptures that belong to the sacred Vedic tradition, are filled with metaphors expressing mystical union: "Even as water becomes one with water, fire with fire, and air with air, so the mind becomes one with the Infinite Mind and thus attains final freedom."[3]

In Hinduism, there are many paths, or yogas, that lead to this union: In our discussion of spiritual discipline, that is, techniques that are practiced in order to transform the person so as to reach a religious goal, one example is Dhyana Yoga, the path of meditation. Along with a primary focus on meditation, ethics and devotion (*Ishvara pranidhana* or "surrender to God") make up this path. In Patanjali's *Yoga Sutra* (1.41), a handbook for yogis, the goal is identified as samadhi, the eighth branch of the "Eight Limbs of the Tree of Yoga."

> the yogi's mind ... becomes clear and balanced and attains the state devoid of differentiation between knower, knowable and knowledge. This culmination of meditation is Samadhi.[4]

This union of "knower, knowable and knowledge" is one step[5] on the way to moksha, or final liberation from samsara—the cycles of life, death, and rebirth. In a state of absolute consciousness and bliss (*satchidananda*), the soul is free for all time. But meditation is not the only path to liberation: other paths are Jnana Yoga, the path of knowledge (or transcendental insight); Bhakti Yoga, the path of loving devotion; and Karma Yoga, the life of selfless service, in which the devotee dedicates his or her actions to God, serving all living beings without any desire for personal gain.

The origins of Buddhism lie also in India, where the teachings of the Buddha Shakyamuni are regarded as yet another path leading to mystical union. The Buddha called his way of attaining the goal the Middle Path, avoiding the extremes of self-mortification (the practice of harsh austerities) and pure pleasure seeking. The Eightfold Path taught by the Buddha has as its eighth and final step samadhi, understood as non-dual consciousness: subject and object become one. When the mind attains this union, it awakens to ultimate reality. This awakening—often translated as enlightenment—

9. Mystical Union

is bodhi, a Sanskrit term that means "wise, intelligent, and fully aware." There are different levels of this awareness, the greatest of which is called sambodhi, or "most completely enlightened." Having attained complete awareness, the buddha enters nirvana ("blow out"), the obliteration of any sense of separate selfhood: "The traveler has reached the end of the journey! In the freedom of the Infinite he is free from all sorrows, the fetters that bound him are thrown away, and the burning fever of life is no more."[6]

Not limited to the traditions of India, the writings of the mystics are both abundant and diverse. In Christianity there is, for example, the autobiography of the Spanish reformer Teresa of Avila. The poetry of the Islamic mystic Rumi comes out of Turkey. Also expressive of mystical experience is the personal journal of Marcus Aurelius, Roman emperor and Stoic philosopher.

Teresa of Avila lived as a nun and a reformer of monasticism in Spain at the time of the European Renaissance.[7] As a young woman, Teresa became a nun in the Carmelite Convent of the Incarnation in Avila. The nuns came from affluent families and followed what was called a "mitigated" (relaxed) rule: they lived in comfortable quarters with servants; daily visitors were entertained in the parlor; and the nuns were free to leave the convent. Teresa was quite content to live this kind of life until she read the *Confessions* of Augustine. Deeply affected by Augustine's description of his spiritual life, she turned her own life around. She began to follow the stricter Carmelite rule of spiritual discipline: prayer, fasting, silence, and retreat.

For seven years after her "conversion," Teresa continued to live at the Convent of the Incarnation while she planned to establish a Carmelite convent for discalced nuns. *Discalced* means "barefoot" and refers to the practice of going without shoes or wearing sandals, symbolic of a simpler life. The reformed convent in Avila became the first of many that she established, both for nuns and later, for monks.

Teresa's life reflects the vitality and creativity associated with the Renaissance: in addition to her religious vocation, Teresa was also a writer and a poet. She intended her writings to serve as aids for young nuns in the life of faith. *The Way of Perfection* is about prayer; *Interior Mansions*, on the other hand, is an account of her practice of spiritual discipline, together with the visions and mystical experiences that accompanied that practice.

Among other things, Teresa explains how the ritual of the Eucharist, or Holy Communion — belonging to the worship and spiritual discipline of the church—can also aid the Christian in her goal to experience union with God: "One day after having received Communion, I truly thought my soul was made one with the most sacred Body of the Lord."[8]

Elsewhere, Teresa uses a metaphor from nature to suggest what it is like when Christ and the soul are united: "One time I understood how the Lord was present in all things, and how in the soul, and I thought of the example of a sponge which absorbs water."[9] Christ is the water; the human soul is the sponge. Filled with the water, the sponge remains a sponge, but at the same time, it is transformed into a wet sponge with new abilities.

Another Western mystic and poet is Jalal al-Din Rumi, who belongs to Sufism, the mystical tradition of Islam. Rumi was born in Central Asia, but when the Mongols invaded their homeland in 1220, his family moved westward to live in present-day Turkey. Rumi grew up to become a teacher; married with many children, he was a highly respected citizen of Konya, the capital city. He then came under the influence of a mendicant mystic by the name of Shams. This religious teacher awakened in Rumi a capacity for mystical knowledge. What followed was an outpouring of poetry expressing this newly found relationship with God. It lasted all his life.

Through his poems Rumi expresses both his union with God and the life that finds this communion as its highest reward. His poetry is filled with metaphors of every kind, taken from all aspects of human life. For example, he uses the image of the human community to convey communion with the divine: it is not a lonely experience that takes the mystic away from fellowship with other people. Quite the contrary.

> There is a community of the spirit.
> Join it, and feel the delight
> of walking in the noisy street,
> and *being* the noise.
> ....
> Why do you stay in prison
> when the door is so wide open?
> Move outside the tangle of fear-thinking.
> Live in silence.[10]

Union with the divine is likened to joining a new company, the fellowship of the spirit. It is also symbolized by the unity of the listener and the sound that is heard: the source of the noise lies outside and apart from the listener, but through attentive listening, it becomes sensation and memory within

9. Mystical Union

the one who listens. The noise enters and occupies the listener. Silence, on the other hand, is a good metaphor for the divine itself as the source of all: only in relation to silence can sound exist. Each sound exists because it is separated from the next sound by silence. To "live in silence" is to be one with God.

For Rumi, union with God is also a state of complete freedom, and this freedom is there for the taking. The prison (isolation from God) does not really exist because it has an open door. It is human "fear-thinking" that turns the wide open room into a prison.

A mystic, who lived in a very different environment, is Marcus Aurelius (121–180), emperor of the Roman Empire from the age of forty until his death at the age of fifty-nine. Born in Rome, Marcus was the son of a Spanish ex-consul. After the death of his father, he received the patronage of the emperor Hadrian, who gave him the nickname Verissimus ("most truthful" or "most sincere"). Hadrian adopted the uncle of Marcus, Antoninus Pius, and required Pius to adopt Marcus. In this way, Marcus stood in line to become emperor, which he eventually did. Meanwhile, he received the best education available in Rome and training in various political roles. His reign was fairly stable, but not without conflict, both within the empire and beyond its borders. Still, "Marcus' lifetime was soon idealized as a Golden Age, partly because of the violent contrast provided by the disastrous reign of his son Commodus (born 161, reigned 180–92), who was eventually assassinated and execrated as a tyrant."[11]

Aurelius found a framework for his worldview in Stoicism, a religious philosophy that flourished throughout the period of both the Greek and Roman empires. A monistic worldview, Stoicism recognizes the presence of the divine in all of creation, regarding the world as the body of the world soul. The Stoics could not conceive of any separation of spirit and matter; they regarded the material world as containing within itself the divine (active and intelligent) principle of creation: Logos Spermatikos, the "creative word of God." Thus, the human being also has the spark of divine intelligence within. Hence, all humans are equal. Stoics condemned slavery and taught that all people should tolerate, forgive, and love one another and think of themselves as brothers and sisters sharing one nature.

For Marcus Aurelius, this cosmological framework serves as the background for his understanding of mystical union. He shares his deepest reflections in his *Meditations*: "Nothing is more wretched than the man who goes round and round everything, and, as Pindar says, 'searches the bowels of the earth,' and seeks by conjecture to sound the minds of his neighbors, but fails to perceive that it is enough to abide with the Divinity that is within himself."[12]

In order to connect with the Divinity that lies within, Aurelius emphasizes the importance of sitting calmly with the mind attentive to the present moment: "Wipe out imagination: check impulse: quench desire: keep the governing self in its own control."[13] "Retreat into yourself."[14]

This ability to withdraw ones attention from all that is in flux and focus on the Divinity within, he calls *apatheia*. It is detachment from what exists only in the mind, memories of the past or imaginings about the future. Modern English *apathy* is a derivative term, but a misleading one. Apathy implies indifference, a lack of caring. But Stoic *apatheia* implies a conscious shift in attention, detaching from thoughts of the past and hopes for the future so as to attach oneself to the divine presence: letting go of what is impermanent to become "mindful of the bond that unites the divine and human."[15]

Teresa of Avila, Rumi, and Marcus Aurelius are just a few examples of mystics in Western history. Clearly mysticism is not limited to Asian cultures, where it is so important. Although it is not a universal type of revelation — it is not found in many small hunting and farming societies — it is widespread. Yet, if mysticism is so common, why is it so hard to understand? It is the nature of the mystical experience that makes it so. Mystics tell us that it is impossible to describe the mystical union because it is unlike anything that is known by the senses of the body. No pictures or feelings drawn from everyday experience can give a sense of what it is like. It is a completely unfamiliar event. The only way that one can understand the mystical experience is to have one!

When Moses heard a voice speaking out of the burning bush, the voice spoke his language. He could share the words with others. When the angel Gabriel appeared to Muhammad as he sat praying in a mountain cave, the vision was one that he could describe to his wife, Khadijah. Even the Siberian shaman who travels to the spirit world can portray what he has seen there. The practice of spirit mediation and divination both take place in the midst of the community and what happens is witnessed by many.

But in the mystical union, the consciousness of the mystic transcends the world of the body (and the imagination) to commune directly with ultimate reality in a way that is somehow very different from knowledge through the senses. Teresa of Avila describes this as a journey into pure spirit: "Getting back to union [with God], I understood that it consists in the spirit being pure and raised above all earthly things so that there is nothing in the soul that wants to turn aside from God's will; but there is such conformity with God in spirit and will, and detachment from everything, and involvement with Him, that there is no thought of love of self or of any creation."[16]

So, the mystics tell us, it is impossible (not just difficult, but impossible) to describe mystical union. And then what do they do? They then go ahead and try to achieve the impossible: they try to describe it. Why? This has more to do with the nature of being human, not the nature of mysticism. Human beings always seem to feel the need to express important inner experience, whether it is possible or not.

Theories About Mysticism

Personal accounts of the mystical experience have attracted the attention of numerous scholars of religion. Three particularly useful theories about mysticism — both its goal of mystical union and also the life that is oriented towards that goal — are found in the writings of American psychologist William James, German scholar of religion Rudolf Otto, and the British writer Evelyn Underhill (1875–1941).

William James. The modern psychologist William James combined science and philosophy in his approach to religion. As a teacher, he originally offered classes in anatomy and physiology as well as philosophy. Before becoming interested in religion, James was drawn to developments in the new field of psychology; in 1890 he published *Principles of Psychology*, a summary of what was going on in the field of psychology at the time. Later, in *The Varieties of Religious Experience* (1902), James discussed religious phenomena with the same methodology that he had developed to describe human anatomy and psychology. For example, he collected and then examined numerous accounts of mystical union to determine their common characteristics. He found that each mystical experience, regardless of the religious tradition in which it occurred, typically displays four essential features:[17]

1. The mystic is passive. The human being cannot make it happen; it is a gift, a revelation.

2. The experience is transient, that is, it usually doesn't last very long, perhaps a few seconds at most.
3. It is ineffable, or indescribable.
4. It is noetic, that is, something is learned about the nature of ultimate reality.

Like all revelations mystical union is a form of communication initiated from the non-human reality, the "spirit world." The human being is always the passive receiver. Even when a mystic has undergone years of training in a spiritual discipline in order to achieve communion with ultimate reality, he or she will admit that in actuality one cannot force it to happen: one prepares oneself and hopes for the revelation.

In addition, most mystics will emphasize the short duration of the mystical experience. Perhaps this has to do with the fact that in order to survive in the physical world, one must be open to bodily sensation, such as hunger, pain, and so forth. During the mystical experience, however, the attention is drawn away from the body. If this state were to last too long, it might cause real physical damage.

The mystical experience is ineffable. We have already touched on this quality. Because the experience is so alien to bodily experience, there is no way to talk about it. It is indescribable. So the mystics must use all sorts of imagery and even paradoxical statements in order to convey their experience to others.

Finally, the noetic quality of the event refers to the knowledge that is received by the mystic. "Seeing from the divine perspective" the mystic becomes aware of much that is hidden to the eyes of the body.

William James cites numerous examples of the mystical experience to illustrate how these different characteristics are expressed. Sometimes the person who has a mystical experience is not even religious. Mystical union may happen spontaneously. This, of course, is further evidence of the passive quality of mystical experience. One example is the account given by a Canadian psychiatrist, R. M. Bucke, in his *Cosmic Consciousness: A Study in the Evolution of the Human Mind*.[18]

> [After a pleasant evening with friends] *I was in a state of quiet, almost passive enjoyment*,[19] not actually thinking, but letting ideas, images, and emotions flow of themselves, as it were, through my mind. All at once, without warning of any kind I found myself wrapped in a flame-colored cloud. For an instant I

thought of fire, an immense conflagration somewhere close by in that great city; but next, I knew that the fire was within myself. Directly afterward there came upon me a sense of exultation, of immense joyousness accompanied or immediately followed by an intellectual illumination *impossible to describe.*

Among other things, I did not merely come to believe, but I saw that the universe is not composed of dead matter, but is, on the contrary, a living Presence; I became conscious in myself of eternal life. It was not a conviction that I would have eternal life, but a consciousness that I possessed eternal life then; I saw that all men are immortal; that the cosmic order is such that without any peradventure all things work together for the good of each and all; that the foundation principle of the world, of all the worlds, is what we call love, and that the happiness of each and all is in the long run absolutely certain.

The experience lasted a few seconds and was gone; but the memory of it and the sense of the reality of *what it taught* has remained during the quarter of a century which has since elapsed.

Bucke did not make the event happen: it happened to him. He even notes that his mental state was one of passive receptivity. The event lasted only a few seconds, and what happened was ineffable, "impossible to describe." But what he learned (the noetic component) from the brief experience was profound, unforgettable. He "knew" that love was the "foundation principle" of all creation and that along with all humankind, he was immortal.

Even though the experience was ineffable, Bucke needed to use some kind of imagery in order to suggest it to others. He draws on the language of sensation. The mystical union is expressed here by means of two related metaphors. First, he feels as if he is wrapped in a flame-colored cloud. Second, he feels that he is filled with fire. In spite of the fire, there is no sense of burning or discomfort. Fire is a common symbol for the divine. The heavenly fire is the sun, which gives us light and life. Earthly fire is one of our great tools: it allows us to see in the dark, cook our food, and heat our homes in winter. In India, fire is known as Agni, the divine transformer, which takes material things and turns them into spiritual reality. In Christianity, fire is a symbol for the Holy Spirit. The new knowledge that Bucke receives is also linked to the symbolism of fire: in this new light he "sees" the true nature of the universe. There is no such thing as dead matter. The world is a living Presence.

Rudolf Otto. The analysis of mystical union into four common characteristics provides us with a tool that we can use to identify this phenomenon even when it is found in diverse cultures where the imagery may differ widely. Another approach is found in the writings of the German theologian and scholar of religion Rudolf Otto. He takes note of the manner in which mystics "locate" the mystical union: for some, God is met within; for others, it seems that the divine is in the world around them, and union with the divine signifies some kind of union with nature.[20] Rudolf Otto was a German Christian theologian, who traveled widely in the Middle East and Asia. A student of Sanskrit, he became interested in the mystical writings of India. These he sought to compare with those of Western mysticism by focusing on two mystics: Shankara, ninth-century proponent of Advaita (non-dualistic) Vedanta; and Johannes Eckhart (Meister Eckhart, c. 1260–1327?), a Christian mystic living in medieval Germany. The results of his study were published in 1926 as *Mysticism East and West: A Comparative Analysis of the Nature of Mysticism.*[21]

When mystics attempt to describe what happens during the mystical union, they draw on different imagery to locate where it happens. For example, when R. M. Bucke says that it seemed as though a flame-colored cloud was wrapped around his body and there was fire inside it, he is identifying the body as the location of the event. Otto might classify this expression as belonging to the Inward Way. The union of the self and ultimate reality feels as if it is taking place within the person. Teresa of Avila uses the imagery of the Inward Way in her poem "Seeking God." Here it is God who speaks to the soul, guiding it towards mystical union[22]:

> And should by chance you do not know
> Where to find Me,
> Do not go here and there;
> But if you wish to find Me,
> In yourself seek Me.

Marcus Aurelius also believed that the divine—what he calls the fountain of good—was to be found within: "Delve within; within is the fountain of good, and it is always ready to bubble up, if you always delve."[23] For both Teresa and Marcus Aurelius, the mystic withdraws attention from the external world, the natural realm of the body. Thus, Otto calls the Inward Path the way of introspection.

The opposite kind of imagery is used to identify the mystical experience as taking place outside the mystic, in the external world. This Rudolf Otto calls the Way of Unity; and there are, in Otto's analysis, four variations, each one presenting a slightly different relationship between the divine reality and the world.

In the first type, the divine reality is everywhere as all that exists. Thus, union with the divine is felt to be the identity of all in all: the many are seen as the One. A good example is found in the notebooks of Jiddu Krishnamurti (1888–1965), a modern mystic who was born in India, raised in England, and lived in California:

> Really the outside is the inside and the inside is the outside and it is difficult, almost impossible to separate them. You look at this magnificent tree and you wonder who is watching whom and presently there is no watcher at all. Everything is so intensely alive and there is only life and the watcher is as dead as that leaf. There is no dividing line between the tree, the birds, and that man sitting in the shade and the earth that is so abundant.[24]

Here, union with the divine is a release from all sense of boundaries and limitation. The man and the tree share the same consciousness. This paradoxical language is very different from that of the Inward Way. Some call it "nature mysticism," but this is misleading if it is meant to suggest the absence of the divine. For Krishnamurti, God is everywhere and union with God is union with all that exists.

In another variation of the Way of Unity, the mystic feels that the divine is not identical with creation but rather pervades all things: the One is seen in the many. For example, the author of the *Shvetashvatara Upanishad* states: "When anyone comes to know God, who is hidden in the heart of all things even as cream is hidden in milk and in whose glory all things have their being, that person is then liberated from bondage."[25] Here there is a slight shift in imagery. It is not that the milk is divine, but it is inhabited by the divine.

A third variation of the Way of Unity sees creation as an illusion and only the Creator as absolutely real. For example, in Hinduism the world is *maya*, the Sanskrit word that means "deception, illusion, and appearance." Maya is the continually evolving, phenomenal world. Time and space and ongoing creation lack the kind of unconditioned independence ascribed to the Creator: "one should know that Nature is illusion and that the mighty Lord is the illusion-maker."[26] So the world is not "real" but rather contingent and impermanent. This is not necessarily a negative view of creation, which is sometimes thought of as divine play (Sanskrit, *lila*) or as a school for the education of souls. The mystic, who regards the world as valuable but not ultimately real, seeks the eternal freedom that results from union with the eternal and unconditioned source of the world.

> God upholds the oneness of the universe: the seen and the unseen, the transient and the eternal. The soul of man is bound by pleasure and pain; but when she sees God she is free from all fetters.[27]

The final variation of the Way of Unity reflects the conviction that creation is not merely an illusion — it is a mistake. This is a negative evaluation, both of the material world and the human body. The divine is felt to be at home somewhere else. Therefore, the mystic seeks a union that will carry him or her out of this world. Gnostic Christianity is a good example of this kind of mysticism. The gnostic sees the world as created by powers that are inferior to a purely spiritual God. In the *Gospel of Thomas*,[28] Jesus says that the world is a vine that was planted without the will of the Father. It is doomed to being uprooted, because it is "dead," that is, the spirit of the divine is not in it. Nevertheless, according to the gnostic Christian view, anyone who perceives the absence of spirit in the world does so only by virtue of his or her own spiritual nature. And this is proof that the person actually comes from the spirit world of the Father. As a spirit being — an alien sojourner in the material world — the gnostic Christian longs to be reunited with the Father, to return to a purely spiritual home.

By clarifying the different locations of the mystical experience as expressed in the writings of mystics in many different cultures, Rudolf Otto helps us see the underlying pattern of mystical union while appreciating its variations. Whether the mystic says that the divine is found within or that it is met in the natural world, the characteristics of the mystical experience and its value for the mystic remain the same.

Evelyn Underhill. Another interpreter of mysticism is the British poet and novelist Evelyn Underhill, whose major contribution in this area was published in 1922 as *Mysticism: A Study in the Nature and Development of Man's Spiritual Consciousness*.[29] Whereas both William James and Rudolf Otto focus on the goal of mysticism (mystical union), Underhill discusses the symbolic imagery that mystics use to describe the life directed towards that goal. According to Underhill, the three themes that are most commonly used to express the life of the mystic are love, the journey, and transmutation.

9. Mystical Union

Some mystics envision themselves as lovers and the divine as a beloved person — child, lover, parent, or friend. Love and longing, tenderness and ecstasy, these are the emotions that convey the mystic's relationship with the divine. Rumi, for example, most often speaks of the mystical union in terms of love:

> You have read in the text where *They love him*
> blends with *He loves them*.
> Those joining loves
> are both qualities of God. Fear is not.[30]

For Rumi, God is the Beloved, or the Friend, and union with God is most clearly conveyed in the language of love.

In Christianity, there is a tradition called Bridal Mysticism.[31] The mystic's soul is the bride and Christ is the bridegroom. The Greek word for soul, *psyche*, is a feminine noun[32]; and so the soul, whether of a man or a woman, can be symbolized as the "bride" of Christ. In her poetry, Teresa of Avila sometimes uses the language of Christian Bridal Mysticism.

> My soul was oned
> With her Creator.
> Other love I want not.
> Surrendered now to my God,
> That my Beloved is for me,
> And I am for my Beloved.[33]

The soul and the Beloved are "oned." This union becomes the total focus of her life; it is enough.

Yet having her center of attention always on God does not result in Teresa's isolation. For in addition to being a mystic, she was also a leader in monastic life, where the theme of marriage with Christ has other associations. Christ is the bridegroom, and the Church as a whole is his bride. In addition, when a woman takes vows to be a nun, she is believed to become a bride of Christ and the profession of vows is celebrated as a wedding. Teresa often wrote poems for women who were about to celebrate this initiation into monastic life.

> Oh what a splendid wedding
> Jesus arranged!
> All of us He loves
> and gives us His light.[34]

At the heart of this poem is the insight that the spiritual wedding is something that can draw people together into community rather than separate them into individual households, as in earthly marriage. So in loving God, one becomes closer to others.

The journey is another symbolic theme that mystics often use to talk about the life that is a search for mystical union. Here the mystic becomes the adventurer, the traveler, the hunter, or the pilgrim. At the same time, the divine is imagined as a place (heaven, Jerusalem, home) or as a precious treasure difficult to find (such as the pearl or the Grail, as in the legends of King Arthur and the knights of the Round Table). Thus, mystical union can be a return to the source, or a return home: "Imagine the time the particle you are returns where it came from! The family darling comes home."[35] Or it can be a journey into new and undiscovered places, such as the Far Mosque in another of Rumi's poems[36]:

> The place that Solomon made to worship in,
> called the Far Mosque, is not built of earth
> and water and stone, but of intention and wisdom
> and mystical conversation and compassionate action.
>
> Every part of it is intelligence and responsive
> to every other. The carpet bows to the broom.
> The door knocker and the door swing together
> like musicians. This heart sanctuary *does*
> exist, but it can't be described. Why try!

Solomon (c. 960–920 BCE) was the son of King David and the third king of Israel. It was he who built the Temple in Jerusalem, a place where the Israelites could go to worship in the presence of their God. In a similar way, the Far Mosque is the place where the mystic meets God. It is not made of wood or stone; it is a "heart sanctuary," a meeting place within. Because it refers to the mystical meeting with God, it is ineffable and cannot be described: "why try!"

The third theme that is found often in the teachings of the mystics is transmutation, or transformation at the deepest level. This imagery expresses a fundamental change in the mystic's state of mind. For example, Islamic mystics often refer to ordinary consciousness as "sobriety" and use the word *drunkenness* to refer to the euphoria of union with God.[37] Hafiz Shirazi, a fourteenth-century Sufi poet, speaks of God's Winehouse and the mystic as one who is drunk on God's wine: "For his lovers, the Teacher poured out so much wine that the scientists became senseless and the philosophers dumb."[38] The silence of the mystics manifests their shift away from ordinary, dual consciousness.

The image of waking up from sleep is another way to express the transmutation of consciousness: it is important image in the language of Buddhism. In fact, the word *buddha* means "the awakened one." Even the word *enlightenment* suggests moving from one state of consciousness to another: filled with light as opposed to filled with darkness. As Citta, one early Buddhist nun, reports: "I ... break through the gloom that boxed me in AHHHHHHH."[39]

The Buddha Was a Mystic

The life of the historical Buddha, Siddhartha Gautama, provides us with an excellent example of mysticism. His teachings about how to attain mystical union demonstrate the importance of the theme of transmutation in the mystical tradition of Buddhism.

Born during the sixth century BCE to King Suddhodana and Queen Mayadevi, whose realm lay among the foothills of the Himalaya Mountains in present-day Nepal, Prince Siddhartha was destined to rule. Their family name was Gautama and they belonged to the Shakya clan. The kings of the small kingdoms that made up India at the time belonged to the warrior class. It is said that when Siddhartha was born, the diviner Asita was invited to examine the markings on his body in order to interpret his destiny. This diviner told the parents that their baby would grow up to be either a universal ruler or a universal savior. If he lived the live of a householder, with wife and children, he would become a great king; if he left the family to join the mendicants living in the forest, he would become a great holy man. It seems that the father preferred his son to become a king and so surrounded Siddhartha with very possible luxury. All forms of suffering were hidden from him, lest feelings of compassion arise and motivate him to take up the life of a holy man in order to help others.

When the boy became a man, he had both wife and child and yet he grew restless: "feeling like an elephant locked up inside a house, he set his heart on making a journey outside the palace."[40] The king arranged everything for this excursion, commanding his guards to keep any person with an affliction away from the path of the prince: the cripples, the elderly, the sick, and the beggars were all driven away. But as recounted in the *Buddhacarita* of Ashvaghosha, the gods sent three separate visions to the young prince.

The first vision was that of an old man. Thereupon, the prince's charioteer explained to Siddhartha the meaning of old age. Shocked, he returned to the palace: "How can I delight to walk about in parks when my heart is full of fear of ageing?"[41]

On the second pleasure trip, the gods sent a vision of a sick man. When his charioteer explained the nature and inevitability of disease, Siddhartha was dismayed and filled with compassion: "Since I have learnt of the danger of illness, my heart is repelled by pleasures and seems to shrink into itself."[42] He returned to the palace once again.

On the third excursion, the two men encountered a vision of a dead man, a corpse that was being carried along the road. Learning about death, Siddhartha wondered how it was that people can carry on their lives of pleasure and forget impending disaster. Returning to the palace, he brooded over the visions and eventually sought solitude under a rose-apple tree. There a fourth vision appeared to him, a religious mendicant. When the prince asked him who he was, the man answered that he was a recluse, terrified by birth and death, living the homeless life in order to win salvation: "the most blessed state in which extinction is unknown."[43]

This last vision was of a shramana, which means "one who strives." Traditionally, the shramana was a homeless person who performed severe austerities, even self-mortification. Irrespective of caste and without the aid of the traditional rites, the mendicant sought to achieve salvation by subduing the body, practicing meditation, and contemplating the divine.

After the fourth vision, Prince Siddhartha left family and home to follow the life of a mendicant. "From then onwards the prince led a religious life, and diligently studied the various systems practiced among ascetics and yogins."[44] For six years Siddhartha fasted until he was nothing more than skin and bone. He felt so exhausted that it became impossible for him to sit in meditation. Realizing the need for inner calm, he gave up such extreme self-torture. He journeyed to the River Nairanjana to bathe. A young girl, Nandabala, daughter of the master cowherder, happened along and seeing him so thin and weak, she offered him her food of rice and milk. Siddhartha ate and strengthened his body, whereupon he sat down under a sacred fig tree to meditate, "intent on discerning both the ultimate reality of things and the final goal of existence."[45] The next morning as the sun appeared above the horizon, Siddhartha awakened to unsurpassed perfect enlightenment: "Unshakeable is the liberation of my mind. This is my last birth. Now there is no more renewed existence." The "awakened one" continued in the state of nirvana for seven days before he returned to ordinary consciousness and took up the task of teaching others his path.

The Buddha's teachings are often referred to as the turning of the wheel, or Dharma. In India the wheel has a long symbolic history, beginning with the wheel of the chariot of the sun, which traveled across the sky every day. The wheel came to represent the course of time itself and eventually, the underlying order of the phenomenal world. So when the Buddha met with five mendicants in the Deer Park at Isipatana, an open space near the city of Benares, he sought to share with them his "enlightened" perspective on the truth of human existence, that is, his Dharma: essentially, the meaning of suffering and the way that leads to the cessation of suffering.

He presented his insights as Four Noble Truths, which if rightly understood can open the way to enlightenment. The first of these identifies the nature of suffering itself:

> Now this, monks, is the noble truth of suffering: birth is suffering, aging is suffering, illness is suffering, death is suffering; union with what is displeasing is suffering; separation from what is pleasing is suffering; not to get what one wants is suffering; in brief, the aggregates subject to clinging are suffering.[46]

The Pali word translated here as suffering is *dukkha* (Sanskrit, *duhkha*), and it refers more broadly to the "frustrating confusion and irritating sense of inadequacy" that runs through all of human experience.[47] We suffer on every level: physical pain, disease, and death; emotional dissatisfaction, trauma, and loss; and spiritual disorientation. Even when everything seems perfectly wonderful and one is happy, it never lasts. Nor is death the end, because in the Buddhist view, there is a "mental continuum"—an individual stream of consciousness—that continues, with the result that one is reborn in a new body and the suffering continues.

Why do we suffer? The second noble truth addresses this question by naming the cause of suffering:

> Now this, monks, is the noble truth of the origin of suffering: it is this craving that leads to renewed existence, accompanied by delight and lust, seeking

171

> delight here and there; that is, craving for sensual pleasures, craving for existence, craving for extermination.

Here the key term is *tanha* (Sanskrit, *trsna*; literally, "thirst), translated as craving. English *crave* refers to a desire that is both strong and beyond ones control. Addictions are cravings. Craving has both a strong physical and a mental component. In Buddhism, this craving is the result of ignorance, which only enlightenment can eradicate. Thus, *tanha* is the craving of creatures that experience everything through the perspective of being a separate self: "My hand goes into the fire; it is I who feel pain. My beloved dies; I feel the loss. My death looms ahead of me causing fear of the unknown." This self-centeredness is not primarily a moral flaw; it is part of the biological foundation that is essential for survival in this world. But from the point of view of the "awakened one," it is also the origin of suffering.

Is there any alternative to this cycle of limited and unhappy existence? The third noble truth is the announcement of the good news: yes, there is a cure.

> Now this, monks, is the noble truth of the cessation of suffering; it is the remainderless fading away and cessation of that same craving, the giving up and relinquishing of it, freedom from it, nonattachment.

If craving is natural and rooted in the perspective of the separate self in contact with the phenomenal world, then the elimination of craving would require a transformation of perspective: a new way of "seeing," or wisdom (Sanskrit, *prajna*). The "awakened one" tells the monks that in order to become wise in this way they must change. By following the spiritual discipline called the Eightfold Path, the person can be transformed into a buddha.

> Now this, monks, is the noble truth of the way leading to the cessation of suffering: it is the Eightfold Path.

This is the spiritual discipline that has as its goal the transmutation of the human being and the attainment of buddhahood.[48]

1. *right vision* (recognize the validity of the Four Noble Truths)
2. *right intention* (dedicate oneself whole-heartedly to attaining enlightenment)
3. *right speech* (use language compassionately)

9. Mystical Union

4. *right action* (practice the Five Precepts: do not kill, do not steal, do not lie, do not indulge in drugs of any kind, and practice chastity)
5. *right livelihood* (earn a living with work that does no harm, to others, to oneself, or to the environment)
6. *right effort* (persevere in following the Eightfold Path)
7. *right mindfulness* (practice meditation regularly)
8. *right concentration* (samadhi, or non-dual awareness)

The foundation of the Eightfold Path is an understanding of the dilemma of the human condition as explained in the Four Noble Truths, the reality of suffering, its cause, and its cessation. This knowledge must be accompanied by the commitment to end suffering. Together they support the daily practice of ethical living and meditation. Persevering on the path, the person finally attains right concentration, or samadhi, the non-dual consciousness that is the doorway to ultimate freedom in nirvana.

Mysticism is a way of life that has as its goal mystical union, a revelation where the boundaries separating the human being and ultimate reality dissolve. Although the mystics all agree that the experience is indescribable, they make use of the many images found in ordinary life to convey the nature of the revelation to others.

Chapter 10

Divine Incarnation

As we look at the world's sacred traditions, we see that sometimes a god or a goddess — or some other spirit being — will choose to be born as a man or woman in order to take up residence in the human community. In contrast to spirit mediation, where the non–human spirit borrows a body for a limited time, divine incarnation implies that the spirit undergoes the entire process of living in the natural world. This is embodiment: the spirit is born as a baby; grows up as a girl or boy; becomes old; and may even suffer the death of the body. Divine incarnation is another way that a deity can reveal itself: living among people, communicating with them and helping them in so many ways.

For example, in spite of the fact that kingship in ancient Egypt lasted for nearly 3000 years, during which time beliefs about the nature of the king underwent many changes, one idea remained constant: the ruler was divine, a living deity.[1] This notion was so deeply ingrained in the worldview of the Egyptians that it survived even after Egypt was conquered by the Greeks and transformed by Hellenistic culture. Interesting is the story of Arsinoe II, who was the daughter of Ptolemaios I and Berenike I. From 178 to 170 BCE, Queen Arsinoe II and her brother-husband, King Ptolemaios II, together governed Egypt. Both the Greek authorities and the Egyptian populace admired the ruling pair because of their active support of religious and artistic pursuits. While they ruled, they were referred to as the Divine Siblings; then, after her death, Arsinoe II was identified with the Greek goddess of sovereignty, Aphrodite Queen of Heaven.

Although the incarnation of a divinity is not a common form of revelation, for many people it is a very meaningful one. How wonderful to be able to live together with an incarnated deity!

The word *incarnation* derives from the Latin *incarnatio*, which means "being in the flesh." Here *flesh*[2] suggests not only the human form but the psychological and biological factors that give rise to human personality: human nature, so to speak. Divine incarnation implies that the incarnated being will know what it feels like to be human: fear, hope, and desire, as well as the sensations of pain and pleasure. Because Christianity developed during the time of the Roman Empire, the term is most often associated with the ways in which Christian theologians understand Jesus of Nazareth as the incarnation of God.

Yet, divine incarnation is found not only in Christianity but also as an important form of revelation in many traditions, especially in the religions of India and Tibet where numerous incarnations are recognized.

Divine Incarnation in Tibetan Buddhism

In Tibetan Buddhism,[3] the closest thing to a divine incarnation is the tulku, a bodhisattva that chooses to live as a human being.

> For one thing, all tulkus are considered to be bodhisattvas who, however high their realization, are still traversing the path toward the full and complete enlightenment of a buddha.[4]

A tulku chooses to be born in the world in order to help others. The power to determine the circumstances of one's rebirth is a special ability of certain transcendent bodhisattvas, as understood in Mahayana Buddhism.

As the teachings and sacred stories about the life of Shakyamuni, the historical Buddha, began to spread beyond India into other lands in Asia, two schools of Buddhism developed. On the one hand, there is Theravada,[5] or the "teachings of the elders." The emphasis in Theravada is on personal striving in order to attain nirvana and liberation from the cycles of rebirth. In Theravada Buddhism, one must be a monk or nun in order to become enlightened. Laypersons can increase their merit by supporting and aiding monasteries, with the hope that in a future life they, too, will have the opportunity to be a monk or nun. Further, in Theravada Buddhism, Shakyamuni (the historical Buddha) is understood to be completely human, the teacher and role model for all others. He is not to be worshipped but emulated. In this tradition, the term *bodhisattva* refers simply to anyone who will become a buddha in the future. Therefore, it refers also to the historical Buddha up to the time of his enlightenment, that is, in previous lives as described in the Jataka Tales as well as in his early life as Siddhartha Gautama. Today, Theravada Buddhism is found primarily among the peoples that originate in Southeast Asia (Sri Lanka, Myanmar, Thailand, Cambodia, Laos, and so forth).

The other school of Buddhism is called Mahayana, which means "great vehicle." It developed largely in northeastern Asia, primarily in China, Korea, Japan, and Tibet. Mahayana Buddhism is called the Great Vehicle, because it recognizes many methods for becoming a buddha, including emphasis on meditation (Chan, or Zen), devotion (as in Pure Land), or ritual techniques (as, for example, in Vajrayana). Mahayana also places less value on monasticism: the layperson can become enlightened with the help of certain transcendent (non-historical) buddhas[6] and bodhisattvas.

In Mahayana, Shakaymuni Buddha acquires something more than human status and can be worshipped. But he is not the first and only buddha: numerous buddhas preceded him in earlier ages, and in the future another will be born and become a buddha in order to teach the Dharma. This future buddha is the bodhisattva Maitreya (Loving One), who abides in Tusita heaven, where he awaits the time for his next and final rebirth.

In addition to Maitreya, other transcendent bodhisattvas exist with the sole purpose of helping others. Moved by compassion, they dedicate themselves to alleviating the suffering of all sentient beings as long as the world endures. The career of the bodhisattva is divided into ten stages, or levels of attainment. Reaching the eighth stage,[7] the bodhisattva acquires the ability for intentional rebirth. The bodhisattva can choose to be born in one of the realms of living beings. There are many slightly different ways to depict these different modes of rebirth. One such image is a nineteenth-century Tibetan tangka depicting the Wheel of Life.[8]

The wheel is divided by spokes into six segments, each one representing one possible mode of existence. At the top is the abode of the gods and goddesses, something like a paradise. Moving clockwise, one arrives at the dwelling place of the demi-gods, beings with superhuman powers who lack the moral perfection of the true gods. Then comes the realm for animals. At the bottom is a depiction of hell, the place of punishment. Closely related is the region of the hungry ghosts, or pretas ("departed ones"). Beings who are afflicted in life by greed, envy, and jealousy may be reborn in a state of frustration: for example, they may suffer the torment of hunger, because

10. Divine Incarnation

their bellies are immense but their mouths are only as big as the eye of a needle. Finally, there is the world of human beings.

Holding the Wheel of Life in his hands and feet is Yama, the Lord of Death. He is not an evil being, but represents the fact that there is no life without death, the transition from one existence to another. When a body dies, the next birth is determined by karma, the universal law of cause and effect. On the simplest level, karma ("deed") is any action; but it implies also that the action will cause other re-actions, which, in turn, have their own effects. Karma operates on each and every level of existence: it is simultaneously material, mental, moral, and spiritual. Thus, each person is free to cause joy or sorrow; but later, in the same or a later life, he or she will receive the same joy or sorrow in return. In this view, it is because of the law of karma — which forces us to know the consequences of our actions — that we learn the meaning of good and evil, compassion and hate, and so on. This is the path of learning that leads to enlightenment, and ultimately to freedom from karma altogether.

At the center of the wheel is the hub, a circle occupied by a pig, a rooster, and a snake. In Tibetan Buddhism, these animals symbolize the three mental states that keep us bound to the cycles of rebirth: the pig represents ignorance, that is, seeing things from the limited perspective of a separate, individual self; the rooster symbolizes greed, wanting more than one really needs; and the snake stands for hate, the inability to care about other living beings. These are called the three poisons. Where there is no hate, no greed, no ignorance, there will be compassion, generosity, and wisdom — the distinctive attributes of the enlightened ones. Free of karma and motivated by compassion, such a one may choose eventually to be born as a tulku.

When a tulku dies, it is always important to find his next incarnation. This is done with the help of various types of revelation: someone who was close to his predecessor or who will be close to him in his new life, such as a parent or friend of the family, will have a dream or a vision indicating the place of the rebirth. Divination may be used to determine whether or not a child is, in fact, the reborn tulku. Even a spirit medium may be consulted. Usually two or three years old at the time of accepted as such, the candidate will be tested to see if he remembers aspects of his last life. Once the incarnation is discovered, he may then be brought into a monastic setting in order to receive training in Buddhist teaching and ritual.

Ever since the Chinese occupation of Tibet, which forced the Tibetan government into exile (1959), the life of all Tibetans has been changed. Today, Tibetan Buddhism is finding new homes in different places all over the world: in New York, in Taiwan, in India, and in England, for example. Forced out of their homeland, Tibetans have begun to share their traditions with others. Two tulkus — Tenzin Gyatso (the fourteenth Dalai Lama) and Khyongla Rato (the tenth Khyongla) — have become teachers in the world beyond Tibet. Their life stories serve as introductions to Tibetan Buddhism and provide us also with excellent accounts of the discovery and training of a Tibetan incarnation.

Tenzin Gyatso. The best known of all Tibetan tulkus is surely the Dalai Lama. *Dalai* is a Mongolian word meaning ocean, suggesting the vast wisdom of the Dalai Lama. The word *lama* is a Tibetan word that translates the Sanskrit term *guru*, or spiritual teacher. This title was first given to Sonam Gyatso (1543–1588), who was recognized as the third incarnation of the Dalai Lama. His two predecessors, the first and second Dalai Lamas, were identified retroactively.

The Dalai Lama is considered to be the incarnation of the patron bodhisattva of Tibet: the Bodhisattva of Compassion, known in Sanskrit as Avalokiteshvara and in Tibet as Chenrezi.[9] According to Buddhist teaching, the home of Avalokiteshvara is located on top of a mythical mountain called Potala. Therefore, the fifth Dalai Lama, Nag-dban-rgya-mtsho (1617–1682), had a palace fortress built on a mountain in the area of Lhasa and named it the Potala. Completed in 1645, the Potala was the home of the Dalai Lama's many incarnations for over three hundred years.[10]

Tenzin Gyatso (1935–) is the fourteenth incarnation of the Dalai Lama. He was born in the province of Amdo as the child named Lhamo Dhondup. Visions and signs pointed to three children as possible incarnations of the Dalai Lama, but Lhamo Dhondup proved to be the best candidate. His mother, Diki Tsering, has described the circumstances surrounding the discovery of her son's identity. A search party headed by Khetsang Rinpoche had visited the family home several times. "This time Khetsang Rinpoche was carrying two staffs as he entered our veranda, where Lhamo Dhondup was playing. Rinpoche put both staffs in a corner. Our son went to the staffs, laid one aside, and picked up the other.[11] He struck Rinpoche lightly on the back with it, said the staff was his and why had Khetsang Rinpoche taken

10. Divine Incarnation

it. The party members exchanged meaningful looks, but I could not understand a word of the Lhasa dialect they spoke."[12] Later on, the child tried to remove a rosary that was hidden under the robes of Khetsang Rinpoche, insisting that it, too, was his. His mother learned that the rosary was a gift that the thirteenth Dalai Lama had once presented to Khetsang Rinpoche.

After many tests, it was determined that Lhamo Dhondup was indeed the incarnation. In 1940, he was enthroned in the Potala at Lhasa. For the next fifteen years, the young Dalai Lama received an education preparing him to be both the political and spiritual leader of Tibet.

The Chinese Communists first invaded Tibet in 1950. For nine years the political situation in Tibet continued to worsen. The Chinese insisted that Tibetan territory belonged to China; furthermore, in line with Marxist condemnation of religion, they sought to eradicate the Buddhist traditions of Tibet. Finally, in March of 1959, the Tibetan people in the capital city of Lhasa made an attempt to overthrow the Chinese occupation, but they were unsuccessful. The Dalai Lama was forced to flee to India, ending more than three hundred years of Tibetan history under the sacred rule of the incarnations of the Bodhisattva of Compassion.

Tenzin Gyatso has written two autobiographies.[13] The first, *My Land and My People*, was published in 1962 shortly after his flight into India. Here he gives an account of all that led to his life in exile. *Freedom in Exile* was published nearly thirty years later in 1990. The title is one of hope. Exile has not meant the end of his role as leader of the Tibetan people. During these years the Dalai Lama has become one of the most respected figures in the modern world. In spite of his busy schedule of travel and teaching, he has found time to write numerous books that render Tibetan Buddhist teachings accessible to modern readers: "as a Buddhist monk, my concern extends to all members of the human family and, indeed, to all suffering sentient beings. I believe that ... suffering is caused by ignorance, and that people inflict pain on others in pursuit of their own happiness or satisfaction. Yet true happiness comes from a sense of inner peace and contentment, which in turn must be achieved through cultivation of altruism, of love, of compassion, and through the elimination of anger, selfishness and greed."[14] His ability to communicate compassionately with people of all faiths, his untiring work in an effort to restore the cultural independence of Tibet, and his great spiritual wisdom have all contributed to making him a world leader.

Khyongla Rato. In October of 1991 the Dalai Lama arrived in New York City to give the Kalachakra Initiation. One of the most important initiations in the Tantric tradition of Tibetan Buddhism, it holds special significance for world peace. Hundreds of New Yorkers attended the lengthy ceremony, since unlike other initiations, the Kalachakra is presented before large audiences. The event was sponsored by New York's Tibet Center, one of whose founders (in 1976) was Tibetan tulku Khyongla Rato. His leadership in bringing Tibetan Buddhism to New York City illustrates the role of an incarnation as spiritual teacher. Khyongla Rato's autobiography, *My Life and Lives: The Story of a Tibetan Incarnation*,[15] offers a good example of the training of a tulku. In addition, it provides readers with a detailed introduction to the role of revelations in Tibetan religion.

Khyongla Rato is believed to be the tenth incarnation of a sixteenth-century enlightened teacher. The parents of the first Khyongla named him Jigme, that is, the Fearless One. Between the ages of 20 and 40, Jigme studied at the most famous Tibetan monasteries. Then, retiring into a hermitage, he remained in seclusion for many years. When he returned to living in society, he soon became known for his sanctity and wisdom. People traveled from all over Tibet to see him and listen to his teachings. He was esteemed far and wide as Lama Khyongla, the lama of Khyong Yul. Sometime after his death at the age of seventy-eight, his disciples began to search for his incarnation. The second Khyongla was as remarkable as the first; he founded, among other things, the Katog Gonpa Monastery and built a labrang, or lama's residence, which became the home of his future incarnations.

When the ninth incarnation passed away, the search for his incarnation involved many types of revelation. In 1928, the searchers found the incarnation in five-year old Norbu Lhamo, who lived in the village of Ophor situated on a high plateau surrounded by the rolling hills of Kham. Norbu's mother had three visions concerning the child before he was born: "It was learned that during the time my mother was carrying me she had once dreamed that the protective deities were pouring water on her head, and this had been interpreted by those she then consulted as meaning that all defilements were being removed from her child, even before its birth. In another dream she appeared to be entering a temple during her final month of pregnancy. She was very heavy and stumbled, and would have fallen had not a protective deity caught her and helped her to stand. This dream at the time was interpreted to mean that the child in her womb was an incarnation, kept safe from harm by his protective deity. In a third dream she saw the moon and sun come together, and this was interpreted to mean that her child would be exceptionally intelligent."[16] She shared her dreams with others, and they were interpreted as messages about the identity of her yet unborn son.

In addition to dreams, there were also many events that were considered to be omens concerning the child's identity: "while she was giving birth, a rainbow appeared over our home. People saw one end of it actually touch the house, which was a very lucky sign. Word eventually reached the Khyongla Labrang that a woman in Ophor had borne a child thought to be an incarnation, and the monks there became interested; for when the Ninth Khyongla had been cremated the smoke of his pyre had drifted westward, which meant that the next incarnation would be found in that direction."[17] The wind moving the smoke from the funeral pyre in a westerly direction was a natural event, and so was the rainbow over Norbu's house at the time of his birth. Diviners, however, interpreted these events as messages from the spiritual world. In the first instance, the smoke moves in the direction where the incarnation will be found; the second sign identifies the child as having a special destiny. Together the signs pointed to the possibility that Norbu Lhamo was the incarnation of Khyongla.

Spirit mediation is also an important type of revelation in Tibetan Buddhism. Since visions and signs pointed to several candidates, the medium at Rato Monastery was consulted. "The oracle went into his trance, during which letters were placed before him describing each of the child candidates. He read them all and then declared in a loud voice: 'The son of Tenzin Lhamo, who was born in the Water Pig Year, is the reincarnation of Khyongla.'"[18]

An astrologer was consulted to ascertain the most auspicious time for the child to begin his education, and so a year later after his sixth birthday, young Norbu Lhamo began a training that lasted for many years. Until the age of 13, he lived in the labrang of his predecessor; then, he went to Lhasa for more advanced studies, which required another twenty years. During the late 1950s, he began to assume more and more responsibility as a teacher and spiritual leader. However, in 1959 he was forced — along with the Dalai Lama and many other Tibetans — into exile, the beginning of a journey that led him first to India, then to Europe, and eventually to the United States. Thus, political conflict and historical conditions have forced Khyongla Rato, like the Dalai Lama, to become a spiritual teacher not only for Tibetans but also for the world.

Divine Incarnation in Hinduism

The idea of karma has its origins in India, where it is the name for the universal law that governs the cycles of rebirth. When we speak of a divine incarnation, we are referring to the birth of a being who is free from karma and willingly chooses to be born in the world. According to the teachings of Buddhism, even the gods are still bound to samsara. Only enlightened beings, buddhas and bodhisattvas, have a choice. In Hinduism, there are at least two ways to view the gods: here, too, we find the notion that even the fate of the gods is determined by karma. For example, the story about the Parade of Ants teaches that a god may be reborn against his will as a lower life form. In the story, Indra, who is the king of the gods and protector of the universe, sees a number of ants walking in single file and learns that each one is a reincarnation of a former Indra.[19] This is for him an unsettling discovery, one that causes him to reflect carefully on his actions.

The more common view in Hinduism, however, is that each god and goddess is a manifestation of the one divine reality and so (like the buddhas and bodhisattvas of Buddhist thought) unaffected by karma and free from the cycles of rebirth. This view integrates monism (the conviction that only one causal principle is at work in the creation) and polytheism (belief in the existence of many gods and goddesses), and it developed under the influence of the mystics of India.

So profound was the impact of mysticism on Indian thought that gradually the devotional traditions were reinterpreted to conform to it. Each god and each goddess was recognized to be but one "face" of the Absolute. Devotional worship, or Bhakti Yoga, became another path to samadhi and liberation. A parallel development was the conviction that work and other worldly activities could also lead to liberation: this is called Karma Yoga. If one's actions are offered as gifts of worship, or sacrifice, to a personal god or goddess, this selfless action can then lead to mystical union and absolute freedom.

In this view, it is possible for ultimate reality to appear to a human being as a god or goddess. Further, a deity can choose to descend into the world of birth and death for the benefit of all creatures: this is the avatar (Sanskrit, *avatara*, literally, "descent"). One example of an historical avatar is Mother Meera, an Indian woman who lives in Germany and who is for her followers an incarnation of the Divine Mother. The Indian synthesis of monism and polytheism allows devotees of individual goddesses to see each

10. Divine Incarnation

one as a manifestation of the Divine Mother (Devi, or "goddess"). And, of course, the Divine Mother is herself a "face" of the Absolute.

Mother Meera. Born on 26 December 1960 in the village of Chandepalle, Andhra Pradesh, as Kamala Reddy, Mother Meera grew up in a family that was not particularly religious; nor did she have spiritual training of any kind. However, at a very early age she began to have spontaneous visions. "At the age of two or three She would go to 'Different Lights' when She was in need of comfort."[20] It is said that at the age of six, Kamala Reddy experienced samadhi. In 1974, she was brought to live in the Aurobindo Ashram in Pondicherry, where she continued to see visions, particularly of Sri Aurobindo and Sweet Mother.

Aurobindo Ghose (1872–1950) was a great yogi, poet, nationalist, and spiritual leader of modern India. Educated in England, he returned to India as a young man to teach English and French, and eventually he served as acting principal of Baroda College. He became involved in India's independence movement, and in 1908, he was imprisoned for a year. It was while he was in jail that his interest in yoga deepened. Upon leaving prison, Aurobindo moved to Pondicherry, where he spent the next forty years formulating his vision of spiritual evolution, which is known as Integral Yoga.

According to this teaching, spiritual development in the individual person is comprised of two stages, or directions. In the first stage, the person withdraws attention from the world and seeks to open up to experience of the divine reality. During the second stage, the same person turns again towards the world in the effort to infuse all creation with the divine presence. These two movements can be suggested using light as a symbol for the divine reality. The yogi attains union with the light; and transformed by this union, he or she then seeks to become a vehicle for bringing the light into the world. Thus, for Aurobindo, samadhi and liberation from rebirth are not the final goals of the religious life. There is still the need to contribute to the transformation of the world itself, rendering it holy, or spiritual.[21]

Sweet Mother is Mother Meera's name for her namesake, Mira Alfassa (1878–1973); the daughter in a Turkish-Egyptian family, Mira Alfassa grew up in France. From 1920 until the time of his death in 1950, she was the constant companion of Aurobindo. In fact, the Aurobindo Ashram owes its inception to her energies, and she, too, is worshipped as an avatar of the Divine Mother.

In her visions, Mother Meera was guided by the figures of Aurobindo and Sweet Mother. "I travelled with Sweet Mother constantly in all the worlds and I saw many beautiful things and beautiful places. But I also saw terrible and frightening things, worlds where the worst forces are at work. I asked Sweet Mother, 'Why are you showing these things when you know I hate them?' Mother said, 'Your work is not just in beautiful places; you are to transform darkness into light, suffering into joy, and death into life.'"[22] Through her visions and her spiritual contact with the divine, Mother Meera has come to see her task in terms of embodying the Divine Mother and purifying the earth so as to prepare it for sanctification. She does this by incarnating the divine and "calling down onto the earth the Light of the Supreme that makes Transformation certain."[23] In other words, she has found her place within the tradition of Integral Yoga, which sees incarnation as part of the process by which humanity will become God; time will become eternity; and the earth will become a paradise.

Krishna. The word *avatar* also refers to certain "mythical" incarnations that are important in the Hindu understanding of the gods. Since all deities are manifestations of the divine, it is common to see one deity as an avatar of another. The language of incarnation is used, but we are not dealing here with historical personages, as in the case of Jesus of Nazareth, Tenzin Gyatso, Khyongla Rato, and Mother Meera. In contrast to the historical incarnations, these are the mythical avatars.

Especially in the worship of the god Vishnu the tradition of avatars is highly developed. In the *Bhagavad Gita* (Song of the Lord, c. 200 BCE), Vishnu's avatar is Krishna, who appears as the charioteer of the young warrior Arjuna during a time of political crisis. Krishna explains to Arjuna why it is he has chosen to enter the world of men and women[24]:

> For whenever of the right
> A languishing appears, son of Bharata,
> A rising up of unright,
> Then I send Myself forth.
> For protection of the good,
> And for destruction of evil-doers,
> To make a firm footing for the right,
> I come into being in age after age.

10. Divine Incarnation

Of all the avatars of Vishnu, Krishna, the god of love, is perhaps the most popular; and many are the myths about Krishna's life: his birth; his childhood; the days of his youth; and his teachings to Arjuna, which make up the *Bhagavad Gita*.

One myth found in the *Bhagavata Purana* describes Krishna as a naughty child growing up in a village among cowherders. He and his young playmates would wallow in the mud, steal good things to eat, set free the cows, and play pranks on their parents. Still, it was impossible for the women of the village to get angry at Krishna; they just laughed and tried to protect him from any danger into which his mischief might lead him. One day, Krishna's playmates ran to his mother to tell her that he had been eating dirt. When his mother confronted him, the little avatar denied this; so she asked him to open wide his mouth and let her have a look. "She then saw in his mouth the whole eternal universe, and heaven, and the regions of the sky, and the orb of the earth with its mountains, islands, and oceans; she saw the wind, and lightning, and the moon and stars, and the zodiac; and water and fire and air and space itself; she saw the vacillating sense, the mind, the elements, and the three strands of matter. She saw within the body of her son, in his gaping mouth, the whole universe in all its variety, with all the forms of life and time and nature and action and hopes, and her own village, and her self."[25] At first Krishna's mother was afraid, but she soon realized joyfully that she was in the presence of God. Then Krishna "spread his magic illusion in the form of maternal affection" over her, and she forgot what she had seen. Once again she was simply the wife of a cowherd and the loving mother of a little boy.[26]

Many of the stories about Krishna as a youth involve his role as divine beloved. The human soul longs for loving union with God, and this is symbolically portrayed in these myths. For example, in Jayadeva's *Gitagovinda* (Song of Govinda), we learn about the love between the boy Krishna, who is sometimes called Govinda ("protector of cows"), and Radha. A young girl of the village, Radha is jealous because her beloved Krishna appears to be unfaithful. All the girls are in love with him. The poem begins with Radha's longing for Krishna and her jealousy, but it ends with their ecstatic union.

In the *Bhagavad Gita*, Vishnu assumes the form of Krishna in order to defeat the demon Kamsa, who is corrupting the world with his evil ways and also to ensure the victory of the Pandava brothers in a war against their cousins, the Kauravas. Arjuna, one of the Pandavas, refuses to fight; he fears that if he kills his relatives — even in a just war — he will incur bad karma. But his charioteer begins to teach him about God and how one can reach God (and liberation) even as a warrior. Krishna thus teaches Arjuna about Karma Yoga and Bhakti Yoga.

First, he reassures Arjuna that it is the gods, not men, who decide who will live and who will die. So, he cannot blame himself as the cause of an opponent's death, should he be victorious in battle. In addition, while doing his duty as a warrior and fighting on behalf of a noble cause, Arjuna can offer his actions as a sacrificial gift to God. This is the path of Karma Yoga that leads to liberation.

Then, after revealing his divine nature to the warrior — appearing before him in his cosmic form — Krishna further teaches Arjuna the path of devotion, or bhakti:

> Further, the highest secret of all,
> My supreme message, hear.
> Because thou art greatly loved of Me,
> Therefore I shall tell thee what is good for thee.
> Be Me-minded, devoted to Me;
> Worshiping Me, revere Me;
> And to Me alone shalt thou go; truly to thee
> I promise it — (because) thou art dear to me.[27]

Here, Krishna appeals to Arjuna's emotional nature, showing a path to spiritual freedom that is closer to what many know in their relationships with parents, lovers, and children. The sacred stories of India show Krishna to be an incarnation of the Divine, choosing to live among human beings in order to invite them into a loving relationship.

Divine Incarnation in Christian Theology

Generally speaking, reincarnation is not part of the cultural matrix out of which Christianity developed. In Western cultures there is the common belief that death is the end of an individual person's life; there is no rebirth in a different body. However, Christians do believe that in Jesus of Nazareth we witness the incarnation of God. It is for them a unique event; there are no other incarnations. How did this view come about?

The question of the Jesus' identity began to preoccupy Christians from the very beginning. When the followers of Jesus witnessed his resurrection, they asked themselves: "Who really is this man who is able to return from the dead?" Among the many interpretations concerning the nature of Jesus, two stand out as central and important to all his followers: Jesus as the Christ (Messiah, King), and Jesus as the incarnation of God.

When early Christians recognized Jesus as the Christ, they were expressing their faith that through him the rule of God enters into the lives of humankind. Jesus fully exemplifies one in whom God's will is at work. Moreover, by submitting to death on the cross, Jesus transforms human destiny. No longer does death have absolute power. Christians believe that in union with Jesus they, too, will be resurrected at the end of time. Thus, Jesus is both king and savior, reconciling humans to their creator and restoring the creation.

Soon, the Christ was understood to be not only a just king chosen by God, not only a savior liberating them from death, but the incarnation of God himself. Although doctrines about the Incarnation have a long and complex history, the germ of the idea is present already in the writings that make up the Christian New Testament.[28] For example, in his Letter to the Philippians,[29] the apostle Paul of Tarsus quotes an early confession of faith that begins as follows: "Let your bearing towards one another arise out of your life in Christ Jesus. For the divine nature was his from the first; yet he did not think to snatch at equality with God, but made himself nothing, assuming the nature of a slave. Bearing the human likeness, revealed in human shape, he humbled himself, and in obedience accepted even death — death on a cross." Here the emphasis lies on the existence of Christ before creation and before his incarnation in history, that is, before his "humbling," or "assuming the nature of a slave."

We find the same kind of language in the opening passage of the late first-century Gospel of John, which states that Jesus incarnates the Logos of God.

> When all things began, the Logos already existed. The Logos was with God, and what God was the Logos was.
> ....
> So the Logos became flesh; he came to dwell among us.[30]

The Greek term *logos* has many meanings, but each usage has a particular connection to the verb *legein*, "to speak." What is spoken must have meaning. Thus, the Logos is God's self-expression, his purpose, and his thought.

According to John the Evangelist, God chose to express himself by entering history through the incarnation as Jesus of Nazareth.

During the first three centuries of Christian history, the missionary goal of spreading the Gospel, that is, the good news of Jesus, led to the establishment of churches all over the Roman Empire.[31] Christian communities developed in the Middle East and as far east as India, in northern Africa, and in southern Europe. One characteristic of the expansion was the emergence of diverse versions of the Gospel. On the one hand, each apostle would have a slightly different way of communicating the story of Jesus; at the same time, the message was received in different cultural contexts and this, too, influenced its expression. Furthermore, during this period, Christians often faced persecution.[32] For example, during the second century Christianity was considered officially a capital offence and many Christians suffered martyrdom. In addition, the non–Christian populace often interpreted natural catastrophes, such as floods or bad harvests, as signs of the gods' displeasure at their neglect under the influence of Christian "atheism." This sometimes led to mob violence against the followers of Jesus, who were believed to be atheists because they did not offer sacrifices to the traditional gods.

During the third century, the Roman Empire began to fragment. Civil war, external invasions, and economic difficulties all contributed to the division of rule. From 284 to 313, either two or four "emperors" shared the role of sovereign. The division of the empire also reflected cultural differences, especially between the Greek-speaking peoples of the east and those living in the western half of the empire, where Latin prevailed.

It was not until the fourth century that the situation changed, allowing Christians to come together from all corners of the empire in order to unify their tradition, both their religious beliefs and their ecclesiastical organization. In 313, Flavius Valerius Aurelius Constantinus (c. 272–337)[33] defeated the last of his opponents and reunified the empire. Constantine I was not baptized a Christian until he lay on his deathbed, but throughout his life, he was attracted to the new religion. His Edict of Milan (313) made religious tolerance the law throughout his realm. The theme of unification is certainly characteristic of Constantine's career, for not only did he seek to unite the empire, he also actively encouraged Christian leaders to meet and find some kind of consensus. This led to the initiation of a series of ecumenical ("all-inclusive") councils, where Christians could begin to find some kind of agreement or unified vision.

10. Divine Incarnation

The Nature of Christ. The first ecumenical council was held at Nicaea in Asia Minor (modern-day Turkey).[34] Approximately 300 bishops, mostly from the Greek-speaking half of the empire, took part, following the procedures and style of the Roman senate. Several matters were considered including the question about the nature of Christ. Fundamental to Jesus and to his followers is the belief that there is only one God. How, then, can one proclaim the divinity of Jesus and remain strictly monotheistic? The council fell into three separate groups in respect to this question: (1) To protect their understanding of monotheism, the followers of Arius of Alexandria (c. 250–336) argued that Christ was a created being, divine but not God. According to this view, God required some kind of mediator in order to create the world, and so, before time and space had come into existence, the Father created the Son, who although divine was subordinate to the Father. (2) Opposed to this thinking were those who followed Athanasius (c. 298–373) and argued that Christ and God were of the same substance (Greek, *homoousios*): like a fountain and the river that flows forth from it. Athanasius argued that Arianism, the teachings of Arius, would lead in practice to polytheism: worshipping God *and* the "divine creature" Jesus. He countered with several questions: Why limit the nature of God? Is it really impossible for God to create without a mediator? If one follows this logic, then how could the Father, lacking a mediator, create the Son? (3) The majority of the bishops were not committed to either position; instead, they were more concerned about maintaining peaceful relations.

The outcome of the council was a creedal statement that was later revised but continued to serve as the basis for the Nicene Creed. It clarified the relationship between God and Jesus, who as the Son of God is eternally "begotten, not made." Indeed, Christ and God are of the same substance: *homoousios*.

During the next sixty years, the debate continued: Athanasius was made bishop of Alexandria in 328 and then subsequently sent into exile again and again by those who opposed his theology. Meanwhile, the followers of Arius grew more and more radical, insisting on the subordination of Christ. This influenced many more conservative bishops to embrace the views of Athanasius. These church leaders were concerned that the three "persons" of God (Father, Son, and Holy Spirit) should be understood as truly distinct and not merely aspects of one divine being. To describe the relationship between God and Christ, they preferred the term *homoiousios*, or "of a similar substance."

Theodosius I, the first emperor to make Christianity the official religion of the Roman Empire, called the second ecumenical council to meet in 381 at Constantinople. Among many decisions, the 150 bishops (from the eastern half of the empire) reaffirmed the language of the Nicene Creed, retaining Athanasius's term *homoousios*: God and Christ are of the same substance. At the same time, the discussion about the nature of the Holy Spirit grew in importance and the creed was amended to state that whereas the Son is generated by the Father, the Holy Spirit "proceeds" from the Father.

One other concern for the bishops was to preserve the belief that although Christ was wholly divine, he was likewise completely human. They thus opposed the teachings of Apollinaris of Laodicea (c. 310–c. 390), who argued that Jesus had a human body, governed by an irrational animal soul, but his mind, or intellect, was the Logos. As a result, he would not experience life in quite the same way as human beings. He was not a true incarnation of God, but rather God's Logos "enfleshed."

The question about the nature of Christ continued to dominate the next two ecumenical councils. At Ephesus in 431, the bishops debated Theotokos ("mother of God") as a title for Mary, mother of Jesus. Nestorius, patriarch of Constantinople (c. 381–c. 451), preferred to refer to her as Christotokos, "mother of Christ," in order to emphasize her role as mother of the human vehicle in which God was incarnated. The meeting ended in chaos; then, in 433 Nestorius was ex-communicated[35] and the more moderate of his followers accepted the title Theotokos for Mary.

The debates about the divinity of Jesus Christ led naturally to questions about the nature of God. If God is incarnated in the historical human being Jesus, what does this tell us about God? Can God feel as humans do? Or is the Divine more like a philosophical ideal, detached and immutable? When Jesus is crucified and dies, is it just the human part that suffers; or is his suffering felt also by God?

The symbolic resolution of these questions is given form in 451 by the bishops who attended the fourth ecumenical Council at Chalcedon (across the Bosporus from Constantinople): Jesus the Christ is one person, the Divine Logos, in whom two natures — the human and the divine — are permanently united before and after the incarnation. The two natures are distinct, not confused or mixed, but fully united.[36] The Logos, or divine Word, becomes incarnated as Jesus the Christ: in this way, God enters fully into human experience and suffering and by virtue of this action transforms the very foundations of human existence.

10. Divine Incarnation

Atonement. Indeed, it is this transformation of the creation that is the very purpose that guides God. The purpose of the Incarnation goes beyond allowing people to know God (although that, too, is achieved). Above all, it is a necessary act in order to reverse the effects of the Fall and to offer a way of reconciling God with all of humanity. Christians understand the Incarnation as part of God's salvation plan: God enters the world to do away with sin, that is, all that separates people from their Creator. We find this notion developed in the Christian teachings of the Atonement.

The religious idea of atonement is part of the Jewish tradition out of which Christianity developed: the most solemn day in modern Judaism is the Day of Atonement (Yom Kippur), an annual day of fasting and repentance. The word *atonement* means the state of being "at one," or reconciliation with God (sometimes referred to as redemption or salvation). Acknowledging sin and feeling remorse, Jews ask God for forgiveness and the healing of any break in their relationship. In ancient times the sacrifice of a lamb (a "guilt offering") could be offered with the goal of atonement, while later prophets emphasized the inner attitude of repentance and mercy towards others.

The various writings found in the Christian New Testament do not present any one doctrine of the Atonement but rather a number of images that express the process of reconciling humans with God. For example, Jesus is called the Son of Man who came into the world to serve and "to give up his life as a ransom for many."[37] The Son of Man is an angel that appears in one of the visions of the prophet Daniel, where God gives the Son of Man sovereignty and kingly power over all nations.[38] *Ransom* refers to the price paid to free a slave. Thus, in Mark's gospel Jesus is God's chosen king, who acts as a servant and gives up his life to pay the ransom that frees humankind from the clutches of the Devil. Here, Jesus is the ransom, the price paid to free humanity.

A second image is found in Matthew's description of the Last Supper, which Jesus shared with his friends on the night that he was taken prisoner. Offering the cup of wine, he says, "this is my blood ... shed for the forgiveness of sins."[39] The symbolism here suggests that Jesus is a "guilt offering" to God, not payment to the Devil. The theme is found also in the Gospel of John. When the holy man John the Baptist sees Jesus for the first time he says, "There is the Lamb of God; it is he who takes away the sin of the world."[40] Here, Jesus is the sacrificial lamb, the guilt offering.

A third image is found in the writings of the apostle Paul: recapitulation.

The life, death, and resurrection of Jesus serve to reverse the effects of the Fall: "For since it was a man who brought death into the world, a man also brought resurrection of the dead. As in Adam all men die, so in Christ all will be brought to life."[41] Here, Jesus is the New Adam. Further, according to this view, the Incarnation affects the entire creation, which suffered flaw because of Adam's disobedience: "The universe itself is to be freed from the shackles of mortality and enter upon the liberty and splendor of the children of God."[42]

Christian theologians have focused on these three images of atonement as they developed their understanding of the meaning of the Incarnation. In *Christus Victor*,[43] Gustaf Aulén points out that there is no one single interpretation of the Atonement but rather many ways to understand God's redemptive work through Jesus. Nevertheless, one important belief that all Christians share is that this redemptive work is accomplished once for all time. Because of the Fall, the children of Adam become slaves subjected to the power of sin, and they live in a flawed world that separates them from God and from eternal life. The Incarnation is God's answer to the Fall — doing away with sin and human alienation. As Paul states in his letter to the Hebrews, "It is by the will of God that we have been made holy through the sacrificial offering of the body of Jesus Christ, once and for all."[44] This is the Atonement; and once it is achieved, it is no longer needed. Hence, in the Christian experience of God, there can be only one Incarnation.

Divine incarnation is a form of revelation that is particularly moving because it shows divinity reaching out to humanity in a very concrete way. Not willing to simply oversee the creation, the divine actively assumes a human life in order to be known and to transform the human condition.

Glossary

Adhan (Arabic): the call to prayer.
Avatar (Sanskrit): literally, "descent"; the incarnation of a divine spirit being.
Babalawo (Yoruba): literally, "master of the mysteries"; the Yoruba word signifying the diviner.
Bhakti (Sanskrit): loving devotion and worship.
Bodhi (Sanskrit/Pali): literally, "awakened"; perfect knowledge.
Bodhisattva (Sanskrit): literally, "awakened being": in Mahayana Buddhism, one who renounces complete entry into nirvana until all sentient beings have been saved.
Buddha (Sanskrit/Pali): literally, "awakened one"; one who has achieved the enlightenment that leads to freedom from reincarnation.
Dao (Chinese): literally, "way"; the principle that underlies the reality of the world of phenomena.
Dharma (Sanskrit): literally, "carrying; holding"; the divine order of creation; and in Buddhism, the teaching about that divine order.
Dhyana (Sanskrit): meditation, a quiet mind in a quiet body.
Eucharist (from Greek, *eucharistia*, "thanksgiving"): the Christian ceremony commemorating the Last Supper, in which bread and wine are consecrated and consumed.
Exodus (from Greek, *exodos*): literally, "road out"; with the help of Moses, God's liberation of the Israelites living as slaves in Egypt.
Guru (Sanskrit): teacher, in particular a spiritual master.
Haggadah (Hebrew): literally, "telling"; the text recited at the Seder on the first two nights of the Jewish Passover.
Jnana (Sanskrit, from the root *jna*, "to know"): knowledge; and in a religious context, intuitive knowledge of ultimate reality.
Lama (Tibetan): literally, "none above"; a religious master.
Logos (Greek): literally, "what is spoken"; word, purpose, meaning.
Mantra (Sanskrit): a sound, word, or phrase embodying sacred power.
Messiah (from Hebrew, *masiah*, "anointed one"): king; savior.

Moksha (from Sanskrit, *moksa*): final liberation from the cycles of birth and death through union with ultimate reality.
Muezzin (Turkish, from Arabic *mu'addin*): in Islam, the one who recites the call to prayer.
Nirvana (Sanskrit): literally, "extinction"; unconditioned reality free from all worldly bonds.
Puja (Sanskrit): ritual worship.
Samadhi (Sanskrit): literally, "to establish"; total absorption in ultimate reality.
Samsara (Sanskrit): literally, "journeying"; the cycle of birth, death, and rebirth.
Seidkona (Old Norse): literally, "woman of the seidr"; ancient Scandinavian spirit traveler.
Seidr (Old Norse): the ancient Scandinavian ritual of spirit travel.
Shaman or **Shamanka** (from Tungus): the leader of the community who is an expert in spirit travel as well as other religious arts (divination, healing, and so forth).
Torah (Hebrew): literally, "law"; the five books of Moses (the first five books of the Hebrew and Christian bibles).
Tulku (Tibetan): literally, "transformation body"; the recognized incarnation of a spiritual being.
Wakan (Lakota): spirit, the divine reality.
Yang (Chinese): literally, "the sunny side of the hill"; the hot, dry masculine energy.
Yin (Chinese): literally, "the shady side of the hill"; the cool, dark, feminine energy.
Yoga (Sanskrit): literally, "yoke"; the process or path of uniting with ultimate reality.

Notes

Preface

1. Mircea Eliade, ed., *The Encyclopedia of Religion*, 16 vols. (New York: Macmillan, 1987).

2. Beverly Moon, "Open House at Martin Buber's: Towards a Typology of Revelation" (26 February 1999 in Arlington, Virginia, at the annual meeting of the American Academy of Religion, Middle Atlantic Region).

3. *Spirit travel* or *spirit journey* is preferred to *shamanism*, which like prophecy, is a complex tradition including more than one form of revelation.

4. Huston Smith, *The World's Religions: Our Great Wisdom Traditions* (San Francisco: HarperSanFrancisco, 1991).

PART ONE

Chapter 1

1. These notions derive from those philosophical theories that see religion as serving primarily psychological or social functions. For example, one still encounters the idea that people create the gods and goddesses in order to assuage their fear of frightening events in nature, such as the destructive powers of lightening, storm, and earthquake, as well as the inevitable experience of suffering, disease, and death. This is not really a modern idea, since it is found already among the writings of the ancient Greek philosophers. According to Epicurus (341–270 BCE) the fabrication of a realm of gods who have control over nature allows the human being to look to these supernatural persons for protection. Religion is nothing more than a way of dealing with innate fears — it is a psychological crutch. The second theory, that religions are created by certain people (rulers or priests) in order to control the masses, is also not that new. For example, the Greek poet Critias (fifth century BCE) writes in his play entitled *Sisyphos* that in the beginning there was no human morality. Therefore, a wise king invented the gods as judges of human behavior. In this view, fear is the result of the creation of religion not its origin: fear of punishment by powerful supernatural beings helps humans control their lawless natures. For a history of these and other theories about the origins of religion, see Jan de Vries's *The Study of Religion: A Historical Approach*, translated with an introduction by Kees W. Bolle (New York: Harcourt, Brace & World, 1967).

2. The Lakota are also called the Sioux, which means "rattlesnake." This is a pejorative name originally coined by their enemies. See Stephen E. Feraca, *Wakinyan: Lakota Religion in the Twentieth Century* (Lincoln, Nebr.: University of Nebraska Press, 1998), xiv.

3. Black Elk converted to Christianity in his later life causing some scholars, as, for example, Damian Costello in his *Black Elk: Colonialism and Lakota Catholicism* (New York: Orbis Books, 2005), to question whether or not his teachings represent Lakota tradition. In response, we have the comments of Lydia Whirlwind Soldier, a fluent Lakota speaker who is the American Indian studies coordinator for the Todd County School District (South Dakota): "*Black Elk Speaks* is the most authoritative account of Lakota 'religion' because the information is from a Lakota who lived, practiced and experienced Lakota culture. There is some controversy over the ways in which Christianity influenced his story, but his vision occurred be-

fore white contact when he was only nine years old. He was raised and lived the Lakota way of life." See David Martinez's review of *Black Elk: Colonialism and Lakota Catholicism* in the *Journal of the American Academy of Religion* 74/4 (December 2006), 1017.

4. *The Sacred Pipe: Black Elk's Account of the Seven Rites of the Sioux*, recorded and edited by Joseph Epes Brown (New York: Penguin, 1971). For further reading about Lakota religion, see also *Dakota Texts*, compiled by Ella C. Deloria (Vermillon, S.D.: Dakota Press, 1978); William K. Powers's *Oglala Religion* (Lincoln, Nebr.: University of Nebraska Press, 1977); and James R. Walker's *Lakota Belief and Ritual* (Lincoln, Nebr.: University of Nebraska Press, 1980).

5. As ultimate reality and the source of all creation, Wakan Tanka is called both Grandfather and Father. Grandfather refers to the divinity that is both unlimited and transcends all qualities, or opposites; Father refers to the spirit's manifestation as creator and within the creation, as the ever-present spirit of life, light, goodness, and mercy.

6. Black Elk, *The Sacred Pipe*, 7.

7. The Seven Sacred Rites of the Lakota are all based on visions: the Sweat Lodge, a place of renewal; Crying for a Vision, a spiritual discipline; Soul Keeping, a ceremony for the dead; the Sun Dance, an annual ceremony; Making Relatives, bonds of friendship; Puberty Ceremony for girls; and Throwing the Ball, a game of luck and good fortune.

8. See *August Comte and Positivism: The Essential Writings*, ed., Gertrud Lenzer (New Brunswick, N.J.: Transaction Publishers, 1998).

9. See *Basic Writings on Politics and Philosophy by Karl Marx and Friedrich Engels*, ed., Lewis S. Feuer (Garden City, N.Y.: Doubleday, 1959).

10. Eschatological teachings express views about the eschaton (Greek, "last"), which refers to the "end of time" or the "end of this age." Marxists—like Jews, Christians, and Muslims—look forward to a future age of peace and justice.

11. As early as 200 BCE, classical Roman writers used the term *superstitio* to condemn "irrational" forms of religion, such as divination and magic. Originally, the term was employed by the educated elite to condemn the religious customs of commoners and country folk. Later, during the period of empire, Romans might call any foreign religion a superstition: the religion of the Egyptians and also that of the Christians, for example.

12. E. B. Tylor, *Primitive Culture* (New York: Harper, 1958).

13. John Lubbock, *Origin of Civilization and the Primitive Condition of Man: Mental and Social Condition of Savages* (Chicago: University of Chicago Press, 1978).

14. Rudolf Otto, *The Idea of the Holy: An Inquiry into the Non-rational Factor in the Idea of the Divine and its Relation to the Rational* (New York: Oxford University Press, 1958).

15. Mircea Eliade, *The Sacred and the Profane: The Nature of Religion* (New York: Harcourt Brace Jovanovich, 1959).

16. Perhaps one way to think of "mythical beings" is to say that they are first known through revelation.

17. *The Classic of the Mountains and Seas*, trans., Anne Birrell (New York: Penguin, 1999), 24.

18. See further, Samuel Noah Kramer's *Sumerian Mythology: A Study of Spiritual and Literary Achievement in the Third Millennium B.C.* rev. ed. (Philadelphia: University of Pennsylvania Press, 1972).

19. G. M. Mullett, *Spider Woman Stories: Legends of the Hopis* (Tucson, Ariz.: University of Arizona Press, 1979), 1.

20. Knud Rasmussen, *Intellectual Culture of the Iglulik Eskimos*, trans., William Worster (Copenhagen: Gyldendal, 1930).

21. Karen McCarthy Brown, *Mama Lola: A Vodou Priestess in Brooklyn* (Berkeley: University of California Press, 1991), 223.

22. See Carolyne Larrington's recent translation of *The Poetic Edda* (New York: Oxford University Press, 1996). For discussions of the *Voluspa*, see E. O. G. Turville-Petre's *Myth and Religion of the North: The Religion of Ancient Scandinavia* (New York: Holt, Rinehart and Winston, 1964); and Hilda R. Ellis Davidson's *Gods and Myths of Northern Europe* (Baltimore: Penguin Books, 1964).

23. Laurens van der Post, *The Heart of the Hunter: Customs and Myths of the African Bushman* (New York: Harcourt Brace Jovanovich, 1961).

24. Revelation 12:3–9.

25. Following Hanyu Pinyin for transliteration.

26. *Dao De Jing*, I.25. D. C. Lau, trans., *Tao Te Ching: A Bilingual Edition* (Chinese University Press: Hong Kong, 2001), 37.

27. For the traditional account, see *Chinese Religions* by Julia Ching (New York: Orbis Books, 1993), 103 f.

28. "Popular Taoism at the End of the Han Dynasty," in *The Ch'in and Han Empires, 221 B.C.–A.D. 220*, vol. 1 of *The Cambridge History of China*, eds., Denis Twitchett and Michael Loewe (Cambridge, U.K.: Cambridge University Press, 1986), 818.

29. During the Six Dynasties Period and later, the movement was also known by its nickname, the Way of Five Bushels of Rice (referring to a tithe placed on members).

30. A good introduction to the life of Muhammad, founder of Islam, is Tor Andrae's *Mohammed: The Man and His Faith* (New York: Harper & Row, 1955).

31. The visions that make up the call of Muhammad to become a prophet are briefly described in the Qur'an (53:1–18).

32. See also the account of Muhammad's call by Muhammad ibn Jarir al-Tabari (838–923), translated by Arthur Jeffery in his *Islam, Muhammad and His Religion* (New York: Liberal Arts Press, 1958), 15–17.

33. Introductions to the life of Jesus of Nazareth include the following: Joachim Jeremias's *New Testament Theology: The Proclamation of Jesus*, trans., John Bowden (New York: Scribner's, 1971); Howard Clark Kee's *Jesus in History: An Approach to the Study of the Gospels*, 2d ed. (New York: Harcourt Brace Jovanovich, 1977); and A. E. Harvey's *Jesus and the Constraints of History* (Philadelphia: Westminster Press, 1982).

34. Accounts of the Easter revelation are found in the Christian New Testament as well as in non-canonical gospels: see, for example, the Gospel of Matthew 28; the Gospel of Mark 16; the Gospel of Luke 24; and the Gospel of John 20–21.

35. Acts of the Apostles 1:7.

36. There are many sacred biographies of the Buddha. One early resource is Ashvaghosha's *Buddhacharita*, partially translated in Edward Conze, *Buddhist Scriptures* (New York: Penguin, 1959). A scholarly overview of the many traditions about the life of the Buddha can be found in *The Life of Buddha as Legend and History*, by Edward J. Thomas (Mineola, N.Y.: Dover, 2000).

37. There are different opinions about the actual dates of the historical Buddha's life. The above dates are favored by scholars in Europe, the United States, and India.

38. Ashvaghosha *Buddhacharita* 12.4. Conze, *Buddhist Scriptures*, 51.

39. *Ibid.*, 13. Conze, *Buddhist Scriptures*, 53 f.

Chapter 2

1. He uses the Latin words *mysterium tremendum* to refer to a complex of feeling responses to revelation. See Otto, *The Idea of the Holy*, 12–40.

2. *Ibid.*, 16.

3. William James, *The Varieties of Religious Experience: A Study in Human Nature* (New York: New American Library, 1958), 64.

4. Eliade, *The Sacred and the Profane*, 28.

5. Akka means "elder sister." Mahadevi is simply Great Goddess. See further, T. N. Sreekantaiya's "Akka Mahadevi," in *Women Saints: East and West*, eds., Swami Ghananda and John Stewart-Wallace (Hollywood, CA: Vedanta Press, 1979), 30–40.

6. *Speaking of Siva*, trans., A. K. Ramanujan (New York: Penguin, 1973). 120.

7. Thérèse of Lisieux, *The Autobiography of Saint Thérèse of Lisieux: The Story of a Soul* (New York: Doubleday, 1989), 61.

8. *Black Elk Speaks: Being the Life Story of a Holy Man of the Sioux*, as told to John G. Neihardt (New York: Washington Square Press, 1959), 15.

9. *Ibid.*, 16.

10. *Ibid.*, 21.

11. *Ibid.*, 36.

12. Feraca, *Wakinyan*, 51 f.

13. *Ibid.*

14. The English word *myth* derives from the Greek *mythos*, which originally referred to both *word* and *story*. Gradually, it came to be associated particularly with the stories about the gods; and in this context, the philosophers reinterpreted the term to mean a story that has no objective truth. I am using the word *myth* for any sacred story, especially those tales that express religious revelation.

15. For general introductions to the theme of the creation myth (also called cosmogony), see Charles H. Long, *Alpha: The Myths of Creation* (New York: G. Braziller, 1963); and Barbara C. Sproul, *Primal Myths: Creating the*

World (San Francisco: Harper & Row, 1979).

16. E. S. Craighill Handy, "Polynesian Religion," *Bernice P. Bishop Museum Bulletin* 34 (1927), 11–12.

17. For example, small medallions (modeled originally on Roman amulets) have been found with runic inscriptions, such as "Luck for Alvin" or "I give luck." See H. R. Ellis Davidson, *Pagan Scandinavia* (New York: Frederick A. Praeger, 1967), 92.

18. Codex Regius. Found in 1643 in an Icelandic farmhouse, the *Poetic Edda* was probably written down about 1300, although the poems are much older.

19. *The Essential Rumi*, trans., Coleman Barks (San Francisco; HarperCollins, 1996), 16.

20. Rumi, *The Essential Rumi*, 132 f.

21. A gopi is a milkmaid, or cowherdess. The gopis were the playmates and devotees of Krishna, and they often serve as symbols for the soul's intense longing for God.

22. See further, Frédérique Apffell-Marglin, *Wives of the God-King: The Rituals of the Devadasis of Puri* (Delhi: Oxford University Press, 1985).

23. Location: no. 8564, Iraq Museum, Baghdad.

24. The term *idol* goes back to Greek *eidolon*, "image."

25. Leviticus 16:1 f.

26. Simone Gaulier and Robert Jera-Bezard, "Iconography: Buddhist Iconography," in *The Encyclopedia of Religion*, ed., Mircea Eliade (New York: Macmillan, 1987), 7:45–50.

27. A. L. Basham, "Asoka and Buddhism: A Reexamination," *Journal of the International Association of Buddhist Studies* 5 (1982): 131–143.

28. Located today in the archaeological Museum at Sarnath.

29. For an introduction to the relationship between revelation (hierophany) and the symbolic determination of sacred places and sacred times, see "Sacred Space and Making the World Sacred" plus "Sacred Time and Myths" in Eliade's *The Sacred and the Profane*, chapters 1 and 2.

30. Genesis 28:10–22.

31. Genesis 28:16 f.

32. The story of Timehin and Osun is found in Jacob K. Olupona's "Yoruba Goddesses and Sovereignty in Southwestern Nigeria," in *Goddesses Who Rule*, eds., Elisabeth Benard and Beverly Moon (New York: Oxford University Press, 2000), 127 f.

33. See Diana L. Eck, "Ganga: The Goddess in Hindu Sacred Geography," in *The Divine Consort: Radha and the Goddesses of India*, eds., John Stratton Hawley and Donna Marie Wulff (Boston: Beacon Press, 1982), 166–183.

34. C. A. Meier offers a good introduction to the ritual of incubation in his study of Asklepios, the Greek god of healing, *Ancient Incubation and Modern Psychotherapy* (Evanston, Ill.: Northwestern University Press, 1967).

35. An introduction to the symbolic meanings of festivals and holy days is found in "Sacred Time and Myths," in Eliade, *The Sacred and the Profane*, 68–113. Here, Eliade suggests that "for religious man time … is neither homogeneous nor continuous. On the one hand there are the intervals of a sacred time, the time of festivals (by far the greater part of which are periodical); on the other there is profane time, ordinary temporal duration, in which acts without religious meaning have their setting. Between these two kinds of time there is, of course, solution of continuity; but by means of rites religious man can pass without danger from ordinary temporal duration to sacred time" (68).

36. See J. B. Segal's *The Hebrew Passover from the Earliest Times to A.D. 70* (London: Oxford University Press, 1963).

37. He is sometimes called Warrior of Deep Dark Heaven.

38. Barbara E. Ward and Joan Law, *Chinese Festivals in Hong Kong* (Hong Kong: The Guidebook Company, 1993), 42.

Chapter 3

1. Thérèse of Lisieux, *The Autobiography of Saint Thérèse of Lisieux*, 46.

2. In the *Encyclopedia of Britannica*, a sacrifice is "a cultic act in which objects [are] set apart or consecrated and offered to a god or some other supernatural power" (1977, 16:128b).

3. For example, see the gold signet ring that depicts a "Goddess Presented with Offerings" (Athens, National Archaeological Museum: no. 6208).

4. For the description of the entire ritual, see Homer, *Odyssey* 11.18–20.

Notes — Chapter 3

5. Olupona, "Yoruba Goddesses and Sovereignty in Southwestern Nigeria," in *Goddesses Who Rule*, 130.
6. *Ibid.*, 119.
7. Carmen Blacker, *The Catalpa Bow: A Study of Shamanistic Practices in Japan* 2nd ed. (London: Umwin, 1986), 79 ff.
8. Deuteronomy 26:1–11.
9. Thomas J. Hopkins, "Puja" in *The Hindu Religious Tradition* (Encino, Calif.: Dickenson, 1971), 110.
10. Bartholomew P. M. Tsui, author of *Taoist Tradition and Change: The Story of the Complete Perfection Sect in Hong Kong* (Christian Study Centre on Chinese Religion and Culture: Hong Kong, 1991).
11. 2 Samuel 6:5.
12. Psalm 148:1–3.
13. Teresa of Avila, *The Life of Saint Teresa* (Baltimore: Penguin, 1958), 46.
14. Acts of the Apostles 3:8.
15. *Ibid.*, 4:24.
16. Matthew 6:9–13.
17. Muzammil H. Sidiqi, "Salat," in *The Encyclopedia of Religion*, 13:22.
18. 1 Timothy 4:7.
19. John Wesley, "On Conscience," 3.2.4.
20. Genesis 1:31.
21. Mark 12:29–31.
22. I am substituting here the Hanyu Pinyin transliteration for consistency.
23. From a commentary on the *Dao De Jing* attributed to Zhang Lu, and translated in John Lagerwey's "Taoism: The Taoist Religious Community," in *The Encyclopedia of Religion*, 14:307.
24. See, for example, Mircea Eliade's *Rites and Symbols of Initiation: The Mysteries of Birth and Rebirth* (New York: Harper & Row, 1965); and Bruce Lincoln's *Emerging from the Chrysalis: Studies in Rituals of Women's Initiation* (Cambridge, Mass.: Harvard University Press, 1981).
25. "It is always the shaman who conducts the dead person's soul to the underworld, for he is the psychopomp par excellence." See Mircea Eliade, *Shamanism: Archaic Techniques of Ecstasy* (New York: Bollingen Foundation, 1964), 182.
26. Originally, the term *fanya* referred only to the soul of the deceased, but eventually it came to be the name for the material vessel in which it was captured by the shaman.
27. Eliade, *Shamanism*, 211.
28. Romans 6:2–4.
29. For the entire myth, see W. Ramsay Smith's *Myths and Legends of the Australian Aboriginals* (London: G. G. Harrap & Company, 1970), 345–350.
30. Brown, *Mama Lola*, 327.
31. An introduction to the Jesus Prayer is found in *The Way of a Pilgrim*, which tells the story of a Russian peasant who seeks to "pray without ceasing." See translation by R. M. French (New York: Seabury, 1965). For a discussion of the Jesus Prayer, see Joseph Wong, "The Jesus Prayer and Inner Stillness," *Religion East and West* 5 (2005), 85–97.
32. Mark 1:6.
33. Matthew 5:44–48.
34. For his account of the pilgrimage, see the chapter "Mecca," in *The Autobiography of Malcolm X*, by Malcolm X and Alex Haley (New York: Ballantine, 1965).
35. See Blacker, *The Catalpa Bow*, 91.
36. For a personal account of Trappist life, see Thomas Merton's *The Seven Storey Mountain* (Garden City, N.Y.: Garden City Books, 1948).
37. For an introduction to contemporary Chinese retreat, see Bill Porter's *Road to Heaven: Encounters with Chinese Hermits* (San Francisco: Mercury House, 1993).
38. Black Elk, *The Sacred Pipe*, 44–66.
39. See Mircea Eliade, *The Forge and the Crucible: The Origins and Structures of Alchemy*, 2nd ed. (Chicago: University of Chicago Press, 1978); and also Nathan Sivin, *Chinese Alchemy: Preliminary Studies* (Cambridge, Mass.: Harvard University Press, 1968).
40. See Mircea Eliade, *Yoga: Immortality and Freedom* (New York: Pantheon Books, 1958).
41. See image #42 (and related discussion on page 168) in Heinrich Zimmer's *Myths and Symbols in Indian Art and Civilization* (New York: Pantheon, 1946).
42. *Katha Upanishad* 2.18.
43. See, for example, *The Yoga Sutras of Patanjali*, translation and commentary by Satchidananda (Yogaville, Va.: Integral Yoga Publications, 1990), II:29.
44. B. K. S. Iyengar with John J. Evans and Douglas Abrams, *Light on Life: The Yoga Journey to Wholeness, Inner Peace, and Ultimate Freedom* (New York: Rodale, 2005), 3.

45. Eastern Christians prefer the language of gradual deification (Greek, *theosis*) through communion with God's divine powers. The process will be complete, however, only at the end of time on the day of judgment.
46. Mark 14:22–25. (Matthew 26:20–29 and Luke 22:14–23)
47. Exodus 12:23.
48. The actual form of baptism varies from total immersion during adulthood to the sprinkling of water on the head during infancy. One rite emphasizes the conscious conversion of the initiate; the other emphasizes the redeeming power of the rite. Rarely is baptism ever repeated.
49. Mark 1:9–11.
50. See Romans 6–8.
51. Acts of the Apostles 8:14–17.
52. See 1 Corinthians 12:1 ff.
53. This practice continues today in the Roman Catholic, Greek Orthodox, Oriental Orthodox, and some Protestant churches. On the other hand, other Protestant churches, because they emphasize the authority of the Bible, limit the number of sacraments to the two that appear in the New Testament accounts of Jesus: Baptism and Eucharist. There are also a few Christian communities, such as the Quakers, for example, that do not have sacraments.
54. Tertullian, *De paenitentia* 4.1
55. Tertullian, *De resurrectione carnis* 8.

Chapter 4

1. Martin Buber, *A Believing Humanism: Gleanings* (New York: Simon & Schuster, 1969), 115.
2. *Ibid.*
3. *Ibid.*
4. *Ibid.*
5. For an introduction to Buber's thought, see Maurice S. Friedman's *Martin Buber: The Life of Dialogue*, 3rd ed. (Chicago: University of Chicago Press, 1976).
6. Martin Buber, *I and Thou* (New York: Scribner, 1970).
7. Buber, *A Believing Humanism*, 115.
8. Genesis 2:15 to 3:24.
9. *Ibid.*, 2:17 f.
10. *Ibid.*, 3:4 f.
11. *Ibid.*
12. *Ibid.*, 3:19.
13. Thus, we are not discussing here "philosophical doctrines of transcendence and metaphysical irreducibility, which are opposed to monistic or pantheistic doctrines of immanence." See Ugo Bianchi, "Dualism," *The Encyclopedia of Religion*, 4:506.
14. Maurice Friedman, *Martin Buber's Life and Work: The Later Years, 1945–1965* (Detroit: Wayne State University Press, 1988), 228.
15. *Sri Swami Satchidananda: Apostle of Peace* by Sita Bordow, et al. (Yogaville, Va.: Integral Yoga Publications, 1986), 350.
16. *Ibid.*, 319 f.
17. Vedanta also includes forms of thinking that some refer to as dualistic. One example is Sankhya (also Samkhya), a doctrine that posits two essentially different principles that underlie all of creation: Purusha (the conscious self) and Prakrti (nature). Nothing exists apart from these two principles. In this Hindu teaching attributed to the sage Kapila (dates unknown), there exist as many Purushas as there are living beings. Liberation from reincarnation is reached only by means of metaphysical knowledge, discriminating awareness that distinguishes the eternal self (pure consciousness) from the psycho-mental activity (belonging to Prakrti) that is often falsely believed to be the self.
18. Two examples of absolute monism in Western religion are found in the writings of Plotinus (204–270) and Baruch Spinoza (1632–1677).
19. *Brihadaranyaka Upanishad* 1.4.10.
20. *Shankara's Crest-Jewel of Discrimination, With a Garland of Questions and Answers*, trans., Prabhavanda and Christopher Isherwood (New York: New American Library, 1970), 75.
21. See Thomas J. Hopkins, "Sectarian Theism: Ramanuja and the Sri-Vaishnava Sect" in *The Hindu Religious Tradition* (Encino, Calif.: Dickenson Publishing Company, 1971), 121–124.
22. Bordow, et al., *Sri Swami Satchidananda*, 345.
23. *Ibid.*, 116.
24. In Hinduism, *sat-chid-ananda* refers to the three qualities of the divine — eternal being, consciousness, and bliss.
25. Bordow, et al., *Sri Swami Satchidananda*, 345.
26. In Hinduism, *swami* is a title of respect for a monk; in Judaism, *rabbi* is a title of respect for a religious leader or teacher.

Part Two

Chapter 5

1. Augustine of Hippo, *Confessions* 10.27.38.
2. *The Vimalakirti Sutra*, translated from the Chinese version by Burton Watson (New York: Columbia University Press, 1997), 112.
3. *Ibid.*, 116
4. *Ibid.*
5. *Ibid.*, 117.
6. Literally, "there is no end," "the endless," or "infinity."
7. *Zohar* 3:26b. Daniel C. Matt, *The Essential Kabbalah: The Heart of Jewish Mysticism* (San Francisco: HarperCollins, 1996), 54.
8. *Journey to the Underworld* (Taichung, Taiwan: Sheng Xian Magazine Association, n.d.), 1.
9. *Ibid.*, 198.
10. *Ibid.*, 199.
11. Sara Sviri, "Dreaming Analyzed and Recorded: Dreams in the World of Medieval Islam," in *Dream Cultures: Explorations in the Comparative History of Dreaming*, eds., David Shulman and Guy G. Stroumsa (New York: Oxford University Press, 1999), 261.
12. *Ibid.*, 267.
13. As per *Webster's Ninth New Collegiate Dictionary*.
14. Morton T. Kelsey, *God, Dreams, and Revelation: A Christian Interpretation of Dreams*, rev. ed. (Augsburg: Minneapolis, 1991), 32.
15. *Ibid.*, 33.
16. See also 1 Samuel 3:5; Isaiah 29:7; and Daniel 2:19, 7:2.
17. Kelsey, *God, Dreams, and Revelation*, 83.
18. *Ibid.*, 23.
19. *Lame Deer, Seeker of Visions: The Life of a Sioux Medicine Man*, by John (Fire) Lame Deer and Richard Erdoes (New York: Simon and Schuster, 1972). A separate account of the vision quest is found in the photographic essay *Lakota Healing: A Soul Comes Home* by Marco Ridomi with Laura Gaccione (Barrytown, N.Y.: Station Hill, 1999). Suffering depression and a life-threatening illness, Ridomi seeks the aid of Lakota healer Godfrey Chipps, who takes him to his home, Pine Ridge Reservation in South Dakota, for a succession of healing ceremonies. Chipps eventually informs him that the spirits want him to perform the Hanblecheyapi. Ridomi, who had been raised as a Roman Catholic Christian, has a vision of God's presence. The vision proves to be the beginning of a spiritual and physical healing: "I am grateful to the Chipps family for restoring this old-time Italian guy to his rightful relationship with the Creator, who is the same Presence that permeates the world in all faiths and is the source of all life and peace" (ibid., 35).
20. Knowing that his grandmother was willing to suffer pain in order to support him in his vision quest must surely have been a powerful comfort to the young boy all alone in the mountain pit.
21. Lame Deer, *Lame Deer, Seeker of Visions*, 15 f.
22. The Chinese character for Immortal unites that for person with that for mountain. In Daoist tradition, the mountains are often believed to be the ideal location for practicing the techniques that lead to immortality.
23. N. J. Girardot, "Hsien," in *The Encyclopedia of Religion*, 6:475–477. See further, *A Gallery of Chinese Immortals*, trans., Lionel Giles (London: J. Murray, 1948).
24. "The Dream of Lu Tung Pin," in *The Eight Immortals of Taoism: Legends and Fables of Popular Taoism*, trans., Kwok Man Ho and Joanne O'Brien (Penguin: New York, 1991), 72 f.
25. For the sake of consistency, Hanyu Pinyin transliteration *passim*.
26. For an introduction to the life and work of Paul of Tarsus, see Leander E. Keck's *Paul and His Letters* (Philadelphia: Fortress Press, 1979).
27. Acts of the Apostles 9:3–6.
28. For a general discussion of biblical prophecy — the foundation of later understandings of this religious type — see Johannes Lindblom's *Prophecy in Ancient Israel* (Philadelphia: Muhlenberg Press, 1962). For a study of individual prophets, see Klaus Koch's *The Prophets*, trans., Margaret Kohn (Philadelphia: Fortress Press, 1983–1984).
29. Jeremiah 20:9.
30. 1 Samuel 10:6.
31. *Ibid.*, 10:11.
32. See 1 Kings 18:46; 2 Kings 3:15; Jeremiah 15:17; and Ezekiel 1:3.
33. For the entire narrative, see 1 Kings 18:17–46.
34. One is a Jew if born of a Jewish mother or if one converts formally to Judaism. For

an introduction to Jewish history, see Raymond P. Scheindlin, *A Short History of the Jewish People from Legendary Times to Modern Statehood* (New York: Oxford University Press, 1998).

35. *Tanakh* is an acronym for the three parts that make up the Bible: the Torah (also called the Five Books of Moses), the Prophets, and the Hagiographa (or Sacred Writings). See Scheindlin, *A Short History of the Jewish People from Legendary Times to Modern Statehood*, 29.

36. Genesis 35:10.

37. Christians call the Jewish (or Hebrew) Bible their Old Testament; the Christian Bible consists of the Old Testament and the New Testament (early Christian texts written in Greek).

38. Some accounts name the mountain Horeb.

39. This name is based on four Hebrew letters, the so-called Tetragammaton, used to refer to God in the Jewish Bible. These letters are often transliterated as YHVH. German scholars are more likely to use a transliteration that corresponds to the sounds in the German alphabet: thus, JHWH (Jahweh).

40. Exodus 1:9–22.

41. Exodus 3:5 f.

42. Exodus 11:4 f.

43. Sometimes translated as Sea of Reeds.

44. Scholars refer to this early Israelite form of religion as henotheism rather than monotheism, which developed later. In henotheism, many gods and goddesses are thought to exist, but one worships only one. Jewish monotheism becomes a reality during the Babylonian Exile (sixth century before the Common Era).

45. Another name for the Five Books of Moses is Pentateuch (from Greek *pentateukhos*, "five books").

46. For an introduction to Islamic ideas about prophecy, see William A. Graham's *Divine Word and Prophetic Word in early Islam: A Reconsideration of the Sources, with special Reference to the Divine Saying or Hadith Qudsi* (The Hague: Mouton, 1977).

47. Karen Armstrong, *Islam: A Short History* (New York: Random House, 2002), 8.

48. Qur'an 33:40.

49. W. Montgomery Watt, "Muhammad," in *The Encyclopedia of Religion*, 10:144.

50. Armstrong, *Islam*, 11.

51. Recorded in the Qur'an (53:1–18).

52. See "Mohammed's Religious Message" in Andrae's *Mohammed*, 53–93.

53. *Ibid.*, 60.

54. See further, Kenneth Cragg, "Worship and Cultic Life: Muslim Worship," in *The Encyclopedia of Religion*, 15:454–463.

55. Armstrong, *Islam*, 13.

56. *Ibid.*, 23.

Chapter 6

1. Manabu Waida, "Jaguars," in *The Encyclopedia of Religion*, 7:506.

2. Jean Rhys Bram, "Sun," in *The Encyclopedia of Religion*, 14:133.

3. For more about Yoruba religious beliefs, see Robert Farris Thompson's *Black Gods and Kings: Yoruba Art at U.C.L.A.*, 2nd ed. (Bloomington: Indiana University Press, 1976).

4. Chinua Achebe, *Things Fall Apart* (New York: Doubleday, 1959), 61.

5. *Ibid.*, 148.

6. Philostratus, *The Life of Apollonios of Tyana* 4.45.

7. *Ibid.*, 1.6.

8. For the entire episode, see Matthew 12:22–28.

9. See Mark Caltonhill, *Private Prayers and Public Parades: Exploring the Religious Life of Taipei* (Taipei: Department of Information, Taipei City Government, 2002), 75–77.

10. Exodus 28:30.

11. Jonah 1:7.

12. Acts of the Apostles 1:26.

13. Lorenz Homberger, "Where the Mouse is Omniscient: The Mouse Oracle among the Guro and Baule," in *Insight and Artistry in African Divination: A Cross-Cultural Study*, ed., John Pemberton III (Washington, D.C.: Smithsonian Institution Press, 2000), 157–167. See also Alisa LaGamma, "Mouse Oracle," in *Art and Oracle: African Art and Rituals of Divination* (New York: Metropolitan Museum of Art, 2000), 40 f.

14. Traditionally, the bones of bats or birds were used; today, the diviner might substitute sticks covered with flour.

15. See further, Thorkild Jacobsen's *The Treasures of Darkness: A History of Mesopotamian Religion* (New Haven: Yale University Press, 1976).

16. Bartel L. Van der Waerden with Peter Huber, *The Birth of Astronomy*, vol. 2 of *Sci-*

ence Awakening (New York: Oxford University Press, 1974), 49.

17. See Samuel Noah Kramer, *The Sacred Marriage Rite: Aspects of Faith, Myth, and Ritual in Ancient Sumer* (Bloomington: Indiana University Press, 1969).

18. Kramer, *The Sacred Marriage Rite*, 64.

19. Kramer, *The Sacred Marriage Rite*, 83.

20. See further, Wilhelm Gundel, *Sternglaube, Sternreligion und Sternorakel: Aus der Geschichte der Astrologie*, 2nd ed. (Heidelberg: Quelle & Meyer, 1959).

21. For an introduction to Ifa divination and photographs of the ritual tools employed by the babalawo, see John Pemberton III, "Divination in Sub-Saharan Africa," in LaGamma, *Art and Oracle*, 17 f.

22. Wande Abimbola, a babalawo and former vice chancellor of the University of Ife, has written extensively about the training of Yoruba diviners. See, for example, his *Ifa Divination Poetry* (New York: Nok Publications, 1977).

23. *The Sacred Ifa Oracle*, translation and commentary by Afolabi A. Epega and Philip John Neimark (San Francisco: HarperCollins, 1995), 379.

24. Through transliteration using the Roman alphabet.

25. Mark Caltonhill, *Private Prayers and Public Parades*, 77.

26. See "Discovery of Oracle Bone Inscriptions," in Hsu Ya-Hwei, *Ancient Chinese Writing: Oracle Bone Inscriptions from the Ruins of Yin*, trans., Mark Caltonhill and Jeffrey Moser (Taipei: National Palace Museum, 2002), 4–7.

27. Hsu Ya-Hwei, *Ancient Chinese Writing*, 29.

28. *Ibid.*

29. Indecipherable ancient Chinese character.

30. "Good Wife." This Good Wife possibly refers to a concubine of the Shang king Wu Ding. She was famous because according to tradition, she had been a successful general, who had won many battles. *Ibid.*, 52.

31. Unpublished brochure entitled "Ancient Writing from the Ruins of Yin: Special Exhibition of Oracle Bone Inscriptions from the Institute of History and Philology, Academia Sinica," (Taipei: National Palace Museum, 2001/2002).

32. Michael Loewe, "The Religious and Intellectual Background," in *The Ch'in and Han Empires, 221 B.C.–A.D. 220*, 675 f.

33. *The I Ching, or Book of Changes*, Richard Wilhelm's translation rendered into English by Cary F. Baynes (Princeton: Princeton University Press, 1950), 4, 6.

34. *Ibid.*, 6 f.

35. *Book of Songs* 3.3.2.8.

36. *Ibid.*, 3.3.2.12.

37. *Ibid.*, 3.3.3.7.

38. See further, Chang Kwang-chih, *Art, Myth, and Ritual: The Path to Political Authority in Ancient China* (Cambridge, Mass.: Harvard University Press, 1983).

39. Robert P. Kramers, "The Development of the Confucian Schools," in *The Ch'in and Han Empires, 221 B.C.–A.D. 220*, 749.

40. Hans Bielenstein, "Wang Mang. the Restoration of the Han Dynasty, and Later Han," in *The Ch'in and Han Empires, 221 B.C.–A.D. 220*, 255 f.

41. Hilda Hookham, *A Short History of China* (New York: New American Library, 1972), 38.

Chapter 7

1. Waldemar Jochelson, *The Yukaghir and the Yukaghirized Tungus* (Leiden: E. J. Brill, 1919–1926), 13:196–199.

2. 2 Corinthians 12:2–4.

3. Julio Cezar Melatti, "Myth and Shaman," in *Native South Americans: Ethnology of the Least Known Continent*, ed., Patricia J. Lyon (Boston: Little Brown, 1974), 275.

4. The word *shaman* has been used to refer to spirit travelers in various societies around the globe: for example, see Eliade, *Shamanism*; and John A. Grim, *The Shaman: Patterns of Siberian and Ojibway Healing* (Norman, Okla.: University of Oklahoma Press, 1983). Concerns about the definition and application of the term are expressed by Alice Beck Kehoe in her *Shamans and Religion: An Anthropological Exploration in Critical Thinking* (Long Grove, Illinois: Waveland, 2000).

5. Anna-Leena Siikala, "Shamanism: Siberian and Inner Asian Shamanism," in *The Encyclopedia of Religion*, 13:209.

6. *Ibid.*, 13:214.

7. *Ibid.*, 13:212.

8. Eliade, *Shamanism*, 41 f.

9. Jochelson, *The Yukaghir and the Yukaghirized Tungus*, 13:210 f.

10. *Spae* means "to divine."
11. *Flateyjarbok*, I:346.
12. Jan de Vries, *Altgermanische Religionsgeschichte*, 2nd ed. (Berlin: W. De Gruyter, 1956–1957), I:330 ff.
13. *Eiriks Saga Rauda*, 4.
14. *Voluspa* 61–63.
15. Lawrence E. Sullivan, *Icanchu's Drum: An Orientation to Meaning in South American Religions* (New York: Macmillan, 1988), 426 ff.
16. Sullivan, *Icanchu's Drum*, 428: translating text found in Curt Nimuendajú, "Die Sagen von der Erschaffung und Vernichtung der Welt als Grundlagen der Religion der Apapocuva-Guarani," in *Mitos de Creación y de Destrucción del Mundo como Fundamentos de la Religión de los Apapokuva-Guaraní* (Lima: Centro Amazónico de Antropología y Aplicación Práctica, 1978), 99.
17. *Ibid.*, 439: translating text found in Marc de Civrieux, *Religión y Magia Kari'ña* (Caracas: Universidad Católica, 1974), 135.
18. Joan Halifax, *Shamanic Voices: A Survey of Visionary Narratives* (New York: Penguin, 1979), 143. Quoted from the story of Manuel Córdova-Rios as presented in Bruce T. Lamb, *Wizard of the Upper Amazon*, 2nd ed. (Boston: Houghton Mifflin, 1975), 86–97.
19. Sullivan, *Icanchu's Drum*, 424–425.
20. Halifax, *Shamanic Voices*, 147.
21. Ioan P. Culianu discusses the theme in a variety of cultural settings in his *Out of this World: Otherworldly Journeys from Gilgamesh to Albert Einstein* (Boston: Shambhala, 1991).
22. Nous.
23. Philo of Alexandria, "Sober Intoxication," in *Philo of Alexandria: The Contemplative Life, the Giants, and Selections* (New York: Paulist Press, 191), 173.
24. For text and discussion, see Hans Jonas, *The Gnostic Religion*, 2nd rev. ed. (Boston: Beacon Press, 1963), 147–173.
25. Culianu, *Out of this World*, 220.
26. See Geo Widengren, *Muhammad, the Apostle of God, and His Ascension* (Uppsala: Lundequista, 1955).
27. Psyche.
28. Pneuma.
29. For studies of early Christian interpretations of the resurrection, see Jürgen Becker, *Auferstehung der Toten im Urchristentum* (Stuttgart: Verlag Katholisches Bibelwerk, 1976); Henry Chadwick, "Origen, Celsus, and the Resurrection of the Body," *Harvard Theological Review*, 41 (1948): 83–102; and Hans-Martin Schenke, "Auferstehungsglaube und Gnosis," *Zeitschrift für die neutestamentliche Wissenschaft und die Kunde der älteren Kirche*, 59 (1968): 123–126.
30. *Gospel of Thomas*, logion 56.
31. Similarly, in a play on words, Plato (c. 428–348/7 BCE) referred to the body (*soma*) as the tomb (*sema*) of the soul. See *Cratylus* (400 C).
32. For the history of the Nag Hammadi library, see James M. Robinson, *Nag Hammadi: The First Fifty Years* (Claremont, Ca.,: Institute for Antiquity and Christianity, 1995).
33. *Exegesis on the Soul*, 134.6–15.
34. The inclusion of Christian writings in the text suggests that the savior is Christ; see *Exegesis on the Soul*, 134.26–135.4.
35. From the song cycle entitled *The Nine Songs*, trans., Deborah Sommer, *Chinese Religion: An Anthology of Sources* (New York: Oxford University Press, 1995), 90. See further, Arthur Waley, *The Nine Songs: A Study of Shamanism in Ancient China* (London: G. Allen and Unwin, 1955).
36. Sommer, *Chinese Religion*, 91–94.
37. See further, Vincent Shih, *The Taiping Ideology: Its Sources, Interpretations, and Influences* (Seattle: University of Washington Press, 1967).
38. Often referred to as Liang Afa.
39. Jonathan D. Spence, *God's Chinese Son: The Taiping Heavenly Kingdom of Hong Xiuquan* (New York: W. W. Norton, 1996), 47.
40. This is actually the second Taiping revolt. The first took place in the second century CE, when a Daoist group similar to that of Celestial Master Daoism tried to overthrow the Han Dynasty. Hong's movement has symbolic affinities to both the earlier Daoist rebellion and to Christian apocalypticism.
41. Spence, *God's Chinese Son*, xxi.
42. *Ibid.*, 325.

Chapter 8

1. Anthony C. Yu, trans., *The Journey to the West*, 4 vols. (Chicago: University of Chicago Press, 1977–1983).
2. Luke 10:19. See further, Dennis Cov-

Notes — Chapter 8

ington, *Salvation on Sand Mountain: Snake Handling and Redemption in Southern Appalachia* (New York: Penguin, 1995).

3. Ericka Bourguignon, "The Self, the Behavioral Environment, and the Theory of Spirit Possession," in *Context and Meaning in Cultural Anthropology*, ed., Melford E. Spiro (New York: Free Press, 1965), 39–60.

4. Blacker, *The Catalpa Bow*, 51–68.

5. *Ibid.*, 51.

6. Literary examples of the transfer of a harmful spirit to a trained medium in Japanese exorcisms are found in the famous *Tale of Genji* by Murasaki Shikibu, a lady of the court living in the eleventh century, and in *The Pillow Book* of Sei Shonagon, from the same period.

7. Sommer, *Chinese Religion*, 35–37.

8. Hugh G. Evelyn-White, trans., *Hesiod, the Homeric Hymns, and Homerica* (New York: Macmillan, 1914), 337 ff.

9. See further, H. W. Parke and D. E. W. Wormell, *The Delphic Oracle*, 2 vols. (Oxford: Blackwell, 1956).

10. Plato, *Apology* 5.21.

11. The male medium is called an *oungan*.

12. *Lwa* is a Yoruba word that refers to a spirit, a saint, a mystery, or even an angel.

13. Brown, *Mama Lola*, 61.

14. In other places in the Americas similar traditions combining African and Christian components continue to thrive, for example, Cuba's Santería and Candomblé in Brazil.

15. For a history of Haiti, see James G. Leyburn's *The Haitian People*, rev. ed. (New Haven: Yale University Press, 1966).

16. Karen McCarthy Brown, "Voodoo," in *The Encyclopedia of Religion*, 15:298.

17. See further, Benjamin C. Ray, *African Religions: Symbol, Ritual, and Community* (Englewood Cliffs, N.J.: Prentice Hall, 1976).

18. A third category of spirit important in Haitian thought is that of the Divine Twins (*lemarasa*).

19. Another source of information about individual Vodou saints is found in Maya Deren's *Divine Horsemen: The Living Gods of Haiti* (New York: McPherson & Co., 1970).

20. *Ibid.*, 114 f.

21. Maria Dolorosa, Mater Salvatoris, and Nuestra Señora de la Caridad dell Cobre. Brown, *Mama Lola*, 221.

22. *Ibid.*, 220–257.

23. For a general introduction to the history of early Christianity, see Henry Chadwick, *The Early Church* (New York: Penguin, 1967).

24. John 11.

25. Mark 1:15.

26. *Ibid.*, 10:23.

27. *Ibid.*, 10:27.

28. *Ibid.*, 10:15.

29. *Ibid.*, 15:18.

30. The Hebrew term *masiah* has its roots in the political history of Israel. Literally, the word means "the anointed one" and it refers to the king, who was anointed during ritual coronation. *Christos* is the Greek word for "anointed."

31. *Gospel* was originally an Old English word that combined *god* ("good") and *spel* ("news").

32. Pentecost refers to the fiftieth day: Jewish Pentecost is fifty days after the Passover Feast; Christian Pentecost is celebrated fifty days after Easter.

33. Acts of the Apostles 2:1–4.

34. Mark 1:10 (Matthew 3:16; Luke 3: 22; and John 1:32).

35. Acts of the Apostles 8:17.

36. Romans 8:14.

37. "The Doctrine of the Trinity," in Otto W. Heick, *A History of Christian Thought*, rev. ed. (Philadelphia: Fortress Press, 1965), 1:143–169.

38. Cappadocia refers to an inland province in Asia Minor (modern Turkey).

39. Karen Armstrong, *A History of God: The 4000-Year Quest of Judaism, Christianity, and Islam* (New York: Ballantine Books, 1993), 117.

40. *Ibid.*, 118.

41. Macrina Wiederkehr, *A Tree Full of Angels: Seeing the Holy in the Ordinary* (New York: HarperCollins, 1995), 24.

42. Acts of the Apostles 9.

43. *Ibid.*, 15:1.

44. *Ibid.*, 15:8–11.

45. My emphasis.

46. *Ibid.*, 15:28 ff.

47. Andrew Reed, "Spirit Divine, Attend Our Prayers," in *Pilgrim Hymnal* (Boston: Pilgrim Press, 1967), hymn 241.

48. Buddhism and Shinto co-exist harmoniously in the lives of the people of Japan.

49. In Tenrikyo, God is also called Oyagami, or God the Parent; likewise, his me-

dium, Nakayama Miki, is often referred to as Oyasama, "honored parent."
50. *The Teachings and History of Tenrikyo*, ed., Translation Section of Tenrikyo Overseas Mission Department (Tenri: Tenrikyo Overseas Mission Department, 1986), 71.
51. *Ibid.*, 72.
52. *Ibid.*, 73.
53. *Ibid.*, 23.
54. Her role as medium then fell to her successor, Iburi Izo (1833–1907). Further revelations were made through him, including a collection of texts known as *Divine Directions* (Osashizu), a large collection of prophecies concerned with salvation as well as individual responses to specific questions concerning problems in daily living.
55. See further, H. J. J. M. van Straelen, *The Religion of Divine Wisdom: Japan's Most Powerful Religious Movement* (Tokyo: Veritas Shoin, 1957).

Chapter 9

1. See, for example, Perle Epstein, *Kabbalah: The Way of the Jewish Mystic* (Boston: Shambhala, 1988).
2. See Livia Kohn, *Early Chinese Mysticism: Philosophy and Soteriology in the Taoist Tradition* (Princeton: Princeton University Press, 1992).
3. *Maitri Upanishad* 6.24. Juan Mascaró, trans., *The Upanishads* (New York: Penguin, 1965), 103.
4. Satchidananda, trans., *The Yoga Sutras of Patanjali*, 64.
5. There are different levels of samadhi, the final one (*nirbija samadhi*) resulting in total liberation.
6. *Dhammapada*, 90. Juan Mascaró, *The Dhammapada* (New York: Penguin, 1973), 48.
7. An introduction to her life is found in John Beevers, *Saint Teresa of Avila* (Garden City, N.Y.: Hanover House, 1961).
8. Teresa of Avila, *The Collected Works of St. Teresa of Avila*, 3 vols. (Washington, D.C.: Institute of Carmelite Studies, 1976, 1980, 1985), 1:411.
9. *Ibid.*, 1:410.
10. Rumi, *The Essential Rumi*, 3. See further, Annemarie Schimmel, *Rumi's World: The Life and Work of the Great Sufi Poet* (Boston: Shambhala, 2001).
11. Aurelius, *The Meditations of Marcus Aurelius*, xxii.
12. *Ibid.*, 2.13.
13. *Ibid.*, 9.7.
14. *Ibid.*, 4.3.
15. *Ibid.*, 3.13.
16. Teresa of Avila, *The Collected Works of St. Teresa of Avila*, 1:398.
17. James, *The Varieties of Religious Experience*, 292–294.
18. R. M. Bucke, *Cosmic Consciousness: A Study in the Evolution of the Human Mind* (Philadelphia: Innes and Sons, 1901), 7 f. Quoted in James, *The Varieties of Religious Experience*, 306–307.
19. My emphasis here and throughout quotation.
20. This has caused some scholars, such as R. C. Zaehner, to define "nature mysticism" as a particular (perhaps lesser) form of mysticism. Otto would disagree and shows that the felt "location" of the experience can vary rather widely without altering our understanding that mysticism is basically one type of revelation.
21. See Rudolf Otto, *Mysticism East and West: A Comparative Analysis of the Nature of Mysticism* (New York: Macmillan, 1963).
22. Teresa of Avila, *The Collected Works of St. Teresa of Avila*, 3:385.
23. Aurelius, *The Meditations of Marcus Aurelius*, 7.59.
24. Jiddu Krishnamurti, *Krishnamurti's Notebook* (HarperCollins: San Francisco, 1976), 215.
25. *Shvetashvatara Upanishad* 4.16. Mascaró, *The Upanishads*, 92.
26. *Shvetashvatara Upanishad* 4.10. *Ibid.*
27. *Shvetashvatara Upanishad* 5.13. Mascaró, *The Upanishads*, 86.
28. *Gospel of Thomas* logion 40.
29. Evelyn Underhill, *Mysticism: A Study in the Nature and Development of Man's Spiritual Consciousness* 12th ed. (New York: New American Library, 1974).
30. Rumi, *The Essential Rumi*, 179–180.
31. See further, Bernard McGinn, "The Language of Love in Christian and Jewish Mysticism," in *Mysticism and Language*, ed., Steven T. Katz (New York: Oxford University Press, 1992), 202–235.
32. The Latin name for soul is also a feminine noun: *anima*.
33. Teresa of Avila, *The Collected Works of St. Teresa of Avila*, 3:380.
34. *Ibid.*, 3:407.

35. Rumi, *The Essential Rumi*, 137.
36. *Ibid.*, 191.
37. Gnostic Christians, on the other hand, used drunkenness as one of the symbols for ordinary consciousness and sobriety for the state of one who had attained mystical union. See Jonas, "Numbness, Sleep, Intoxication," in *The Gnostic Religion*, 68–73.
38. Hafiz Shirazi, *Drunk on the Wine of the Beloved*, trans., Thomas Rain Crowe (Boston: Shambhala, 2001), 27.
39. Anne Waldman and Andrew Schelling, eds., *Song of the Sons and Daughters of the Buddha* (Boston: Shambhala, 1996), 45.
40. Ashvaghosha, *Buddhacarita*, 4. Conze, *Buddhist Scriptures*, 39.
41. *Ibid.*
42. *Ibid.* Conze, *Buddhist Scriptures*, 40.
43. *Ibid.*, 7. Conze, *Buddhist Scriptures*, 43.
44. *Ibid.*, 9. Conze, *Buddhist Scriptures*, 45.
45. *Ibid.*, 11. Conze, *Buddhist Scriptures*, 49.
46. *Dhammacakkappavattana Sutta* 5. 420–24. Bhikkhu Bodhi, ed., *In the Buddha's Words: An Anthology of Discourses from the Pali Canon* (Boston: Wisdom Publications, 2005), 75–78.
47. Samuel Bercholz and Sherab Chödzin Kohn, eds., *Entering the Stream: An Introduction to the Buddha and His Teachings* (Boston: Shambhala,1993), 57.
48. See further, Bhikkhu Bodhi, *The Noble Eightfold Path: The Way to the End of Suffering* (Onalaska, Wa.: Pariyatti, 2000).

Chapter 10

1. See, for example, D. P. Silverman, "The Nature of Egyptian Kingship," in *Ancient Egyptian Kingship*, eds., D. O'Connor and D. P. Silverman (Leiden: E. J. Brill, 1995), 49–92.
2. The Latin *carne* translates the Greek *sarx*: flesh, physical body, human nature, etc.
3. For a succinct but thorough introduction to Tibetan Buddhism, see Tenzin Gyatso, the Fourteenth Dalai Lama, *Opening the Eye of Awareness*, trans., Donald S. Lopez, Jr., with Jeffrey Hopkins (London: Wisdom, 1985).
4. Reginald A. Ray, "Rebirth in the Buddhist Tradition," in *Entering the Stream: An Introduction to the Buddha and His Teachings*, eds., Samuel Bercholz and Sherab Chödzin Kohn (Boston: Shambhala, 1993), 309.

5. Sometimes referred to as Hinayana Buddhism.
6. The transcendent buddhas include Amitabha (Boundless Light), Akshobhya (Immovable), Vairochana (He Who is Like the Sun), Ratnasambhava (Jewel-born One), and Vajrasattva (Diamond Being).
7. Achala-bhumi, the Immovable Land.
8. Robert A. F. Thurman, trans., *The Tibetan Book of the Dead: Liberation Through Understanding in the Between* (New York: Bantam Books, 1994), plate 4.
9. Tibetan, *Spyan-ras-gzigs*. In Chinese Buddhism, the Bodhisattva of Compassion underwent a transformation that resulted in the feminine figure known as Guan Yin. See Yü Chün-fang, *Kuan-Yin: The Chinese Transformation of Avalokitesvara* (New York: Columbia University Press, 2001).
10. For a history of the first thirteen Dalai Lamas, see Günther Schulemann's *Die Geschichte der Dalailamas* (Heidelberg: C. Winter, 1911).
11. The second staff had belonged to the thirteenth Dalai Lama.
12. Diki Tsering, *Dalai Lama, My Son: A Mother's Story* (New York: Penguin, 2000), 91.
13. Tenzin Gyatso, the Fourteenth Dalai Lama, *My Land and My People: The Original Autobiography of His Holiness the Dalai Lama of Tibet* (New York: Warner Books, 1997) and also *Freedom in Exile: The Autobiography of the Dalai Lama* (New York: HarperPerennial, 1991),
14. Tenzin Gyatso, *Freedom in Exile*, 270.
15. Khyongla Rato, *My Life and Lives: The Story of a Tibetan Incarnation*, 2nd ed. (New York: Rato Publications, 1991).
16. *Ibid.*, 21.
17. *Ibid.*
18. *Ibid.*
19. See Heinrich Zimmer's *Myths and Symbols in Indian Art and Civilization*, (New York: Harper & Row, 1962), 3–11.
20. Adilakshmi, *The Mother* (Dornburg-Thalheim, Germany: n.p., 1995), 9.
21. See further, Beatrice Bruteau's *Worthy Is the World: The Hindu Philosophy of Sri Aurobindo* (Rutherford, N.J.: Fairleigh Dickinson University Press, 1971).
22. Adilakshmi, *The Mother*, 12.
23. *Ibid.*, 4.
24. *Bhagavad Gita* 4.7–8. Franklin Edger-

ton, trans., *The Bhagavad Gita* (Cambridge, Mass.: Harvard University Press, 1974), 23.

25. Wendy Doniger O'Flaherty, *Hindu Myths* (New York: Penguin, 1975), 220.

26. *Ibid.*, 221.

27. *Bhagavad Gita* 18.64–65. Edgerton, *The Bhagavad Gita*, 90.

28. See J. N. D. Kelly, *Early Christian Creeds*, 2nd ed. (New York: Harper & Row, 1960).

29. Philippians 2:6–11.

30. John 1.1, 1.14.

31. See Adolf Harnack, *The Mission and Expansion of Christianity in the First Three Centuries* (Gloucester, Mass.: Peter Smith, 1972).

32. Ste. Croix, G. E. M. de, "Why Were the Early Christians Persecuted?" *Past and Present* 26 (November 1963), 6–38.

33. See Hermann Dörries, *Constantine the Great* (New York: Harper & Row, 1972).

34. See Heick, *A History of Christian Thought*, 1:154–159.

35. Nestorius was exiled to live in the Egyptian desert; his followers continued to thrive and expanded eastward into India, Central Asia, and China (arriving in China as early as 636). Geoffrey Parrinder, ed., *World Religions: From Ancient History to the Present* (New York: Facts on File, 1985), 431.

36. The churches that reject the Chalcedonian Christology insist that Jesus the Christ has one nature only (wholly divine). This is called monophysitism, "the idea of one nature only." Monophysite communities separated from the other Christian churches and continue to exist in Egypt, Ethiopia, Armenia, Syria, and elsewhere. See further, W. H. C. Frend, *The Rise of the Monophysite Movement: Chapters in the History of the Church in the Fifth and Sixth Centuries* (Cambridge: Cambridge University Press, 1972).

37. Mark 10:45.

38. The Son of Man will share his power with the saints, according to Daniel 7:27.

39. Matthew 26:28.

40. John 1:29.

41. 1 Corinthians 15:21 f.

42. Romans 8:21.

43. Gustaf Aulén, *Christus Victor: An Historical Study of the Three Main Types of the Idea of Atonement* (London: Society for Promoting Christian Knowledge, 1931).

44. Hebrews 10:10.

Select Bibliography

Primary Sources in English Translation

Birrell, Anne, trans. *The Classic of the Mountains and Seas*. New York: Penguin, 1999.
Black Elk. *Black Elk Speaks: Being the Life Story of a Holy Man of the Sioux*. With John G. Neihardt. New York: Washington Square Press, 1959.
_____. *The Sacred Pipe: Black Elk's Account of the Seven Rites of the Sioux*. Ed., Joseph Epes Brown. New York: Penguin, 1971.
Conze, Edward, trans. *Buddhist Scriptures*. New York: Penguin, 1959.
Deloria, Ella C., comp. *Dakota Texts*. Vermillion, S.D.: Dakota Press, 1978.
Doniger O'Flaherty, Wendy, trans. *Hindu Myths*. New York: Penguin, 1975.
_____. *The Rig Veda: An Anthology*. New York: Penguin, 1981.
Edgerton, Franklin, trans. *The Bhagavad Gita*. Cambridge, Mass.: Harvard University Press, 1974.
Hume, Robert Ernest, trans. *The Thirteen Principal Upanishads Translated from the Sanskrit with an Outline of the Philosophy of the Upanishads*. Rev. ed. New York: Oxford University Press, 1971.
The I Ching, or Book of Changes. Richard Wilhelm's trans. rendered into English by Cary F. Baynes. Princeton: Princeton University Press, 1950.
Khalidi, Tarif, trans. *The Qur'an*. New York: Penguin, 2008.
Khyongla Rato. *My Life and Lives: The Story of a Tibetan Incarnation*. 2nd ed. New York: Rato, 1991.
Krishnamurti, Jiddu. *Krishnamurti's Notebook*. San Francisco: HarperCollins, 1976.
Larrington, Carolyne, trans. *The Poetic Edda*. New York: Oxford University Press, 1996.
Lau, D. C., trans. *Lao Tzu: Tao Te Ching*. New York: Penguin Books, 1963.
Long, Charles. *Alpha: The Myths of Creation*. New York: G. Braziller, 1963.
Malcolm X. *The Autobiography of Malcolm X*. With Alex Haley. New York: Ballantine, 1965.
Marcus Aurelius. *The Meditations of the Emperor Marcus Aurelius Antoninus*. Trans., George Long (1873). Garden City, N.Y.: Doubleday, n.d.
Mascaró, Juan, trans. *The Dhammapada: The Path of Perfection*. New York: Penguin, 1973.
Matt, Daniel C. *The Essential Kabbalah: The Heart of Jewish Mysticism*. San Francisco: HarperCollins, 1996.
Merton, Thomas. *The Seven Storey Mountain*. Garden City, N.Y.: Garden City Books, 1948.

Mullett, G. M. *Spider Woman Stories: Legends of the Hopis.* Tucson: University of Arizona Press, 1979.
The New English Bible with the Apocrypha: Oxford Study Edition. New York: Oxford University Press, 1976.
Philo Judaeus. *Philo of Alexandria: The Contemplative Life, the Giants, and Selections.* New York: Paulist Press, 191.
Rumi, Jalal al-Din. *The Essential Rumi.* Trans., Coleman Barks. San Francisco: HarperCollins, 1996.
The Sacred Ifa Oracle. Trans., Afolabi A. Epega and Philip John Neimark. San Francisco: HarperCollins, 1995.
Satchidananda, trans. *The Yoga Sutras of Patanjali.* Yogaville, Va.: Integral Yoga Publications, 1990.
Smith, W. Ramsay. *Myths and Legends of the Australian Aboriginals.* London: G. G. Harrap, 1970.
Sommer, Deborah, ed. *Chinese Religion: An Anthology of Sources.* New York: Oxford University Press, 1995.
Sproul, Barbara C. *Primal Myths: Creating the World.* San Francisco: Harper & Row, 1979.
Tenzin Gyatso, the Fourteenth Dalai Lama. *Freedom in Exile: The Autobiography of the Dalai Lama.* New York: HarperPerennial, 1991.
———. *My Land and My People: The Original Autobiography of His Holiness the Dalai Lama of Tibet.* New York: Warner Books, 1997.
Teresa of Avila. *The Collected Works of St. Teresa of Avila.* 3 vols. Washington, D.C.: Institute of Carmelite Studies, 1976, 1980, 1985.
Thérèse of Lisieux. *The Autobiography of Saint Thérèse of Lisieux: The Story of a Soul.* New York: Doubleday, 1989.
Thurman, Robert A. F., trans. *The Tibetan Book of the Dead: Liberation through Understanding in the Between.* New York: Bantam, 1994.
Waldman, Anne, and Andrew Schelling, eds. *Songs of the Sons and Daughters of the Buddha.* Boston: Shambhala, 1996.
Watson, Burton, trans. *The Vimalakirti Sutra.* New York: Columbia University Press, 1997.

Secondary Sources

Andrae, Tor. *Mohammed: The Man and His Faith.* New York: Harper & Row, 1955.
Bhikkhu Bodhi. *The Noble Eightfold Path: The Way to the End of Suffering.* Onalaska, Wa.: Pariyatti, 2000.
Brown, Karen McCarthy. *Mama Lola: A Vodou Priestess in Brooklyn.* Berkeley: University of California Press, 1991.
Caltonhill, Mark. *Private Prayers and Public Parades: Exploring the Religious Life of Taipei.* Taipei: Department of Information, Taipei City Government, 2002.
Chang Kwang-chih. *Art, Myth, and Ritual: The Path to Political Authority in Ancient China.* Cambridge, Mass.: Harvard University Press, 1983.
Culianu, Ioan P. *Out of this World: Otherworldly Journeys from Gilgamesh to Albert Einstein.* Boston: Shambhala, 1991.
Davidson, Hilda R. Ellis. *Gods and Myths of Northern Europe.* Baltimore: Penguin, 1964.

Select Bibliography

Eliade, Mircea. *Rites and Symbols of Initiation: The Mysteries of Birth and Rebirth.* New York: Harper & Row, 1965.

———. *The Sacred and the Profane: The Nature of Religion.* New York: Harcourt Brace Jovanovich, 1959.

Feraca, Stephen E. *Wakinyan: Lakota Religion in the Twentieth Century.* Lincoln: University of Nebraska Press, 1998.

Grim, John A. *The Shaman: Patterns of Siberian and Ojibway Healing.* Norman: University of Oklahoma Press, 1983.

James, William. *The Varieties of Religious Experience: A Study in Human Nature.* New York: New American Library, 1958.

Jochelson, Waldemar. *The Yukaghir and the Yukaghirized Tungus.* Leiden: E. J. Brill, 1919–1926.

Jonas, Hans. *The Gnostic Religion*, 2nd rev. ed. Boston: Beacon, 1963.

Kee, Howard Clark. *Jesus in History: An Approach to the Study of the Gospels.* 2d ed. New York: Harcourt Brace Jovanovich, 1977.

Kelsey, Morton T. *God, Dreams, and Revelation: A Christian Interpretation of Dreams.* Rev. ed. Minneapolis: Augsburg, 1991.

Kramer, Samuel Noah. *The Sacred Marriage Rite: Aspects of Faith, Myth, and Ritual in Ancient Sumer.* Bloomington: Indiana University Press, 1969.

———. *Sumerian Mythology: A Study of Spiritual and Literary Achievement in the Third Millennium B.C.* Rev. ed. Philadelphia: University of Pennsylvania Press, 1972.

Lincoln, Bruce. *Emerging from the Chrysalis: Studies in Rituals of Women's Initiation.* Cambridge, Mass.: Harvard University Press, 1981.

Otto, Rudolf. *The Idea of the Holy: An Inquiry into the Non-rational Factor in the Idea of the Divine and its Relation to the Rational.* New York: Oxford University Press, 1958.

———. *Mysticism East and West: A Comparative Analysis of the Nature of Mysticism.* New York: Macmillan, 1963.

Porter, Bill. *Road to Heaven: Encounters with Chinese Hermits.* San Francisco: Mercury House, 1993.

Powers, William K. *Oglala Religion.* Lincoln: University of Nebraska Press, 1977.

Schimmel, Annemarie. *Rumi's World: The Life and Work of the Great Sufi Poet.* Boston: Shambhala, 2001.

Spence, Jonathan D. *God's Chinese Son: The Taiping Heavenly Kingdom of Hong Xiuquan.* New York: W. W. Norton, 1996.

Sullivan, Lawrence E. *Icanchu's Drum: An Orientation to Meaning in South American Religions.* New York: Macmillan, 1988.

The Teachings and History of Tenrikyo. Ed., Translation Section of Tenrikyo Overseas Mission Department. Tenri: Tenrikyo Overseas Mission Department, 1986.

Tenzin Gyatso, the Fourteenth Dalai Lama. *Opening the Eye of Awareness.* London: Wisdom, 1985.

Thomas, Edward J. *The Life of Buddha as Legend and History.* Mineola, N.Y.: Dover, 2000.

Turville-Petre, E. O. G. *Myth and Religion of the North: The Religion of Ancient Scandinavia.* New York: Holt, Rinehart and Winston, 1964.

Underhill, Evelyn. *Mysticism: A Study in the Nature and Development of Man's Spiritual Consciousness.* 12th ed. New York: New American Library, 1974.

van der Post, Laurens. *The Heart of the Hunter: Customs and Myths of the African Bushman.* New York: Harcourt Brace Jovanovich, 1961.

Bibliography

Vries, Jan de. *The Study of Religion: A Historical Approach.* Trans., Kees W. Bolle. New York: Harcourt, Brace & World, 1967.

Walker, James R. *Lakota Belief and Ritual.* Lincoln: University of Nebraska Press, 1980.

Widengren, Geo. *Muhammad, the Apostle of God, and His Ascension.* Uppsala: Lundequista, 1955.

Women Saints: East and West. Eds., Swami Ghanananda and John Stewart-Wallace. Hollywood, Calif.: Vedanta, 1979.

Yü Chün-fang. *Kuan-yin: The Chinese Transformation of Avalokitesvara.* New York: Columbia University Press, 2001.

Index

Aaron 96, 131
Abraham 36, 95, 97–98, 131
Abu 'Abdallah Muhammad ibn 'Ali al-Halim al-Tirmidhi *see* al-Tirmidhi
Acts of the Apostles 24, 50, 64, 145, 149
Adam 131, 192
Adam and Eve 66, 71–73, 134
adhan 51, 193
advaita 74, 164
Aeneas (the paralytic) 149
Aesir 17
agape 58
Agni 163
Ahab (king of Israel) 93
ajami 124
Akka Mahadevi *see* Mahadeviyakka
alchemy 60, 70
Alfassa, Mira *see* Mira Alfassa
Allah (God) 22, 39, 99–100
Almagest 17, 129
al-Tirmidhi: *The Way of the Friends of God* 86
Amahuacan religion: Córdova-Rios, Manuel 128–129; hallucinogenic plants 128; Xumu 128–129
Amitabha Buddha 152
Ananias of Damascus 91
androgyne 132–133
angels 18–19, 22–24, 36, 49, 72, 130, 142–143, 191; *see also* Gabriel
Ani 103
aniconic religion 34
anima 11
animism 11–12
anrita 54
apatheia 160
Aphrodite 109, 132, 174
Apocalypse of John *see* Revelation of John
Apollinaris of Laodicea 190
Apollo 78, 139–141
Apollonios of Tyana 103–104
Aquarius 110
Ares 109

Arius of Alexandria 189–190
Arjuna 184–186
Armstrong, Karen: *A History of God: The 4000-Year Quest of Judaism, Christianity and Islam* 147–148
Aroko 111
Arsinoe II 174
Arthur 168
Arugba 46
asceticism *see* spiritual discipline
Ashoka 35
Ashvaghosha: *Buddhacarita* 170
Asita 169
Asklepios 39
astral religion 16, 107–110
astrology 16, 102, 105, 107–110
Athanasius 189–190
atheism 11
atman 61
atonement 191–192
Augustine of Hippo 83–84, 148; *Confessions* 157
Aulén, Gustaf: *Christus Victor* 192
Aurobindo Ghose 183–184
Australian religion: Pleiades 56–57
Avalokiteshvara 178; *see also* Bodhisattva of Compassion
avatara 182
avatars 182–186, 193

Baal 93
babalawo 110–112, 193
Babylonian Exile 94
Baha' Allah 21
Bahá'í: Baha' Allah 21
baptism 56, 64, 91, 132, 147, 149
Barnabas (saint) 150
Basil of Caesarea 147
Baule religion: mouse oracle 107; Queen Aura Poku 107
benei ha-nevi' im 94
Bertolucci, Bernardo: "The Little Buddha" 35

Index

Beth-El 36
Bhagavad Gita 184–186
Bhagavata Purana 185
Bhagiratha 38
bhakti (devotion) 75, 156, 193
Bhakti Yoga 156, 182, 186
Bian Cheng Wang 85
Bianchi, Ugo 72
Bible 86–87, 92, 94, 101, 105, 130, 134, 149, 151–152
Black Elk 7–8, 12, 29–30, 60, 77–78
"Blessing of Shulgi" 108–109
bodhi 157, 193
Bodhi Tree 25, 35, 67
bodhisattva 175, 193
Bodhisattva of Compassion 79, 178–179; see also Avalokiteshvara; Dalai Lama
bodhisattvas 15, 50, 79, 84, 175–176, 178–179, 182; see also Avalokiteshvara; Chenresi; Maitreya
Boehme, Jacob 70
Bondye (God) 143
Book of Changes 112, 115–117
Book of Jonah 105–106
The Book of Rites 139
Book of Songs 117
Bourguignon, Ericka 137
brahman 19, 45
bridal chamber 132–133
Bridal Mysticism 167
Brihadaranyaka Upanishad 74
Brodsky Jochelson, Dina 120
Brown, Karen McCarthy 57
Buber, Martin 68–73, 75; *I and Thou* 70
Bucke, R. M. 162–164; *Cosmic Consciousness: A Study in the Evolution of the Human Mind* 162–163
buddha 169, 193
Buddha (historical) 21, 24, 34–35, 37, 41, 54, 58, 67, 84, 156, 169, 171; see also Shakyamuni; Siddhartha Gautama
Buddhacarita 170
buddhas 15, 25, 49, 157, 172, 175; see also Amitabha; Buddha (historical); Fragrance Accumulated Buddha
Buddhism: Amitabha Buddha 152; aniconic religion 34; Ashoka 35; Ashvaghosha 170; Asita 169; Avalokiteshvara 178; Bertolucci, Bernardo 35; bodhi 157, 193; Bodhi Tree 25, 35, 67; *bodhisattva* 175, 193; Bodhisattva of Compassion 79, 178–179 (*see also* Avalokiteshvara; Dalai Lama); bodhisattvas 15, 50, 79, 84, 175–176, 178–179, 182 (*see also* Avalokiteshvara; Chenresi; Maitreya); *buddha* 169, 193; Buddha (historical) 21, 24, 34–35, 37, 41, 54, 58, 67, 84, 156, 169, 171 (*see also* Shakyamuni; Siddhartha Gautama); *Buddhacarita* 170; buddhas 15, 25, 49, 157, 172, 175 (*see also* Amitabha; Buddha [historical]; Fragrance Accumulated Buddha); casting lots 112; Chan 84, 176; Chenresi 178; Citta 169; *dalai* 178; Dalai Lama 79, 178–179 (*see also* Tenzin Gyatso); demi-gods (asuras) 176; devotion 176; Dharma 35, 54, 85, 171, 176, 193; *duhkha* 171; Eightfold Path 156, 172–173; enlightenment 24, 59, 67, 84–85, 152, 156, 169, 171–173, 175–176 (*see also* liberation; nirvana; samadhi); ethics 173; fasting 170; Five Precepts 173; Four Noble Truths 171–173; Fragrance Accumulated Buddha 84–85; *Freedom in Exile* 179; Great Stupa at Sanci 38; hell 176; hungry ghosts (pretas) 176; initiation 180; Jataka Tales 176; *The Journey to the West* 137; Kalachakra Initiation 180; karma 177; Katog Gonpa Monastery 180; Khetsang Rinpoche 178–179; Khyongla Jigme 180; Khyongla Rato 178, 180–181, 184; *lama* 178, 193; liberation 171, 175; "The Little Buddha" 35; Mahabodhi Temple 58; Mahayana 152, 175–176; Maitreya 176; Mayadevi 169; meditation 24, 59, 84, 170–171, 173, 176; Middle Path 156; *My Land and My People* 179; *My Life and Lives: The Story of a Tibetan Incarnation* 180; Nag-dban-rgya-mtsho 178; Nandabala 170; nirvana 19, 24–25, 157, 171, 173, 175, 194; non-duality 156, 173; paradise 152, 176; *parinirvana* 35; Potala 178–179; Pure Land 152, 176; Rato Monastery 181; reincarnation 171; ritual 176; Rock and Pillar Edicts 35; Ryoan-ji 35; samadhi 84–85, 156–157, 173, 194; Shakyamuni 58, 156, 175–176 (*see also* Buddha [historical]; Siddhartha Gautama); shramanas 170; Siddhartha Gautama 21, 24–25, 35, 37, 41, 67, 84, 169–173, 176 (*see also* Buddha [historical]; Shakyamuni); Sonam Gyatso 178; stupa 37–38; Suddhodana 169; Tantra 180; Tenzin Gyatso 178–181, 184; Tenzin Lhamo 181; Theravada 175–176; *trsna* 172; Tsering, Diki 178–179; tulkus 35, 175–181, 194; Tusita Heaven 176; Vajrayana 176; *Vimalakirti Sutra* 84–85; Western Paradise 152; Wheel of Life 176–177; Yama 177; Zen 84, 176
Bun Festival 41–42

Cancer 110
Carmelites 28, 43, 157
casting lots 104–107, 112, 116
Celestial Master Daoism 21, 23, 54
Celtic religion: Samhain 40
Chan 84, 176

Index

chanting 57–58
chaos 53
charity 58, 100
Chenresi 178
Chest 88–89
chiromancy *see* palm reading
Christ 21–24, 28, 56, 63–64, 66, 91, 137, 146, 151, 167, 187, 189–190, 192; *see also* Jesus of Nazareth; Messiah
Christian Tradition 151–152
Christianity: Acts of the Apostles 24, 50, 64, 145, 149; Adam 192; Adam and Eve 66; Aeneas (the paralytic) 149; Ananias of Damascus 91; Apollinaris of Laodicea 190; Arius of Alexandria 189–190; Arthur 168; Athanasius 189–190; atonement 191–192; Augustine of Hippo 83–84, 148, 157; Aulén, Gustaf 192; baptism 56, 64, 91, 147, 149; Barnabas (saint) 150; Basil of Caesarea 147; Bible 149, 151–152 (*see also* New Testament and specific books of the Bible); Bridal Mysticism 167; Carmelites 28, 43, 157; charity 58; Christ 21–24, 28, 56, 63–64, 66, 91, 137, 146, 151, 167, 187, 189–190, 192 (*see also* Jesus of Nazareth; Messiah); Christian Tradition 151–152; Christmas 41; *christos* 146; Christotokos 190; *Christus Victor* 192; circumcision 150; *Confessions* 157; Confirmation 64; Constantine I 188; Council of Chalcedon 190; Council of Constantinople I 190; Council of Ephesus I 190; Council of Florence 65; Council of Jerusalem 150; Council of Nicaea I 189; creeds 189–190; crucifixion 187, 190; Devil 19, 104, 191; dragons 19; Easter 23; Eckhart, Johannes 164; Edict of Milan 188; Eucharist 41, 47, 63–66, 150, 157–158, 193; Extreme Unction 64–65; Fall 191; Feast of All the Saints 40; Gabriel 22; Garden of Eden 17; gnosticism 65 (*see also* Gnostic Christianity); god-man 104; godhead 19; Gospel 147, 149, 188; Gospel of John 145, 187–188, 191; Gospel of Mark 23, 146, 191; Gospel of Matthew 191; Grail 168; Gregory of Nazianzos 147; Gregory of Nyssa 147; Halloween 40; Hebrews, Letter to the 150; Holy Orders 64–65; Holy Spirit 50, 64, 145–152, 163, 189–190; *homoiousios* 189; *homoousios* 189–190; *incarnatio* 174; initiation 167; inspiration 4, 64, 145–152; *Interior Mansions* 157–158; James (brother of Jesus) 91, 150; Jesus of Nazareth 10, 15, 21, 24, 28, 41, 43, 47, 50–51, 54, 56, 58, 63–65, 67, 91–92, 99, 104–106, 109, 145–147, 149, 151, 167, 175, 184, 186–192 (*see also* Christ); John the Baptist 22, 64, 191; John the Evangelist 50, 64, 188; Joseph Justus 106; Judas Iscariot 106; kingdom of God 10, 23–24, 64, 104, 145–147; Lamb of God 63, 191; Letter to the Philippians 187; Letter to the Romans 56; *logos* 187, 193; Logos 187, 190; Lombard, Peter 65; Lord's Prayer 50; Mary (mother of Jesus) 22, 43, 109, 190; Mary of Magdala 24; Matrimony 64–65; Matthias 106; meditation 58–59; Messiah 187, 193 (*see also* Christ); Methodism 53; monotheism 189; Nestorius 190; New Adam 192; New Testament 22, 50, 58, 87, 92, 104, 151, 187, 191; Nicene Creed 189–190; Old Testament 151; paradise 121; Paul the Apostle 17, 53, 56, 91–92, 121, 147, 150–151, 187, 191–192; Penance 64–65; Pentecost 145; Peter the Apostle 17, 50, 64, 149–150; polytheism 189; prayer 67, 152, 157; Prayer of the Heart 58; Queen of Heaven 109; resurrection 23–24, 67, 145–147, 187, 192; Revelation of John 19; sacraments 64–66; Satan 104; Second Coming 146; sin 191–192; Son of God 23, 104, 146, 189; Son of Man 191; Tabitha 149; Taiping *see* Taiping Christianity; Teresa of Avila 50, 157–158, 160–161, 164, 167; Tertullian 65–66; Theodosius I 140, 189; Theotokos 190; Thérèse of Lisieux 28, 43; I Timothy 53; Trappists 59; Trinity 147–149, 189–190; Vodou *see* Vodou Christianity; *The Way of Perfection* 157; Wesley, John 53; Zachariah 22
Christmas 41
christos 146
Christotokos 190
Christus Victor 192
circumambulation 38–39, 48
circumcision 150
Citta 169
Classic of the Mountains and Seas 15–16
Communion *see* Eucharist
Comte, Auguste 9
Confessions 157
Confirmation 64
Confucianism 41, 118, 139
Confucius 41, 118
Constantine I 188
Conyers, Claude B. 1
Córdova-Rios, Manuel 128–129
Cosmic Consciousness: A Study in the Evolution of the Human Mind 162–163
cosmogony *see* creation myth
cosmology 15, 115, 126, 129–130, 159
cosmos 53; *see also* kosmos
Council of Chalcedon 190
Council of Constantinople I 190
Council of Ephesus I 190
Council of Florence 65
Council of Jerusalem 150

215

Index

Council of Nicaea I 189
Covenant 97–98, 147
creation myths 32, 53–54
creeds 100, 189–190
crucifixion 187, 190
Cusa, Nicholas of 70

dalai 178
Dalai Lama 79, 178–179; *see also* Tenzin Gyatso
Danbala Wedo 143–144
Daniel 22, 191
Dao 20, 54, 89, 193
Dao De Jing 20, 23
Daoism: Bian Cheng Wang 85; *Book of Changes* 112, 115–117; *Book of Songs* 117; Bun Festival 41–42; casting lots 112, 116; Celestial Master Daoism 21, 23, 54; *Classic of the Mountains and Seas* 15–16; cosmology 115; Dao 20, 54, 89, 193; *Dao De Jing* 20, 23; Doctrine of the Orthodox One [Resting on] the Authority of the Alliance 20; Dragon Boat Festival 45; dragons 21, 45, 113, 133; Gong Sun Shu 119; Guang Wu Di 119; Han Zhong Li 90; Heaven 78, 118–119; Hell 85–86; Hungry Ghost Festival 45; Immortals 89–90, 92; incense 112–113; Jade Emperor 85; Ji Gong 85; *jia-gu* 113; *Journey to the Underworld* 85–86; Lantern Festival 45; Lao Zi 20–21, 23, 54; Lu Dong Bin 89–92; Mandate of Heaven 78. 117–119; Mazu 45, 105; meditation 89–90; Mid-Autumn Festival 45; New Year 44–45, 48–49, 115; oracle bones 113–114; Pak Tai 42; Paradise 85–86; prayer 112, 117; Queen Mother of the West 16, 19; scapulomancy 113–114; Shang Di 117–119; Son of Heaven 118; *Songs of the South* 133; Yang Sheng 85–86; yin and yang 105, 115–116, 194; Zhang Ling 20–22, 54; *Zhuang Zi* 20
David (king of Israel) 49, 168
Deism 10
Delphic Oracle 139–141
Demeter 155
demi-gods (asuras) 176
Demiurge 132
Devi 183–184
Devil 19, 72, 104, 191
devotion 176; *see also* bhakti
dharma 35, 54, 85, 171, 176, 193
dhyana 61, 193; *see also* meditation
Dhyana Yoga 61–63, 73, 156
Doctrine of the Orthodox One [Resting on] the Authority of the Alliance 20
Dome of the Rock 37, 131
Dorcas *see* Tabitha
Dragon Boat Festival 45
Dragon Demon of the Eastern Sea 135

dragons 19, 21, 45, 113, 133–135, 140
dualism 72–73
duhkha 171

Earth-Owner 125
Easter 23
Eckhart, Johannes 164
ecstasy 127
Eden 71–73
Edict of Milan 188
Egyptian religion: Hathor 18; pyramids 37
Eight Limbs of the Tree of Yoga 61, 156
Eightfold Path 156, 172–173
ekstasis 127
Eland 18
Elder Edda see *Poetic Edda*
Elegba (Esu) 112
Eliade, Mircea 1–2, 13, 27, 55; *The Encyclopedia of Religion* 1
Elijah 93
The Encyclopedia of Religion 1
Enlightenment 24, 59, 67, 84–85, 152, 156, 169, 171–173, 175–176; *see also* liberation; nirvana; samadhi
Enlightenment (European) 10, 12
Epega, Afolabi A. 112
Esau 36
eschatology 99–100
Eskimo religion *see* Inuit religion
Esu *see* Elegba (Esu)
ethics 12, 53–55, 156, 173
Eucharist 41, 63–66, 150, 157–158, 193
Evil Forest 103
Evolutionism 10–11
Exegesis on the Soul 132
Exodus 41, 47, 63, 94–97, 193
exorcism 138–139
Extreme Unction 64–65
Ezili Danto 144
Ezili Freda 144
Ezili Lasyrenn 16, 144

Fall 71–73, 191
Falling Star 8
fasting 58, 100, 170
Father of Majesty 72
Feast of All the Saints 40
Feraca, Stephen E.: *Wakinyan: Lakota Religion in the Twentieth Century* 31
Five Pillars of Islam 51, 100
Five Precepts 173
Flood 134
Four Noble Truths 171–173
Fragrance Accumulated Buddha 84–85
Freedom in Exile 179
Freyja 126

216

Index

Gabriel 22–23, 27, 99–100, 131, 160
Ganga 38
Garden of Eden 17
Gelberman, Joseph 76
Genesis 53–54
geomancy 105
Germanic religion: Aesir 17; cosmology 126; Freyja 126; Gimlé 127; Hel 17; Norna-Gest 125; Odin 126; Olaf the Holy 32; Olaf Tryggvason 32, 126; *Poetic Edda* 32; *The Saga of Eric the Red* 126; seidkona 125–127, 194; seidr 125–127, 194; Snorri Sturluson 32; *Voluspa* 17, 126–127; World Snake 17; Yggdrasill 17, 126; Ymir 32, 53, 126
Gimlé 127
Ginen 16
Gitagovinda 185
Gnostic Christianity 65, 129, 131–133, 136; androgyne 132–133; Aphrodite 132; baptism 132; bridal chamber 132–133; Demiurge 132; *Exegesis on the Soul* 132; Gospel 151; Gospel of Luke 151; *Gospel of Thomas* 132, 166; Jesus of Nazareth 131–132, 166; Marcion 151; Paul the Apostle 151; Psyche 132–133; resurrection 131–133; tripartite anthropology 131; Venus (planet) 132
God, Dreams, and Revelation: A Christian Interpretation of Dreams 86–87
god-man 103–104
godhead 19
gohei 153
Goldi religion *see* Siberian religions
Gong Sun Shu 119
Good Words for Exhorting the Age 134
Gospel 147, 149, 151, 188
Gospel of John 145, 187–188, 191
Gospel of Luke 151
Gospel of Mark 23, 146, 191
Gospel of Matthew 191
Gospel of Thomas 132, 166
Gounder, C. K. Ramaswamy *see* Satchidananda (Swami)
gourd rattle 88, 127
Grail 168
Great Stupa at Sanci 38
Greek religion: Aphrodite 109; Apollo 78, 139–141; Ares 109; Asklepios 39; Delphic Oracle 139–141; Demeter 155; dragons 140; Hermes 109; Homeric Hymn to Pythian Apollo 140; incubation 39; initiation 155; Meilichios 48; mysteries 155; Odysseus 46; Plato 140; *pythein* 140; Pythia 78, 140; Pytho 140; Socrates 140–141; Teiresias 46; Zeus 109
Gregory of Nazianzos 147
Gregory of Nyssa 147
Guang Wu Di 119

Guarani religion: gourd rattle 127
guru 178, 193

Hafiz Shirazi 168–169
Haggadah 41, 193
hajj 39; *see also* pilgrimage
Halloween 40
hallucinations 87
hallucinogenic plants 128
Han Zhong Li 90
Hanblecheyapi 59–60, 88–89
haruspicy 105
Hathor 18
Heaven 78, 118–119; *see also* Paradise
Heavenly Kingdom of Great Peace 134–135
Hebrews, Letter to the 192
Das Heilige 12
Hel 17
Hell 85–86, 176
Hellenistic religions: Aphrodite 174; Apollonios of Tyana 103–104; Arsinoe II 174; cosmology 129–130; god-man 103–104; Jupiter 130; Mars 130; Mercury 130; Ogdoas 130–131; *Poimandres of Hermes Trismegistos* 131; Queen of Heaven 174; resurrection 103–104; Saturn 130; Venus 130; Zeus 104
hepatoscopy 104
Hermes 109
hierophany 2, 13, 27
hieros gamos see sacred marriage
Hinduism: *advaita* 74, 164; Agni 163; *anrita* 54; Arjuna 184–186; atman 61; Aurobindo Ghose 183–184; *avatara* 182; avatars 182–186, 193; *Bhagavad Gita* 184–186; *Bhagavata Purana* 185; Bhagiratha 38; bhakti (devotion) 75, 156, 193; Bhakti Yoga 156, 182, 186; brahman 19, 45, 61, 74–75; *Brihadaranyaka Upanishad* 74; circumambulation 48; Devi 183–184; dharma 193; Dhyana Yoga 61–63, 73, 156, 193; Eight Limbs of the Tree of Yoga 61, 156; ethics 156; Ganga 38; *Gitagovinda* 185; *guru* 178, 193; Indra 182; Integral Yoga 75, 183–184; Iyengar, B. K. S. 61; Jayadeva 185; Jhana Yoga 156; jnana 74–75, 193; Kamsa 185; Kapila 38; karma 182, 186; Karma Yoga 156, 182, 186; Krishna 34, 184–186; liberation (moksha) 74, 156, 165–166, 182, 186, 194; *lila* 165; Mahadeviyakka 27; mantra 193; *maya* 165; meditation 27, 38, 61–63, 75, 156, 170–171; Mira Alfassa 183–184; moksha 156, 194 (*see also* liberation); monism 74, 182; Mother Meera 182–184; Nirguna-Brahman 19; nirvana 19; non-duality 61–62, 74, 164; Pancha Mahayajna 45; Patanjali 61, 156; polytheism 182; *pradakshina* 48; prayer 38; puja 48, 194; purusha

217

61; Radha 34, 185; Ramanuja 75; reincarnation 182; *Rigveda* 54; *rita* 54; samadhi 61, 156, 182–183, 194; samsara 156, 182, 194; *satchidananda* 156; Satchidananda (Swami) 73–76; Shankara 74, 164; Shiva 27–28, 38; Shivananda 75; *Shvetashvatara Upanishad* 165; Upanishads 74, 156; Vedanta 74; Vedas 74, 156; Vishnu 75, 184–185; *yoga* 60, 194; yoga 60–62, 75, 156, 183 (*see also* Bhakti Yoga; Dhyana Yoga; Integral Yoga; Jnana Yoga; Karma Yoga); *Yoga Sutra* 61, 156
A History of God: The 4000-Year Quest of Judaism, Christianity and Islam 147–148
Holy Orders 64–65
Holy Spirit 50, 64, 145–152, 163, 189–190
Homeric Hymn to Pythian Apollo 140
homoiousios 189
homoousios 189–190
Hong Xiu Quan 129, 133–136
Hopi religion: Spider Woman 16; Tawa 16
horama 87
Horse Dance 30–31
hozeh 94
Hugo, Victor: *Hunchback of Notre-Dame* 69
Hunchback of Notre-Dame 69
Hungry Ghost Festival 45
hungry ghosts (pretas) 176

I and Thou 70
Icanchu's Drum: An Orientation to Meaning in South American Religions 127
Ichibei 153
ideology 9
Idris-Enoch 131
Ifa *see* Orunmila (Ifa)
Ifa oracle 110–112, 115
Igbo religion: Ani 103; Evil Forest 103; twins 103; Week of Peace 103
Iglulik *see* Inuit religion
Iko 37
imam 52
Immortals 89–90, 92
Imori 111
Inanna 108–109
incarnatio 174
incense 112–113
incubation 38–39
Indra 182
initiation 55–57, 155, 167, 180
inspiration 1–2, 4, 64, 78, 141, 145–154
Integral Yoga 75, 183–184
Intellectual Culture of the Iglulik Eskimos 16
Interior Mansions 157–158
Inuit religion: shaman 16; Takánakapsâluk 16
Isaac 36, 95
ish ha-Elohim 94
islam 100

Islam: Aaron 131; Abraham 131; Adam 131; adhan 51, 193; Allah (God) 22, 39, 99–100; al-Tirmidhi 86; charity 100; circumambulation 39; creed 100; Dome of the Rock 37, 131; eschatology 99–100; *fana* 32; fasting 100; Five Pillars of Islam 51, 100; Gabriel 23, 27, 99–100, 131, 160; Hafiz Shirazi 168–169; *hajj* 39 (*see also* pilgrimage); Idris-Enoch 131; imam 52; Jesus of Nazareth 98–99, 131; John the Evangelist 131; Joseph (son of Jacob) 131; judgment 99; Ka'bah 22, 39, 51, 99–100; Khadijah 22, 99, 160; monotheism 99; Moses 131; muezzin 51, 194; Muhammad 21–23, 27, 39, 67, 86, 92, 94, 98–101, 131, 160; Muhammad's "night journey" 37, 131; Nation of Islam 59; pilgrimage 39, 58, 100; polytheism 22; prayer 39, 100; Qur'an 22, 50–51, 94, 100–101; Ramadan 58, 99–100; resurrection 99; Rumi, Jalal al-Din 32, 59, 157–160, 167–168; Salat 51; Shams 32, 158; Shi'ah 51; Sufism 32, 86, 158, 168; Sunni 51; Umm 'Abdallah 86; *ummah* 101; *The Way of the Friends of God* 86
Israelites 41, 47, 63, 87, 93–97, 105
Iyengar, B. K. S. 61

Jacob (Israel) 36, 94–95
Jade Emperor 85
James (brother of Jesus) 91, 150
James, William 26, 161–163, 166; *Principles of Psychology* 161; *The Varieties of Religious Experience* 26, 161–163
Jataka Tales 176
Jayadeva: *Gitagovinda* 185
Jeremiah 92
Jesus of Nazareth 10, 15, 21, 24, 28, 41, 43, 47, 50–51, 54, 56, 58, 63–65, 67, 91–92, 99, 104–106, 109, 145–147, 149, 151, 167, 175, 184, 186–192; *see also* Christ
Jewish-Roman War (First) 91, 145
Ji Gong 85
jnana 74–75, 193
Jnana Yoga 156
Jochelson, Waldemar 120
John the Baptist 58, 64, 191
John the Evangelist 50, 64, 131, 188
Jonah 105–106
Joseph (son of Jacob) 131
Joseph Barsabbas *see* Joseph Justus
Joseph Justus 106
Journey to the Underworld 85–86
The Journey to the West 137
Judaism: Aaron 96; Abraham 36, 95, 97–98; Adam and Eve 71–73; Ahab (king of Israel) 93; aniconic religion 34; Baal 93; Babylonian Exile 94; *benei ha-nevi' im* 94; Beth-El

36; Bible 86–87, 92, 94, 101, 105, 130 (*see also* specific books of the Bible); Book of Jonah 105–106; circumcision 150; Covenant 97–98, 147; Daniel 22, 191; David (king of Israel) 49, 168; Eden 71–73; Ein Sof 85; Elijah 93; Esau 36; Exodus 41, 47, 63, 94–97, 193; Fall 71–73; Gabriel 22; Genesis 53–54; Haggadah 41, 193; *hozeh* 94; Isaac 36, 95; *ish ha-Elohim* 94; Israelites 41, 47, 63, 87, 93–97, 105; Jacob (Israel) 36, 94–95; Jeremiah 92; John the Baptist 58; Jonah 105–106; Leviticus 34; Messiah 193; Moses 21, 37, 41, 54, 92, 94–99, 101, 106, 150, 160; *navi'* 94; Passover 41, 63, 65, 97; Pentecost 147; Philo of Alexandria 130; prayer 93; Rebecca 36; *ro'eh* 94; Sabbath 23, 34, 44; Samuel 93; Saul (king of Israel) 93, 105; Seder 41; Solomon (king of Israel) 49, 168; Temple in Jerusalem 37, 49–50, 91, 105, 145, 149, 168; Torah 37, 54, 94, 98, 100, 147, 150, 194; Urim and Thummin 105; Yahveh (God) 94; Yom Kippur 191
Judas Iscariot 106
judgment 99
Julius Caesar 109
Jupiter 109, 130

Ka'bah 22, 39, 51, 99–100
Kalachakra Initiation 180
kami 46
Kamsa 185
Kapila 38
Kaplan, Jeremiah 1
karma 177, 182, 186
Karma Yoga 156, 182, 186
Katog Gonpa Monastery 180
Kelsey, Morton T.: *God, Dreams, and Revelation: A Christian Interpretation of Dreams* 86–87
Khadijah 22, 99, 160
Khetsang Rinpoche 178–179
Khyongla Jigme 180
Khyongla Rato 178, 180–181, 184; *My Life and Lives: The Story of a Tibetan Incarnation* 180
kingdom of God 23–24, 64, 104, 145–147
Kingdom of Shadows 120–121
kosmos 15
Kowalski, Alourdes 142–145
Krahó religion: Tir'kre 122; Zezeinho 122
Krishna 34, 184–186
Krishnamurti, Jiddu 165

Lakota religion: Black Elk 7–9, 12, 29–30, 60, 77–78; Chest 88–89; Falling Star 8; gourd rattle 88; Hanblecheyapi 59–60, 88–89; Horse Dance 30–31; Lame Deer 88–89, 91–92; prayer 8, 60; sacred pipe 7–9, 13–14, 18, 29–30, 60, 67, 88; Standing Hollow Horn 8; *wakan* 8, 194; Wakan Tanka 7–9, 60, 194; White Buffalo Calf Woman 7–9, 12–14, 18, 22, 29, 60, 83, 88
lama 178, 193
Lamb of God 63, 191
Lame Deer 88–89, 91–92
Lantern Festival 45
Lao Zi 20–23, 54
Laroye 36–37
Lasyrenn *see* Ezili Lasyrenn
law *see* ethics
Leviticus 34
Lhamo Dhondup *see* Tenzin Gyatso
Liang Fa: *Good Words for Exhorting the Age* 134
liberation (moksha) 74, 156, 165–166, 171, 175, 182, 186, 194; *see also* enlightenment
lila 165
Lin Moniang *see* Mazu
"The Little Buddha" 35
logos 15, 187, 193
Logos 187, 190
Logos Spermatikos 159
Lombard, Peter 65
Lord's Prayer 50
Lord's Supper *see* Eucharist
Lu Dong Bin 89–92
Lubbock, John 11–12

magic 11
Mahabodhi Temple 58
Mahadeviyakka 27
Mahayana 152, 175–176
Maitreya 176
Malcolm X 59
Mama Lola *see* Alourdes Kowalski
manbo 142
Mandate of Heaven 78, 117–119
Mani 72
Manichaeism: Father of Majesty 72; Mani 72; Prince of Darkness 72
Mantis 18
mantra 58, 193
Marcion 151
Marcus Aurelius 157, 159–160, 164; *Meditations* 159–160
Mars 109, 130
Marx, Karl 10
Marxism 9–10
Mary (mother of Jesus) 22, 43, 109, 144, 190
Mary of Magdala 24
masiah 146
Mass *see* Eucharist
Matrimony 64–65
Matthias 106
maya 165

Index

Mayadevi 169
Mazu 45, 105
mbaraká see gourd rattle
meditation 24, 27, 38, 58–59, 61–63, 75, 84, 89–90, 156, 159, 170–171, 173, 176; *see also* Chan; Dhyana Yoga; Zen
Meditations 159–160
Meilichios 48
Meister Eckhart *see* Eckhart, Johannes
Mercury 109, 130
mermaid 16, 144
Messiah 187, 193; *see also* Christ
Methodism 53
Mid-Autumn Festival 45
Middle Path 156
Mira Alfassa 183–184
Mirza Husayn 'Ali Nuri *see* Baha' Allah
moksha 156, 194; *see also* liberation
monism 74, 159, 182
Monkey King 137
monotheism 11–12, 72, 99, 143, 152, 189
monster 18
Moon (Nanna) 108
morality *see* ethics
Morning and Evening Star *see* Venus (planet)
Moses 21, 37, 41, 54, 92, 94–99, 101, 106, 131, 150, 160
Mother Meera 182–184
mouse oracle 107
muezzin 51, 194
Muhammad 21–23, 27, 37, 39, 67, 86, 92, 94, 98–101, 131, 160
My Land and My People 179
My Life and Lives: The Story of a Tibetan Incarnation 180
mysteries 155
mysterion 63, 155
mystes 155
mysticism 155
Mysticism East and West: A Comparative Analysis of the Nature of Mysticism 164–166
Mysticism: A Study in the Nature and Development of Man's Spiritual Consciousness 166

Nag-dban-rgya-mtsho 178
Nakayama Miki 152–154
Nakayama Shuji 153
Nanai religion *see* Siberian religions
Nandabala 170
Nanna *see* Moon
Nation of Islam 59
"nature worship" 11
navi' 94
Neimark, Philip John 112
Nelbosh 120–121
Nestorius 190
New Adam 192

New Jerusalem 135
New Testament 22, 50, 58, 87, 92, 104, 151, 187, 191
New Year 40, 44–45, 48–49, 108, 115
Nicene Creed 189–190
Nirguna-Brahman 19
nirvana 19, 24–25, 157, 171, 173, 175, 194
non-duality 61–62, 74, 156, 164, 173
Norbu Lhamo *see* Khyongla Rato
Norna-Gest 125
Norse religion *see* Germanic religions
numen 12

Odin 126
odu 110–111
Odu Ifa 110–112, 115
Odysseus 46
Ogdoas 130–131
Oladipupo 111
Olaf the Holy 32
Olaf Tryggvason 32, 126
Old Testament 151
Olorun 103
oracle bones 113–114
ornithomancy 105
Orunmila (Ifa) 110–111
Osogbo 36–37, 46
Osun 36–38, 46
Otto, Rudolf 13, 26–27, 161, 163–166; *Das Heilige* 12; Inward Way 164–165; *Mysticism East and West: A Comparative Analysis of the Nature of Mysticism* 164–166; Way of Unity 164–166

Pak Tai 42
palm reading 102, 104
Pancha Mahayajna 45
Paradise 10, 17, 37, 66, 71–72, 85–86, 89, 121, 152, 176, 184
parinirvana 35
Passover 41, 63, 65, 97
Patanjali: *Yoga Sutra* 61, 156
Patrick (saint) 144
Paul the Apostle 17, 56, 91–92, 121, 147, 150–151, 191–192; Letter to the Philippians 187; Letter to the Romans 56; I Timothy 53
Penance 64–65
Pentateuch *see* Torah
Pentecost 145, 147
"personator of the dead" 139
Peter the Apostle 50, 64, 149–150
Philo of Alexandria 130
phrenology 105
pilgrimage 38–39, 58, 100
Pindar 160
Plato 140
Platonism 65, 131

Index

Pleiades 56–57
Poetic Edda 32
Poimandres of Hermes Trismegistos 131
Polynesian religion: Rumia 32; Ta'aroa 31–32
polytheism 11–12, 22, 143, 182, 189
positivism 9
Potala 178–179
pradakshina 48
prayer 8, 15, 38–39, 44–45, 49–52, 57–58, 60, 67, 93, 100, 112, 117, 138, 144, 152–153, 157; *see also* adhan
Prayer of the Heart 58
Primitive Culture 11
Prince of Darkness 72
Principles of Psychology 161
prophet 92
prophetes 92
prophets 92–101, 105–106, 134
Prose Edda 32
psyche 167
Psyche 132–133
Ptolemaeus, Claudius: *Almagest* 17, 129
puja 48, 194
Pure Land 152, 176
purusha 61
pyramids 37
pythein 140
Pythia 78, 140
Pytho 140

Queen Aura Poku 107
Queen of Heaven 108–109, 174
Queen Mother of the West 16, 19
Qur'an 22, 50–51, 94, 100–101

Radha 34, 185
Raja Yoga *see* Dhyana Yoga
Ramadan 58, 99–100
Ramanuja 75
Rasmussen, Knud: *Intellectual Culture of the Iglulik Eskimos* 16
rational and non-rational forms of religion 12–13; *see also* subjective experience
Rato Monastery 181
reason 10, 152
Rebecca 36
rebirth 124; *see also* reincarnation
Reddy, Kamala *see* Mother Meera
reincarnation 171, 182
resurrection 23–24, 67, 99, 103–104, 131–133, 145–147, 187, 192
Revelation of John 19, 134
Rigveda 54
rita 54
rites of passage *see* initiation
Rock and Pillar Edicts 35
ro'eh 94

Roman religion: Julius Caesar 109; Jupiter 109; Mars 109; Mercury 109; Sol 41; Venus 109
Rumi, Jalal al-Din 32, 59, 157–160, 167–168
Rumia 32
Ryoan-ji 35

Sabbath 23, 34, 44
sacrament 63–66
sacred marriage 108–109
sacrifice 45–48
The Saga of Eric the Red 126
Saint Lorenz Cathedral, Nuremberg, Germany 67
saints 142–145
Salat 51
Salvation Dance Service 154
samadhi 61, 84–85, 156–157, 173, 182–183, 194
Samhain 40
Samoyed religion *see* Siberian religions
samsara 156, 182, 194
Samuel 93
San religion: Eland 18; Mantis 18
Satan 104; *see also* Devil
satchidananda 156
Satchidananda (Swami) 73–76
Saturn 130
Saul (king of Israel) 93, 105
Saul of Tarsus *see* Paul the Apostle
Scandinavian religion *see* Germanic religions
scapulomancy 113–114
Second Coming 146
Seder 41
seidkona 125–127, 194
seidr 125–127, 194
Septuagint 151
Shakyamuni 58, 156, 175–176; *see also* Buddha (historical); Siddhartha Gautama
shaman 122, 194
shamans 55, 122–125, 160
Shams 32, 158
Shang Di 117–119
Shankara 74, 164
Shavu'ot *see* Pentecost
Shi'ah 51
Shiism *see* Shi'ah
Shinto: exorcism 138–139; *kami* 46; prayer 138
Shiva 27–28, 38
Shivananda 75
shramanas 170
Shulgi (king of Ur) 108–109
Shvetashvatara Upanishad 165
Siberian religion: *ajami* 124; Earth-Owner 125; Kingdom of Shadows 120–121; Nelbosh 120–121; rebirth 124; shaman 122, 160, 194; shamans 55, 122–125
Siddhartha Gautama 21, 24–25, 35, 37, 41,

Index

67, 84, 169–173, 176; *see also* Buddha (historical); Shakyamuni
sin 91–192
Smith, Huston: *The World's Religions* 4
Snorri Sturluson: *Prose Edda* 32
Socrates 140–141
Sol 41
Solomon (king of Israel) 49, 168
Solomon's Temple *see* Temple in Jerusalem
Son of God 23, 104, 146, 189
Son of Heaven 118
Son of Man 191
Sonam Gyatso 178
Songs for the Sacred Dance 154
Songs of the South 133
Soyo 153
Spider Woman 16
spirit possession 138–139, 141
spiritual discipline 34, 44, 52–66
Standing Hollow Horn 8
Stoicism: *apatheia* 160; cosmology 159; Logos Spermatikos 159; Marcus Aurelius 157, 159–160, 164; Meditation 159; *Meditations* 159–160; monism 159
stupa 37–38
subjective experience 10, 13, 27, 152; *see also* rational and non-rational forms of religion
Suddhodana 169
Sufism 32, 59, 86, 158, 168
Sukhavati *see* Western Paradise
Sullivan, Lawrence E.: *Icanchu's Drum: An Orientation to Meaning in South American Religions* 127
Sumerian religion: astral religion 16, 107–110; astrology 16, 107–110; "Blessing of Shulgi" 108–109; Inanna 108–109; Moon (Nanna) 108; New Year 108; Queen of Heaven 108–109; sacred marriage 108–109; Shulgi (king of Ur) 108–109; Sun (Utu) 108
Sun (Utu) 108
Sunni 51
Superior Divinity of the Deep Dark Heaven, true Soldier of the North *see* Pak Tai
superstition 10, 12
"The Swami and the Rabbi" 76

Ta'aroa 31–32
Tabitha 149
Taiping Christianity: Adam and Eve 134; Bible 134; Dragon Demon of the Eastern Sea 135; dragons 134–135; Flood 134; *Good Words for Exhorting the Age* 134; Heavenly Kingdom of Great Peace 134–135; Hong Xiu Quan 129, 133–136; Jesus of Nazareth 129, 134–135; Liang Fa 134; New Jerusalem 135; prophets 134; Revelation of John 134; Xiao Chao Gui 135

Takánakapsâluk 16
Tanakh *see* Bible
tanha see *trsna*
Tantra 180
Tarot cards 102, 104
Tatar religion 103, 123
Taurus 110
Tawa 16
Teiresias 46
Temple in Jerusalem 37, 49–50, 91, 105, 145, 149, 168
Tenri O no Mikoto 153
Tenrikyo Shinto 21; *gohei* 153; Ichibei 153; inspiration 152–254; monotheism 152; Nakayama Miki 152–154; Nakayama Shuji 153; prayer 153; Salvation Dance Service 154; Songs for the Sacred Dance 154; Soyo 153; Tenri O no Mikoto 153; Tip of the Divine Writing Brush 154; Tsukihi (God) 153
Tenzin Gyatso 178–181, 184; *Freedom in Exile* 179; *My Land and My People* 179
Tenzin Lhamo 181
Teresa of Avila 50, 157–158, 160–161, 164, 167; *Interior Mansions* 157–158; *The Way of Perfection* 157
Tertullian 65–66
Theodosius I 140, 189
theos aner see god-man
Theotokos 190
Theravada 175–176
Thérèse of Lisieux 28, 43
Tian Hou *see* Mazu
Tian Ming *see* Mandate of Heaven
Timehin 36–37
Tip of the Divine Writing Brush 154
Tir'kre 122
Titus Flavius Vespasianus 91
Todaiji, Nara, Japan 67
Torah 37, 54, 94, 98, 100, 147, 150, 194
Trappists 59
Trinity 147–149, 189–190
tripartite anthropology 131
trsna 172
Tsai Chih Chung: *Chinese Philosophies in Comics* (series) 35
Tsering, Diki 178–179
Tsukihi (God) 153
tulkus 35, 79, 175–181, 194
Tungus religion *see* Siberian religions
Tusita Heaven 176
twins 103
Tylor, Edward Burnett 12; *Primitive Culture* \ 11

Umm 'Abdallah 86
ummah 101

Index

Underhill, Evelyn 161, 166–169; *Mysticism: A Study in the Nature and Development of Man's Spiritual Consciousness* 166
Upanishads 74, 156, 165
Urim and Thummin 105
Utu *see* Sun (Utu)

Vajrayana 176
van der Post, Laurens 18
The Varieties of Religious Experience 26, 161–163
Vedanta 74, 164
Vedas 74, 156
Venus 109
Venus (planet) 16, 108, 130, 132
Vimalakirti Sutra 84–85
Virgin Mary *see* Mary (mother of Jesus)
Vishnu 75, 184–185
vision quest *see* Hanblecheyapi
Vodou Christianity: Bondye (God) 143; Danbala Wedo 143–144; Ezili Danto 144; Ezili Freda 144; Ezili Lasyrenn 16, 144; Ginen 16; initiation 57; Kowalski, Alourdes 142–145; *manbo* 142; Mary (mother of Jesus) 144; mermaid 16, 144; monotheism 143; Patrick (saint) 144; polytheism 143; prayer 144; saints 142–145; *vodu* 142
Voluspa 17, 126–127

wakan 8, 194
Wakan Tanka 7–8, 60
Wakinyan: Lakota Religion in the Twentieth Century 31
The Way of Perfection 157
The Way of the Friends of God 86
Week of Peace 103
Wesley, John 53
Western Paradise 152
Wheel of Life 176–177

White Buffalo Calf Woman 7–9, 12–14, 18, 22, 29, 60, 67, 77, 83, 88
World Snake 17
The World's Religions 4
worship 44–52

Xiao Chao Gui 135
Xumu 128–129

Yahveh (God) 94
Yama 177
Yang Sheng 85–86
Yggdrasill 17, 126
yin and yang 105, 115–116, 194
Ymir 32, 53, 126
yoga 60, 194
yoga 60–62, 75, 156, 183; *see also* Bhakti Yoga; Dhyana Yoga; Integral Yoga; Jnana Yoga; Karma Yoga
Yoga Sutra 61, 156
Yom Kippur 191
Yoruba religion: Aroko 11; Arugba 46; babalawo 110–112, 193; Elegba (Esu) 112; Ifa oracle 110–112, 115; Iko 37; Imori 111; Laroye 36–37; *odu* 110–111; Odu Ifa 110–112, 115; Oladipupo 111; Olorun 103; Orunmila (Ifa) 110–111; Osogbo 36–37, 46; Osun 36–38, 46; prayer 112; Timehin 36–37; twins 103
Yukaghir religion *see* Siberian religions

Zachariah 22
Zen 84, 176
Zeus 104, 109
Zezeinho 122
Zhang Ling 20–22, 54
Zhuang Zi 20
zodiac 109–110

www.ingramcontent.com/pod-product-compliance
Ingram Content Group UK Ltd.
Pitfield, Milton Keynes, MK11 3LW, UK
UKHW041949140426
5217IPUK00014B/716